Publications in Librarianship no. 55

The Digital Reference Research Agenda

Compiled from the Digital Reference Research Symposium
August 2002
Harvard University

Editors

D1570908

R. *David Lankes*
Scott Nicholson
Abby Goodrum

Association of College and Research Libraries
A Division of the American Library Association
Chicago 2003

The paper used in this publication meets the minimum requirements of American National Standard for Information Sciences-Permanence of Paper for Printed Library Materials, ANSI Z39.48-1992.

Library of Congress Cataloging-in-Publication Data

Digital Reference Research Symposium (2002 : Harvard University)
    The digital reference research agenda / compiled from the Digital
Reference Research Symposium, August 2002, Harvard University ; editors,
R. David Lankes, Scott Nicholson, Abby Goodrum.
        p. cm. -- (ACRL publications in librarianship ; no. 55)
Includes bibliographical references.
    ISBN 0-8389-8231-X (alk. paper)
    1. Electronic reference services (Libraries)--Congresses. 2. Digital
libraries--Congresses. I. Lankes, R. David. II. Nicholson, Scott. III.
Goodrum, Abby. IV. Title. V. Series.

    Z674.A75 no. 55
    [Z711.45]
    025.5'24--dc21
                                                          2003011041

Printed on recycled paper.

Printed in the United States of America.

07 06 05 04 03   5 4 3 2 1

Acknowledgments
The editors would like to acknowledge the participants and supporters of the
Digital Reference Research Symposium, which is the origin of this work.

Sponsored by
The Information Institute of Syracuse
The National Library of Canada
The Association of College & Research Libraries
Harvard University
QuestionPoint
Gemstar

with participation by
The Institute of Museum and Library Studies and the Library of Congress

Symposium Participants
- William Arms, Cornell University
- Joan Bartlett, University of Toronto
- Fiona Black, Dalhousie University
- John Collins, Harvard University
- Paul J. Constantine, University of Washington
- Martha Crawley, Institute of Museum and Library Services
- Bruce Croft, University of Massachusetts Amherst
- Ann Curry, University of British Columbia
- Mary Ellen Davis, Association of College & Research Libraries
- Blane Dessy, U.S. Department of Justice Law Library
- Donna Dinberg, National Library of Canada
- Carol Farber, University of Western Ontario
- Luanne Freund, University of Toronto
- Catherine Friedman, MIT/Reference and User Services Association
- Deborah Garson, Harvard University
- Franceen Gaudet, National Library of Canada
- Laura Gottesman, Library of Congress
- Maurita Holland, University of Michigan
- Joseph Janes, University of Washington
- R. David Lankes, Information Institute of Syracuse, Syracuse University
- Anna Maria Lankes, Information Institute of Syracuse
- Clifford Lynch, Coalition for Networked Information (CNI)
- Marcia Mardis, Michigan Teacher Network
- Michael McClennen, Internet Public Library
- Lynne McKechnie, University of Western Ontario
- Peter McNally, McGill University
- Jeff Penka, OCLC/QuestionPoint.
- Jeff Pomerantz, Syracuse University

- Matt Saxton, University of Washington
- Joanne Silverstein, Information Institute of Syracuse
- Linda Smith, University of Illinois at Urbana Champaign
- Helen Tibbo, University of North Carolina at Chapel Hill
- Carolyn Watters, Dalhousie University
- Marilyn D. White, University of Maryland
- Jo Bell Whitlatch, San Jose State University

Special thanks to Franceen Gaudet and Donna Dinberg at the National Library of Canada, Mary Ellen Davis of ACRL, Blane Dessy at the Department of Justice, John Collins of Harvard University, Diane Kresh at the Library of Congress, Jeff Penka at OCLC, and Charlie Hill at Gemstar. These individuals championed the symposium idea in their organizations and helped make it a reality. Also thanks to Charles McClure of Florida State University, who provided a great deal of thinking into the structure of the symposium and this book. The editors also would like to acknowledge Eric Plotnick, Joan Laskowski, and Joanne Silverstein at the Information Institute of Syracuse for their invaluable assistance.

Finally, the editors would like to especially acknowledge Anna Maria Lankes, who not only pulled together the symposium but also contributed greatly to the creation of this book. Without Anna Maria, this book would not be a reality.

Table of Contents

Introduction

R. David Lankes, A. Goodrum, S. Nicholson
School of Information Studies, Syracuse University

Overview

The past several years have brought about advances in network computing and digital library technology that have immediate and permanent consequences for the provision of reference services. As a result, digital reference practice has grown at an exponential rate and is fast becoming a part of routine library operations. Sessions at the American Library Association Conference, the Annual Virtual Reference Desk Conference, and regional library conferences are overflowing with librarians seeking education and direction in the provision of services to their online patrons. Funding agencies, commercial entities, and libraries of all types are investing substantial monies (often from limited resources) to support digital reference and, in doing so, are setting priorities for funding that will impact library services for years to come.

At the same time, there has emerged a small, but dedicated, cadre of researchers providing scholarship in this area. Unlike the domain of traditional reference, the scholarship of digital reference lacks a comprehensive framework for understanding where the field is going and for informing best practices for the future. A further problem has been the lack of interaction between the digital reference and digital library research communities. Although digital reference can be seen as a subfield of digital libraries, few cases exist where research or development in these areas has been coordinated.

This book has its origin in the 2nd Annual Virtual Reference Desk Conference in Seattle, Washington. It was at this conference that two concepts were expressed: (1) There is a great need for empirical research in the burgeoning field of digital reference, which up to this point has been dominated by isolated ad hoc case studies; and (2) there are few scholarly and research-oriented participants in digital reference conferences and activities. We saw a need to engage the scholarly and research communities in digital reference not to a make up for a perceived lack of quality but, rather, to supplement the outstanding grassroots work with more generalizable and grounded research understanding. In essence, the research community needed to be engaged in an exploration of the issues surrounding digital reference in order to enrich the field.

To encourage participation by the research community (in universities, libraries, and beyond), Syracuse University's Information Institute organized a symposium on digital reference research to be held at Harvard University. The symposium was sponsored by the National Library of Canada, the American Library Association's Association of College & Research Libraries, the Online Computer Library Center Inc. (OCLC), the Harvard Graduate School of Education, and the Library of Congress.

The stated objective of the symposium was to create a research agenda in digital reference that bridged the areas of digital reference, library practice, digital libraries, and computer science. The symposium also sought to foster a cohort of collaboration among researchers who had often worked apart or in competition with each other. In order to generate wide discussion, white papers were commissioned on topics that emerged from the 3rd Annual Virtual Reference Desk Conference. The authors were asked to present their papers and to facilitate discussion to ferret out the hard questions surrounding digital reference research.

What emerged from this symposium provides us with a clearer understanding of the field along with its research priorities and shared knowledge. The white papers have been revised and augmented, where necessary, and an initial research agenda has emerged from the symposium's rich tapestry of papers, presentations, and discussions.

Structure of This Book

The digital research agenda presented by R. David Lankes in chapter 1 of this book builds on the white papers submitted for the symposium and provides a high-level overview of the origins and scope of the interdisciplinary relationships that foster and feed digital reference research and practice. It identifies the central research questions surrounding digital reference and points to gaps in our understanding of this phenomenon. Using the metaphor of conceptual lenses, the author discusses how different disciplines approach and build on the core framework of questions and assumptions surrounding digital reference. The discussion is not intended to represent a definitive map of digital reference research but, rather, should be seen as an early attempt to document the evolution of an emerging field of research and practice, to foster discussion and debate, and to advance the work of scholars in this area.

Following the research agenda established in chapter 1 are eight unique papers exploring specific facets of digital reference research, namely:

- Chapter 2, Integrating Digital Reference Service into the Digital Library Environment, by Jeffrey Pomerantz
- Chapter 3, Question Negotiation in an Electronic Age, by Joseph Janes

- Chapter 4, Software, Systems, and Standards in Digital Reference: A Research Agenda, by Michael McClennen
- Chapter 5, Policies for Digital Reference, by Jo Bell Whitlatch
- Chapter 6, Impact and Opportunity of Digital Reference in Primary and Secondary Education, by R. David Lankes
- Chapter 7, Image Intermediation: Visual Resource Reference Services for Digital Libraries, by Abby A. Goodrum
- Chapter 8, Education for Digital Reference Services, by Linda C. Smith
- Chapter 9, Exploring the Future of Digital Reference through Scenario Planning, by Scott Nicholson

The final chapter was not part of the symposium but constitutes another form of synthesis from the papers. Where chapter 1 presents the research agenda as it currently stands, chapter 9 explores how the field of digital reference might move forward. In this paper, the author uses Schwartz's model of scenario planning to explore the feasibility of the proposed research agenda, the placement of the work presented here, and other opportunities for researchers in digital reference.

Taken as a whole, this book is part of a living process. It represents both an artifact of a point in time, a beginning, as well as an implied promise to innovate and understand for the future. Although the current research agenda identifies more gaps in our understanding than areas of agreement, it is hoped that this book will provide a starting point, one that will lay a foundation for great things to come. Now the hard work begins.

Chapter 1
The Digital Research Agenda

R. David Lankes
School of Information Studies, Syracuse University

This chapter represents the digital reference research agenda. It defines digital reference and states the central question in digital reference research as: How can human expertise be effectively and efficiently incorporated into information systems to answer user questions? This central question is broken down into question components and assumptions, which then are used to contract a research agenda in the form of a matrix with significant areas of needed research identified.

Introduction
For the purposes of this book, a research agenda is defined as a reference document that seeks to indicate:

- the scope and scale of a phenomenon;
- what is known about a given phenomenon under investigation;
- what gaps are recognized in the understanding of a phenomenon; and
- a common belief of the priorities of filling in the gaps in understanding.

It is at once an objective description of a field of inquiry and a political document that seeks to focus the attention of the research and practitioner community.

Throughout this book, the reader will find thoughtful explorations of aspects of digital reference, and associated research topics and approaches. Chapter 1 seeks to take these inputs, in combination with the resulting discussions of the scholarly and practitioner community, and create a cohesive framework for exploration. It further seeks to operationalize this framework into a series of relations to other domains of knowledge, theory and practice, and a series of specific research questions.

A Working Definition of Digital Reference

Many terms are used to describe the study and practice of digital reference (e.g., virtual reference, real-time reference, chat reference, real-time chat reference, and live reference), all of which share a central concept: the use of software and the Internet to facilitate human intermediation at a distance. This centrality can be seen in the definitions of digital reference in use within this book:

> "Digital Reference Services are Internet-based services that employ human experts or intermediaries to provide information to users." Whitlatch

> "Digital reference is a service that provides users with answers to questions in a computer-mediated environment." Pomerantz

> "Digital reference services seek to enhance the ability of users to locate needed information through the work of reference librarians providing both direct and indirect services. While one aspect of digital reference services involves assisting users in accessing digital library resources, digital reference services encompass any reference services provided over the Internet and can involve use of print as well as digital resources." Smith

> "Digital reference refers to a network of expertise, intermediation, and resources put at the disposal of a person seeking answers in an online environment." Lankes

Although these definitions vary, they have common themes. The first is the concept of intermediation. The second is the concept of question answering. The third, naturally, is that this question answering and intermediation occurs in a digital environment. What is not self-evident in these quotes, and yet is apparent in both the practice of digital reference and the conduct of research studies and methods in digital reference, is the necessity of human intermediation. Digital reference does not refer to so-called self-help searching or to the field of automated question answering as seen in the TREC Question Answering track (http://trec.nist.gov/). Although these areas certainly are related (as is discussed later), they do not encompass the unique nature of digital reference, human-intermediated question answering in a digital environment. This, then, is the working definition used throughout this agenda: the use of human intermediation to answer questions in a digital environment. It should be noted, however, that this definition does not rule out partial automation of the question-answering process, as discussed by McClennen and Pomerantz; rather, it places automation in service of human answering.

The Central Question in Digital Reference

A definition is necessary, but insufficient, to create a research agenda. A definition is sufficient to identify a field or practice but lacks analytical ability to define the shape and direction of the field. Any domain of inquiry is predicated on a central question. This question both provides boundaries to the unique nature of a discipline and situates the domain in the realm of other streams of exploration. In the specific case of digital reference, this central question must identify why digital reference is different from both traditional library-based reference research and digital library research. Of course, it also must define how it is related to these domains (as well as to information retrieval and computer-mediated communication).

A Thought Experiment for Digital Reference

At the research symposium that is the basis of this book, William Arms posed the issue of a central question in the form of a provocative "thought experiment" that I will replicate here.

Suppose a prestigious academic institution has just hired a new president. To welcome the president, each discipline within the university selects its outstanding, world-class researchers to extol the accomplishments of the schools. In the fields of chemistry or physics, the university may select Nobel Prize winners that have unlocked fundamental operations in nature. The economics department may select a scholar who has forwarded the understanding of complex markets; the education school selects a researcher who has forwarded the understanding of language acquisition. The point is that not only can each school determine a "star" who has made a fundamental contribution to knowledge in their field, that contribution can also be recognized by the other disciplines.

Now, hypothetically speaking, the "school of digital reference" selects a scholar who has not only made a fundamental contribution to digital reference, but whose contribution is recognized across the whole of the university as meaningful and important.

The question—What was that contribution? What question did that scholar answer that was fundamental enough to define a field and powerful enough to be recognized as significant beyond the field of digital reference? It is this challenge that must lie at the center of digital reference, or it is simply a practice or an application of existing knowledge.

Digital Reference: The Central Question

The central question of digital reference is how can human expertise be effectively and efficiently incorporated into information systems to answer user questions. This central question has several components and assumptions to be examined.

Question Components
Question components are defined as key areas of understanding needed to

explore digital reference and from which deeper understanding can be drawn and studies can be conducted to further the understanding of the central question. They are the atomic units of inquiry that may be shared by many disciplines but, in combination, are unique to the study of digital reference. For example, the "Question" and "Answer" components certainly have great relevance to the field of information retrieval, and "Efficiency" and "Effectiveness" are core to the study of economics. The combination and specific application create a unique question, whereas their application to other domains situates the field of digital reference within the larger edifice of human knowledge. The author identifies five question components for digital reference:

Component 1: Human Expertise
What is the nature of human expertise in a system? It is proposed, for further exploration, that expertise exists on a continuum from subject knowledge to process knowledge. *Subject knowledge* is the understanding of a core collection of facts and their interrelations, such as the field of chemistry where the facts range from natural laws to molecular structures. *Process knowledge* is defined as the ability to manipulate a system to achieve a desired result where core understanding of the system's content is not required. In digital reference practice, these two extremes are often typified as scientists with ready and extensive knowledge of a domain and librarians with information-seeking skills to inform that domain. It is assumed that the placement of a given individual, or even knowledge domain, may shift on the continuum of subject to process knowledge based on context of application. Certainly, in the field of library and information science, as an example, the process knowledge of librarians constitutes the subject knowledge of the field.

Component 2: Efficiency and Effectiveness
How can the costs and benefits of digital reference be measured and assessed? In this context, efficiency and effectiveness are defined in economic terms where an ideal state may be defined (the most effective service) against the most parsimonious use of available resources (e.g., time, money, staff, and so on). This intertwined relationship between outcome and resources expended makes this issue particularly difficult. It is posited for further examination that the proper balance between these two variables is context dependent. The central research issue related to effectiveness and efficiency seems to be identifying cogent variables in both measuring these variables and identifying relevant context conditions to arrive at an optimal balance.

Component 3: Information Systems
What is the proper configuration of technologies and resources to produce a required output? The concept of information system used in the digital reference definition can be characterized as a special case of a general system

(Bertalanffy 1968), where the input to the system is a user question, the process involves human expertise, and the output is an answer. The author restricts the examination of information systems in the realm of digital reference to networked and digital systems. That is to say that, although so-called analog resources may be used in part of a digital reference system, as a whole the system is seen in the context of a digital interaction where, at the very least, the input to the system is digital. Although, to date, digital reference research has approached the information systems in digital reference as both rational systems (as typified in chapter 4 by McClennen) and complex systems (Lankes 1998), no position is taken in this research agenda. Rather, this question component refers generally to discovery of the necessary and sufficient architecture of an information system (in respect to digital reference) and the means of interrelating the structural aspects of that architecture.

Component 4: Questions

What is the nature of user input to a digital reference system? The analysis of "questions" as expressions of a user need or cognitive gap is a rich area of exploration (Dervin and Nilan 1986). This question component refers specifically to the identification, classification, and use of questions. It is posited that questions are an imperfect representation of an information need by the user (Taylor 1968). Research on questions, then, seek to identify the sufficiency of questions as expression of need (their isomorphism to cognitive state), the inherent nature of question types (an ontology of user needs and/or their expressions), and the means by which true information needs can be discovered and/or bounded (i.e., question negotiation).

Component 5: Answers

What set of information and in what form can that information be bundled to satisfy an information need? Like questions, answers are an imperfect medium used in knowledge transfer from a recognized source of expertise to a recognized point of information need. Unlike a question (operationalized as a user expression), however, answers involve two parties: the transmitter (the "expert") and the receiver (the "user"). As such, answers would seem to be extremely context sensitive. If *answer* is defined as "information that meets a user need," it is operationalized by user determinations and evaluations. On the other hand, if *answer* is defined as "accurate data produced in response to user need," it is the transmitter of information (human or automated) that operationalizes and evaluates system results. This dichotomy of definition is often referred to as user perspectives versus system perspectives. This agenda notes the issue for further research without supporting one stance over the other.

Question components are derived from the expression of the question itself. As such, they are explicit. The next section explores the implicit facets of the central question in digital reference, the assumptions.

Assumptions
Assumptions are implicit components of the central research question in digital reference: How can human expertise be effectively and efficiently incorporated into information systems to answer user questions? Assumptions are the necessary conditions to ask the question or, at the very least, to see the question itself as significant. Just as with question components, assumptions should be both testable and provocative. That is, they should be susceptible to theoretical and empirical scrutiny as well as provide a departure point for further research and examination. The author identifies two assumptions in the central question of digital reference:

Assumption 1: Human Expertise Is Useful to Incorporate into Information Systems

If human expertise is not necessary in the ongoing functions of an information system, there is no need for the exploration of digital reference. A few bounding elements are needed in this assumption. The assumption is not that all information systems require ongoing participation of human expertise. This would be false on its face. Clearly, the majority of information systems function without the inclusion of experts. From search engines to automatic teller machines, users are clearly able to successfully engage systems without the guidance or presence of a human intermediary.

This assumption is specific in the means of inclusion of human expertise. In the exploration of digital reference, human expertise is the object of the system (users engage an information system to gain access to human expertise) and a means of providing information to users, not in the design of the system. Every system utilizes human expertise in its design and construction; in digital reference, human expertise is exposed to the user for access and engagement.

With this assumption in place, research questions are needed that seek to uncover the utility of human expertise. What value does ongoing inclusion of human expertise add to the system? Some proposed values for further exploration include:
- Providing a familiar, human touch in a complex, overwhelming, or intimidating computing environment, where the value is not simply in the information provided, but the mode in which it is presented.
- Taking advantage of the human ability to provide synthesis, where the user is able to span systems, information sources, opinions, and presentations in order to provide context provision. The two aspects of this value would be operational, where humans can simply span system boundaries, and cognitive, a human's ability to match a user's cognitive framework to a system's framework.
- Using digital means to elicit tacit knowledge held by an expert. Tacit knowledge refers to information (facts, opinions, procedures, and so on) that has no documented form that is normally gained from human experience.

• Providing instruction and restatement, where a human can offer a wide range of information coding and depth that a system may be unable to replicate. This includes the ability not only to decode information provided by a system, but also to impart the methods of system operation to the user and relate that operation to some larger context or user pursuit.

This list does not seek to be exhaustive. Rather, it lays out current hypothesis and beliefs concerning values. It is anticipated this list will be refined, augmented, and possibly prioritized with future research. It also is assumed that the value will shift based on system context and that research is needed to identify cogent contextual variables that relate to the value of human intermediation and expertise.

Assumption 2: The Digital Nature of Digital Reference Systems Provides a Significant Differentiating Context

As will be discussed, there is a close relationship between the domain of digital reference and other allied domains such as information retrieval, digital libraries, and reference theory. In many ways, digital reference was born out of the marriage of several lines of investigation and practice, but this assumption implies that digital reference provides a unique set of questions, components, and approaches. In essence, the whole of digital reference is greater than, or in this case different from, its component progenitors.

This assumption does not preclude the adoption of knowledge from analog systems (so-called traditional library-based reference). It recognizes, instead, that digital reference differs from traditional reference in three significant ways:

• Whereas traditional reference work is founded primarily on an oral tradition with little concern for reference artifacts, digital reference is centrally concerned with reference artifacts from a primarily textual context. As such, much of digital reference explores the creation of reference artifacts (previously asked questions, knowledge bases, questions as quanta that can be transferred between institutions).

• Digital reference research and systems are defined and bounded by human participation and intermediation. Whereas traditional reference (primarily operationalized in library settings) spans intermediation, collection development (building and maintaining the reference collection), and resource creation (pathfinders), digital reference focuses on human intermediation, perhaps more accurately referred to as human answering. This is not to say that digital reference systems and services do not include aspects of collection development and product development (discussed in chapter 2) but, rather, that the domain of digital reference is centered and bounded by human intermediation.

• Digital reference expands on the central concept of traditional reference practice's emphasis on referral to include subject expertise and primary knowledge. Whereas reference research has concentrated on evaluation and question negotiation, particularly with regard to human intermediation, there has been an implicit assumption that reference sources (the human expertise of the system) are process experts guiding users through a collection (a library collection, the Internet, electronic databases, and so on). Digital reference, in large part because of the participation of the AskA community, has expanded on and, in some cases, supplanted these assumptions to where the user interacts directly with the collection, but that the collection is a collection of human subject experts. Although this is not a fundamental difference of theory, it is a significant departure in practice.

The assumption of significant difference should be testable through a comparison of significant variables in analog human-intermediated systems and digital reference systems. The author does not take a strong stance that digital reference is a fully distinct field from reference. Clearly, operation systems have demonstrated that existing reference services can migrate and cofunction in digital systems. Rather, the author argues that defining digital reference as a subdiscipline of reference provides little analytic power and ignores the stated sustentative differences in reference and digital reference practice as well as the ability to see digital reference in light of other "parent" domains, such as digital libraries. Ultimately, every field can be seen as related to virtually any other domain of inquiry. (After all, many would argue that biology is a subdiscipline of chemistry and chemistry is a subdiscipline of physics, which may well have its roots in philosophy.) This complex relationship will soon be explored.

Another community may ask what the difference is between digital reference and traditional customer service. The author posits that the primary difference between these two fields is the existence of a common referent. In customer service, there is some common, third-party referent that is a vital part of the conversation. Whether a product (software, furniture, electronics, and so on) or a service (cellular service, a performance, plumbing, and so on), both user and expert share a common experience that bounds their interaction. In digital reference, on the other hand, the only shared framework is the question being asked. In many cases, the use of the information must be negotiated along with the question itself. Digital reference must have at its center the creation of a common context, whereas in customer service this framework is assumed. This has led to customer service work's concentration on efficiency and answer reuse, whereas digital reference has focused on issues of intermediation and question negotiation. Certainly, methods of efficiency gains may be shared by these two domains (particularly in terms of software development), but the core assumptions between the two fields diverge significantly.

A Digital Reference Research Framework

The combination of question components and assumptions constitutes a digital reference research framework. This framework differs from a model of the digital reference process (Pomerantz et al. [forthcoming]) or the systems view outlined by McClennen in chapter 4. Instead, it serves as a scaffolding from which models, system, research questions, methods, and studies can be derived, compared, and, in some cases, combined to further the larger understanding of digital reference.

This framework can be further refined in two ways, indicating significant approaches to the framework and the relation of the framework to other domains of inquiry

The Construction of Conceptual Lenses

The author adopts the metaphor of conceptual lenses to discuss how different researchers and different communities might reflect and build on the core framework of question components and assumptions. A "lens," then, embodies the values and concerns of a given community through which it acts. The action may be in research, in systems building, or simply in discussion.

The lenses presented in this section are meant to be significant, but by no means complete. It is assumed that there is effectively a limitless number of lenses defined by the nature of concern or preoccupation of a community, where a community may well be a single person. Thus, there are geographical lenses ("how does this question component work in Canada"), institution lenses ("what is the relationship of these assumptions to the work of Syracuse University"), personal lenses ("how can I incorporate these research questions in my study"), and so on.

Significant lenses in this document represent a set of clear and pressing issues (and values) in digital reference (as expressed by researchers and the practice community). They also represent broad concerns across a large potential audience of scholars, funding institutions, and practitioners.

Lens 1: Policy
In chapter 5, Jo BellWhitlatch defines policy as follows:

> Policy can be defined as how an organization sets its rules under which services are offered. You can also define policy as guiding principles or a course of action thought to be advantageous.

We see in this quote two aspects to policy: process and product. Policy as a process is the series of events and decisions that guide the operation and governance of a system (what McClennen calls a procedure). Policy as product is the outcome of this procedure and constitutes the implicit and/or explicit rules by which system components are held accountable. Products are seen as instruments and artifacts that represent the end point of a deliberative process. The policy lens is concerned with both the process and effect of organizational decision making and the actual products. For example, privacy has been expressed as a policy concern in digital reference (Whitlatch). The policy community seeks to understand the needed concepts to protect privacy as well as privacy statements (policies) that explain an organization's stance on privacy to its user base.

Lens 2: Systems

The systems lens seeks to understand the means by which technologies can be used to improve both the efficiency and effectiveness of digital reference. Note that this lens differs from the evaluation lens in that efficiency and effectiveness measures are often seen as secondary to the actual implementation of systems, standards, and procedures.

Two system models have been put forward as general means of understanding digital reference systems. McClennen seeks to define a digital reference system as a series of roles and the interaction among them. Lankes, on the other hand, presents a General Digital Reference Model modeled as a special case of a complex system. (See figure 1.)

Another central concern of the systems lens in digital reference relates to the mode of user–expert interaction. This discussion has been characterized as synchronous systems, where user and expert interact in real time, versus asynchronous systems, where users forward a question to a system where it can be processed by an expert at some later point (Pomerantz et al. [forthcoming]). This document posits that this distinction is an artificial dichotomy. This assertion is based on Bruce Croft's point raised at the Digi-

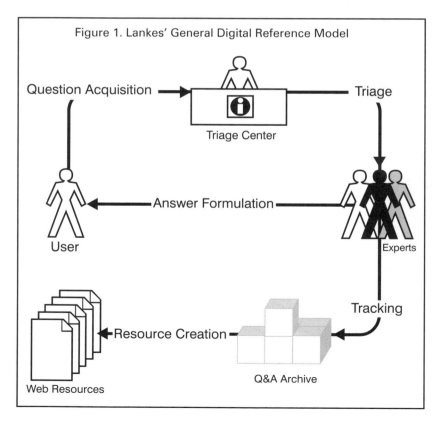

Figure 1. Lankes' General Digital Reference Model

tal Reference Research Symposium. In any digital reference system, there are real-time components regardless of whether the human component of that system is available in real time. In a Web-based system, the user enters a question in real time and the digital reference system processes it (saving it to a file, transforming it into an e-mail, or entering it into a database) in real time as well. The fact that an expert component of the system may not answer the question for some time can be seen as merely a lag in the total processing time of the system.

This view seems supported by Lankes and Shostack's (2002) examination of asynchronous systems, in which they sought to empirical-test an assertion made by Peters (2000):

> Although all reference service involves some sort of time delay, it appears to be true that, for most users and most reference needs, delays of more than a few minutes significantly diminish both the usefulness and use of a reference service that routinely incorporates such delays into its service architecture.

Lankes and Shostack found both high use and utility in at least one system, AskERIC, which involves delays of up to two business days.

The true question asked in a system lens is, What are the interaction requirements of the user in any given context? Does the nature of the question require real-time interaction with an expert? Do users need some form of immediate feedback (such as a "question received" message), regardless of expert interaction mode?

Lens 3: Evaluation

Evaluation in this document is defined as the means of determining value, with value being defined as the effect (impact either intended or unintended) of a given entity (a service, product, idea, and so on) as compared to its cost (resources consumed such as money, time, and space). At the center of evaluation is the determination of current balance between efficiency and effectiveness as discussed earlier in the section on question components.

The means of evaluating are assumed to be both qualitative and quantitative. They also are assumed to be (1) behavioral in attempting to assess the impact of human behavior and change in both user and expert abilities; (2) technical in the ability of a system to perform as designed and expected; and (3) economic in a digital reference system's ability to account for, and be an effective steward of, the resources used in delivering service.

There are currently several exemplars of an evaluative lens approach to digital reference. The largest is the quality study conducted by McClure et al. (2002). This study developed a series of metrics, performance measures, and quality standards to be used in the evaluation of digital reference services at a local level.

Lens 4: Behavior

The behavioral lens focuses on human attitudes and interactions with and within a digital reference system. These behaviors may relate to affective conditions or determine trends in digital reference usage. Janes (2000) provides an exemplary behavioral digital reference study. In his work, he studied librarians' attitudes toward digital reference work, finding a significant link between positive attitudes toward digital reference and time spent engaged in answering questions online.

As with question components, lenses are not unique to digital reference. It is even believed that their combination and approaches will be found in many contexts. For example, a grade school could be examined through the policy lens ("the utility of high-stakes testing"), a systems lens ("the role of instructional management systems"), and evaluative lens ("performance on high-stakes testing as influenced by the use of instructional management systems"), instruction (" the pedagogical approaches used in instructional management systems"), and behavior ("students attitudes to being required to use instructional management systems and then tested"). Because of the general nature of lenses and question components, these elements of the building framework provide excellent points of connection with other domains of inquiry.

Relation of Digital Reference to Other Domains

All fields have their progenitors and relationships to existing domains. These linkages (to past practice and current research) situate the investigation of digital reference. This section of the research agenda quickly lays out these linkages.

Progenitors

The digital reference field has two progenitors. The first is library and information science (LIS), particularly LIS practice. The second major contributor to digital reference is the category of Internet services known as AskA services, or expert question/answer sites.

Progenitor 1: Library Reference

Digital reference as an examination of the librarian's role in a digital environment began with e-mail reference efforts. These efforts extended the traditional core reference function of the library past the reference desk to the desktop. Users were able to ask reference questions and consult with trained librarians through e-mail. Still and Campbell (1993) provide an excellent example of early e-mail reference studies. This thread of digital reference concerns issues, such as the role of the librarian in cyberspace, the impact of distance service on the traditional reference interview, evaluation (McClure et al. 2002), and new skills needed by the information professional (Mardikian and Kesselman 1995).

Progenitor 2: AskA Services

The second progenitor to the current digital reference arena is that of AskA services (Lankes 1999). AskA services (so-called because services tend to take on names such as Ask-A-Scientist, Ask-A-Teacher, and so on) are expert-based question-and-answer services. They use networked communities of experts to answer questions via the Internet. AskA services have been extremely popular on the Internet and have given rise to a separate set of issues concerning system development and scalability.

Although these two lines of examination began in isolation, the author argues that the fields have effectively merged into a single research domain. Even though the practice of AskAs and libraries may still be somewhat distinct, these differences tend toward staffing, business models, and marketing. In terms of their core questions, they are emphases on common themes and both should find their issues addressed in this document.

Domain Linkages

Fields with a strong link to digital reference are defined in pragmatic and opportunistic terms. A strongly aligned field is one where a clear linkage or application of research results has been demonstrated (such as digital libraries) or one where core theory is essential for examination of digital reference research questions (such as systems theory). The author places digital reference in the context of six domains of inquiry:

Domain 1: Digital Libraries

Collier (National Science Foundation 2003) defines a digital library as "a managed environment of multimedia materials in digital form, designed for the benefit of its user population, structured to facilitate access to its contents, and equipped with aids to navigate the global network ... with users and holdings totally distributed, but managed as a coherent whole." In his paper, Pomerantz sees the domain of digital libraries as focused primarily on the process, tools, and theories in collections of digital materials. Certainly, recent digital library efforts, most notably the National Science Foundation's National Science Digital Library (NSDL), are operationalized as a set of distributed collections of resources with an available set of services that can provide functionality (at its most basic access to the resource) and context to the collections. In this framework, digital reference can be seen as a service available to builders and users of digital libraries.

Digital reference both draws from and influences digital library research. Certainly, fundamental digital library concepts such as metadata, networked information discovery and retrieval, and protocols have been adopted in digital reference (NISO 2003 and Pomerantz et al. [forthcoming]). Recent events seem to indicate that digital reference concepts also are having an impact on digital libraries. This includes adopting digital reference as a core service of the NSDL as well as the subtle redefinition of digital library as a set of collections and services operating virtually in parallel to a digital library as a set of resources accessed through services (from simple browsing services to complex visualization services). Discussions of this have happened within NSDL as well as within the advent of so-called Web services architectures.

Domain 2: Information Retrieval

The *World Book Dictionary* defines information retrieval (IR) as "the science that is concerned with the gathering, manipulation, classification, storage, and retrieval of recorded knowledge." In operation, IR research has focused on the use of inherent textual and/or media elements of documents for location and manipulation. It also has been solely concerned with the automation of this process through the use of software algorithms. Certainly, there are strong parallels between the fields of IR and digital reference. The difference between IR and digital reference has already been explored under the central question of digital reference (specifically, the inclusion of human expertise). However, much of the intermediation provided by digital reference requires the use of IR tools, and thus these fields are closely akin. In addition, a portion of the digital reference literature (primarily using the systems lens outlined previously) is devoted to appropriate levels of automation. That is to say, whereas digital reference is founded on the principle of human intermediation (versus IR's focus on computer mediation), many researchers are seeking to isolate the unique human contribution to the system and use computing to handle repetitive or programmable functions within a digital reference system.

Domain 3: Reference and Library Science

As has been previously discussed, digital reference is closely aligned to library science and the reference practice. Certainly, key concepts in reference research can be brought to bear on digital reference. Most notable of these concepts are the question negotiation (Taylor 1968) and open-ended questioning (Dervin and Nilan 1986). This open approach is one of the strong differences between digital reference and traditional closed systems such as help desks and customer support systems.

Moreover, there is some guidance from library science practice and evaluation. Certainly, RUSA's Behavioral Guidelines (1996) provide a template for the development of new online behavioral norms and studies. Likewise, library evaluation (Hernon and McClure 1986) has already provided the basis for research in the digital reference environment (McClure et al., 2002).

Domain 4: Computer Mediated Communication

Some groundbreaking work on digital reference in a multimodal reference environment has been done using Computer Mediated Communication theory (Southwick 2001). This study points the way to looking at digital reference within the broader concepts of computer-mediated communication with reference intermediation as a special case of guided communication (versus free-form conversation). It is believed that such expansive views of digital reference as one means of either communication or help will prove ripe for exploration and research.

Domain 5: Systems Theory

To date, significant work has been done to tie digital reference into systems theory. This includes special cases of systems such as complex systems (Lankes 1998). Much more work can be done looking at subsets of the digital reference system as a complex and dynamic system. For example, research is already under way (Croft, Lankes, and Koll 2002) on using complex inductive techniques to model expert profiles in digital reference. It is believed that similar approaches deserve investigation in the digital reference knowledge bases and routing systems.

Domain 6: Education

As stated in Lankes, education has been a widely supported arena for digital reference. However, there is much work to be done in tying digital reference practice to education theory and evaluation. For example, can inquiry-based learning take advantage of digital reference research to improve learner performance? Can digital reference research aid in a constructivist paradigm?

There are some ties to other fields that are either self-evident or have been identified as existent. These include looking at digital reference as a social and behavioral activity (for example, Janes's studies of librarians' attitudes toward digital reference). They also include linkage of digital reference research to the fields of economics, psychology, and law. These areas are mentioned briefly in the section on conceptual lenses in this chapter and throughout this book.

An Initial Digital Reference Research Framework

Taken as a whole—the question components, assumptions, conceptual lenses, and domain linkages, the author presents an Initial Digital Reference Research Framework. This framework seeks to map out an initial set of investigations concerning digital reference. It is assumed that this framework will be both augmented and revised as more work is done. The initial framework is shown in figure 2

The Research Agenda

The previous sections have created a map of ideas and relationships in digital reference. They represent the intellectual effort of synthesis, synthesizing what is currently known and sought in digital reference research. This final section seeks to list immediately identified research questions. These questions come from the chapters of this book, issues identified at the Digital Reference Research Symposium, and from the general field (primarily through

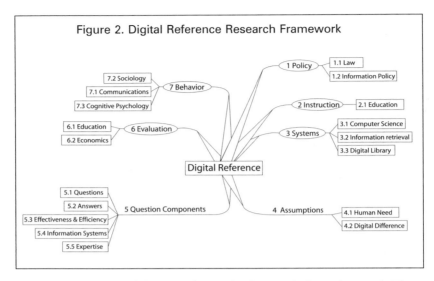

Figure 2. Digital Reference Research Framework

DIG_REF Listserv and the annual virtual reference desk conferences). These questions are meant to be relatively short term, operationalizable, and subquestions of the primary research question in digital reference: how can human expertise be effectively and efficiently incorporated into information systems to answer user questions.

They are organized in a matrix drawn from the Digital Reference Research Framework constructed previously. (See table 1.) Although domain interconnections are not explicitly stated, it is assumed that these domains will aid in the determination of methodology, reporting, and, potentially, theory development.

This matrix is far from complete. It represents an opportunistic view. Empty cells do not represent a lack of research potential but, rather, a lack of immediately identifiable research projects. It is assumed that this matrix will change over time as some research questions are answered and new questions are identified. Further discussion of these research areas and questions can be found throughout the remaining chapters of this book.

Moreover, it is hoped that this matrix can be converted into a sort of road map, filling in the cells with citation and data as digital reference research proceeds.

Conclusion

This chapter has built a map of uncertain terrain. This map to existing concepts and work in digital reference, as well as the fuzzy borders to the broader world of information and computer science, is a first step toward understanding digital reference at a deep and fundamental level. Although it does not provide an answer to Dr. Arms's thought experiment, it does provide a start point for arriving at that answer.

Table 1. Research Agenda Matrix, Organized by Question Component and Conceptual Lens

	Policy	Systems	Evaluation	Behavior
Human Expertise				
The Value of Human Expertise What does a user and/or system gain by the inclusion of human expertise and mediation?	What level of staff expertise and training is required to provide high-quality digital reference services?	How can the output of digital reference be incorporated into digital collections?	What are the perceived values of human expertise by the users (e.g., familiarity of a human voice, content expertise, process expertise, instruction)?	Do users phrase questions differently when they know a human intermediary is involved?
The Functions of Human Expertise What is the scale and scope of human involvement in digital reference services?		What is the relation of question answering to other roles such as knowledge-based construction?	How are non-question-answering functions of human expertise measured and evaluated?	
Efficiency and Effectiveness				
Cost What is the cost of human expertise in a digital reference system?	What are the limits to service provided to the users (e.g., providing answers versus citations)? What are the methods for determining these limits (e.g., are these limits context dependent or universal to digital reference services)?		What are the metrics and standards needed to evaluate costs in digital reference? What factors must be considered in a cost equation (e.g., staff time, resource expense)? Do these measures change with the digital reference setting (e.g., library, AskA) or scale (e.g., local settings versus consortium services)?	Does the knowledge of cost effect use of the system (e.g., are users willing to pay for digital reference services)? How can a digital reference market or service assign cost to a question as a priory (i.e., before a question is answered)?

Table 1. Research Agenda Matrix, Organized by Question Component and Conceptual Lens

	Policy	Systems	Evaluation	Behavior
Efficiency and Effectiveness				
Benefits — What are the benefits of human involvement in digital reference systems?			What are the metrics and standards needed to evaluate benefits in digital reference (e.g., return use, satisfaction)?	
Value — What is the necessary level of value demanded by users in digital reference systems?		What level of automation can be brought to bear in digital reference services?		Can users make value judgments in digital reference services?
Information Systems				
System Components — What is the proper configuration of technologies and resources to produce a required output?	What policies are needed to ensure the appropriate use of digital reference systems? How can digital reference systems be constructed to protect individual privacy and licensing while achieving maximum benefit for an intended community?	What are the required components of a digital reference system?	What are appropriate performance metrics for system evaluation?	How do experts and users interact in a digital reference system? What are the needed skills and training for digital reference system acquisition?
System Models and Architectures — How can digital reference systems be represented and conceptualized?		Is there a single high-level architecture that represents both real-time and asynchronous systems? What is the value of inductive versus deductive system construction?		

Table 1: Research Agenda Matrix - Organized by Question Component and Conceptual Lens

	Policy	Systems	Evaluation	Behavior
Information Systems				
Interoperability How can digital reference services find and ensure proper levels of interoperability?	What policies and policy instruments are need for service collaboration?	What technical standards are needed to ensure service interoperability (e.g., NISO Networked Reference Committee[2])?		
Questions				
Questions as Input What is the nature of user input to a digital reference systems?		Are there identifiable taxonomies of questions? Do these taxonomies provide functional and computational power in digital reference systems (e.g., for automatic question routing)?	Do questions to a digital reference service qualitatively change in nature over time (e.g., become harder or more synthesis oriented)?	What digital aids can be provided to users to better phrase their information need?
The Reference Interview[3] What is the role of the reference interview in digital reference?		How do digital reference systems best elicit the information need of users (e.g., through human-to-human reference interviews, Web forms, or serial e-mail)? Does this method change based on information need?	What is the current state of practice in digital reference question negotiation? What are the best indicators and measures of success of the reference interview?	

Table 1: Research Agenda Matrix - Organized by Question Component and Conceptual Lens

	Policy	Systems	Evaluation	Behavior
Answers				
Satisfaction What set of information and in what form can that information be bundled to satisfy an information need?	What policies are needed to bound answer types in a service (e.g., copyright)?	How can systems automatically match user questions to appropriate answer types?	What measures are needed to evaluate "right" and "wrong" answers in digital reference?	What are the necessary components of an answer needed to meet a user's information need?

1. See McClure et. al. (2002) for an example
2. See http://www.niso.org for more information
3. It has been a long-standing practice of librarians to conduct an interview constituted of a series of open- and closed-ended question to identify the compromised information need (cite Taylor). In a digital environment, some services have attempted to replicate this human-to-human exchange in so-called real-time systems. Other services, primarily asynchronous services, have sought to replicate this process through the use of Web forms or iterative e-mails.

Digital reference is important. This is based on literally thousands of hours and millions of questions from the field. It is an area that is rooted and expanding in practice. It is vital that the research community keep pace and bring its unique perspective to the field. Without careful, patient, and thoughtful examination of digital reference by scholars and action researchers, practice will continue to leap and lurch without full realization of the digital reference implications and contributions.

The time has come to put digital reference to the test. This test is twofold: Does digital reference improve the information lives of its users, and can the research community aid practice? The first question is obvious; the second is more political in nature. It reflects not only the continued tension between doing and understanding, it also touches at the often-tense relationship between practice and research. If the research community ignores the trends and resource allocation of practice (in both libraries and the digital library communities), it will find itself marginalized. Such a divorce between practice and research hurts both.

References

Bertalanffy L. 1968. *General System Theory: Foundations, Development, Applications.* New York: Braziller.

Croft, B., R. D. Lankes, and M. Koll. 2002. "Question Triage for Experts and Documents: Expanding the Information Retrieval." Unpublished article, funded proposal to NSF. Available online from https://www.fastlane.nsf.gov/servlet/showaward?award=0226144.

Function of the NSDL. National Science Foundation–funded research project. Available online from https://www.fastlane.nsf.gov/servlet/showaward?award=0226144.

Dervin, B., and M. Nilan. 1986. "Information Needs and Users." *Annual Review of Information Science and Technology* 21: 3–31.

Hernon, P., and C. McClure. 1986. "Unobtrusive Reference Testing: The 55 Percent Rule." *Library Journal* 111(7): 37–41.

Janes, J. 2000. "Digital Reference: Services, Attitudes, and Evaluation." *Internet Research* 10(3): 256–58.

Lankes, R. David. 1998. *Building & Maintaining Internet Information Services: K–12 Digital Reference Services.* ERIC Document Reproduction Service no. ED 427778. Syracuse, N.Y.: ERIC Clearinghouse on Information & Technology.

Lankes, R. David. 1999. "As KA's: Lesson Learned from K–12 Digital Reference Services. "Reference and User Services Quarterly 38 (1).

Lankes, R. D., and P. Shostack, P. 2002. "The Necessity of Real-time: Fact and Fiction in Digital Reference Systems." *Reference and User Services Quarterly* 41(4).

Mardikian, J., and M. Kesselman. 1995. "Beyond the Desk: Enhanced Reference Staffing for the Electronic Library." *Reference Services Review* 23(1): 21–28.

McClure, C., R. David Lankes, M. Gross, and B. Choltco-Devlin. 2002. *Statistics, Measures and Quality Standards for Assessing Digital Library Services: Guidelines and Pro-*

cedures. Syracuse, N.Y.: ERIC Clearinghouse on Information & Technology.

National Science Foundation. 2003. National Science, Technology, Engineering, and Mathematics Education Digital Library (NSDL). Available online from http:// www.ehr.nsf.gov/ehr/due/programs/nsdl/. (Accessed 25 March 2003).

NISO. 2003. Networked Reference Services. Available online from http:// www.niso.org/committees/committee_az.html.

Peters, T. A. 2000. "Current Opportunities for the Effective Meta-assessment of OnlineReference Services." *Library Trends* 49(2) 334–49.

Pomerantz, J., S. Nicholson, Y. Belanger, and R. D. Lankes. Forthcoming. "The Current State of Digital Reference: Validation of a General Digital Reference Model through a Survey of Digital Reference Services." *Information Processing &* Management.

RUSA. 1996. "Guidelines for Behavioral Performance of Reference and Information Services Professionals." Available online from http://www.ala.org/rusa/ stnd_behavior.html.

Still, J., and F. Campbell. 1993. "Librarian in a Box: The Use of Electronic Mail for Reference." *Reference Services Review* 21(1): 15–18.

Southwick, S. B. 2001. *Understanding Intermediation in a Digital Environment.* Ann Arbor, Mich.: UMI.

Taylor, R. 1968. "Question Negotiation and Information Seeking in Libraries." *College & Research Libraries* 29: 178–94.

Chapter 2
Integrating Digital Reference Service into the Digital Library Environment

Jeffrey Pomerantz
School of Information and Library Science, the University of North Carolina at Chapel Hill

The difference between a digital library and a library with which a digital reference service is affiliated is discussed, and digital reference in these contexts is defined. Several issues are involved in integrating digital reference service into a digital library environment, but two that are unique to the intersection between digital libraries and digital reference: collection development of previously answered questions, and presentation of specialized subsets of the materials in the digital library's collection. These two issues are explored.

Introduction

Digital libraries have traditionally been defined primarily as collections of electronic resources, with little thought to services that may be offered to increase the usability of those collections. On the other hand, digital reference has traditionally been defined primarily as a service, with little thought to ways in which that service can contribute to and increase the value of a library collection. As both digital libraries and digital reference services mature, both are coming to realize the benefit of joining forces and integrating digital reference service into the digital library environment.

Physical libraries and desk reference services have been inseparable for more than a century. There can be little argument that a library's collection makes it possible to provide reference service and that reference service increases the value of that collection for the library's patrons. Both digital libraries and digital reference are mature services in their own right: A number of technologies to support both of these services have developed and are continuing to evolve, and both have spawned well-established communities of research and practice. To date, however, these two mature services have matured independently of one another. As both digital libraries and digital reference services continue to evolve, it has become increasingly clear that, as physical libraries and desk reference services are necessary counterparts, each maximizing the utility of the other, so, too, digital libraries and digital reference services seem to be necessary counterparts. This chapter explores the issue of integrating digital reference service into digital libraries.

Before any discussion of integrating digital reference service into a digital library can proceed, one point needs to be clarified: The difference between a digital library and a library with which a digital reference service is affiliated. This may seem an obvious distinction, but if it were indeed so, this discussion would be unnecessary. There is quite a bit of inconsistency in the literature concerning just what exactly both a digital library and a digital reference are. Before this discussion can address integrating digital reference into digital libraries, it is necessary to understand what is being proposed to be integrated into what.

Digital Libraries Defined

Buckland (1992, 5–6) makes a distinction between three types of libraries: the paper, automated, and electronic library. The distinction among these types of libraries rests on both the materials in the collection and the means by which technical services functions are performed. The paper library contains primarily a paper collection and is administered primarily via paper; the automated library contains primarily paper, but administration is performed electronically; and in the electronic library, both the collection and the administration are electronic. This distinction is shown in table 1, reproduced from Buckland.

Table 1. Technological Bases of Library Operations and Materials		
	Technical Operations	Library Materials
Paper Library	Paper	Paper
Automated Library	Computer	Paper
Electronic Library	Computer	Electronic media

These days, most libraries in the developed world are automated libraries; more and more libraries are utilizing computing to perform technical services functions, but the primary collection of most libraries is still a print collection. Indeed, the paper library may be on its way to extinction in the developed world: Few libraries these days do not offer at least electronic access to their catalog, and many libraries maintain digital collections—or at least access to others' digital collections—in addition to their physical collections. On the other hand, the electronic library is yet to come: Many libraries maintain digital collections, but there are few entirely digital libraries, with no physical counterpart.

Buckland's distinction between types of libraries is according to the amount of technology used, and for what purpose. Greenstein and Thorin

(2002) differentiate between types of digital libraries according to the age and sophistication of the digital library project. They make a distinction between three types of digital libraries as well: the young, maturing, and adult digital library. The young digital library is just being launched, is in the planning and experimentation phase, and is "at some level deploying innovative technologies to deliver very traditional library services" (p. 4). Although every digital library project develops differently, Greenstein and Thorin state that there are patterns to this development. The maturing digital library, then, is no longer as experimental as in its younger days, has "acquired core competencies and technical understanding," and is focused primarily on "integrating digital materials into the library's collections and on developing... the policies, technical capacities, and professional skills needed to sustain it" (p. 12). Greenstein and Thorin argue that all digital libraries currently in existence are of one of these two types; they claim that the adult digital library, one that is in no way "organizationally or functionally distinct from the library as whole," has yet to arrive.

The difference—or lack thereof—between a digital collection and a digital library needs to be clarified at this point. A digital library might be taken to be equivalent with Buckland's electronic library: technical services performed electronically, and an entirely electronic collection. However, this describes an extremely small set of libraries at this point in time. In practice, the term "digital library" is generally used synonymously with the term "digital collection" to describe any aggregation of electronic materials, whatever the format and whatever the electronic materials' relationship to physical materials. Take, for example, some of the larger and older digital libraries. The Association for Computing Machinery's Digital Library (http://www.acm.org/dl/) is a collection of all ACM journals, magazines, and proceedings—a digitization of preexisting print materials. The Perseus Digital Library (http://www.perseus.tufts.edu/) is actually a collection of several collections and includes collections of texts (including transcriptions of papyri) and digitizations of maps, photographs, and other media. The Alexandria Digital Library Project (http://www.alexandria.ucsb.edu/) is based on existing maps and geospatial information but expands on those materials through the use of variety of media and technologies. The American Memory Project (http://memory.loc.gov/) contains electronic versions of materials in the Library of Congress archives. These collections (1) are all collections of electronic materials, (2) are all based (to different degrees) in preexisting physical media, and (3) all refer to themselves as digital libraries.

The upshot is that there is no meaningful distinction between the terms "digital collection" and "digital library." At present, there are few exclusively electronic collections (that is, with no corresponding physical collection); moreover, electronic collections based on physical collections are referred to as digital libraries. For the purposes of this discussion, the terms "digital library" and "digital collection" are treated as equivalent. The definition of digital library used in this discussion is just this: A digital library is any collection of electronic resources that patron can access electronically. A digital library may therefore be exclusively electronic, with no physical counterpart, or it may be a digital supplement to, or extension of, a physical library or library collection.

Levy and Marshall, presaging Greenstein and Thorin's adult digital library, suggest that "the better word for these evolving institutions is 'libraries,' not 'digital libraries'" (1995, 83) because there is no function that a digital library serves that is not served by a physical library. In addition, physical libraries have always contained information objects of a variety of media in their collections. Levy and Marshall suggest that the rise of digital libraries is simply the latest historical development in the several-thousand-year history of developments in libraries: The media in which information objects are stored and accessed is largely irrelevant; and what fundamentally makes a library is the existence of a collection and mechanisms for accessing it.

Borgman makes Levy and Marshall's point for them—that there is no meaningful distinction between physical and digital libraries—by offering perhaps the broadest definition of digital library in the literature. She states that digital libraries are (1) "a set of electronic resources and associated technical capabilities" (1999, 234) that are (2) designed to serve a specific user community. Remove the word "electronic" from this definition, and Borgman could be describing a physical library, which is almost certainly her point.

In addition, Borgman raises an important point: the existence of a user community. All libraries serve a community of patrons: Public libraries serve the local neighborhood, town, or city community; academic libraries serve the community of faculty, staff, and students of an educational institution; special libraries serve the community of employees and users of the organization of which they are a part. No library can be all things to all people; due to constraints on both physical space and budgets, a collection can only contain a finite amount of material, so any library must selectively choose what materials to acquire and maintain. Such decisions are performed "within the context of the institution's missions and programs and the needs of the user populations served by the library" (Association for Library Collections & Technical Services 2002, ¶ 2). This selective collection development is as true for digital libraries as for physical libraries. (The major difference between physical and digital libraries in this regard is that the "space" in which a digital library's collection is stored is virtual and not physical. A digital library has no concerns about the cost of shelf space; instead, a digital library must be concerned with the cost of disc space. Even digital collections are necessarily finite.)

Digital Reference Defined

The foundations of modern reference work were laid by Samuel Swett Green in 1876 in his seminal essay, "Personal Relations between Librarians and Readers." Since then, the practices involved in providing reference service have been refined, but there has never been much disagreement about the central purpose of reference service, which is to answer questions and to provide resources to enable patrons to answer their own questions.

In a physical library, reference question answering is most often performed face-to-face at a reference desk. Telephone reference has been offered for decades by many desk reference services, so a tradition of providing reference service in the absence of a face-to-face interaction with a patron is well established. In digital reference services, face-to-face service is obviously unfeasible (at least until videoconferencing starts being used in reference). Early digital reference services discovered, however, as had telephone reference services, that face-to-face interaction is not necessary for answering patrons' questions; this function could be performed perfectly well in a mediated environment. Perhaps even more important than the existence of technological mediation, however, is the fact that many digital reference services utilize asynchronous communication media: early services were entirely e-mail based, whereas many services nowadays continue to utilize e-mail and also use the Web. Patrons may submit a question to an asynchronous service at any time, and that question can be answered when a librarian is available to answer it.

Indeed, it did not take early digital reference services long to realize that asynchronous reference offered decided advantages. Specifically, the librarian could take his or her time in composing a complete answer (rather than being held to an impatient patron's time constraints) and the question could be forwarded to the individual best qualified to answer it (rather than the librarian who happened to be at the desk when the patron walked up).

In the early to mid-1990s, reference services began to appear on the Internet that were not affiliated with a library, either physical or digital. Lankes (1998) refers to services of this type as AskA services, "such as Ask-A-Scientist" (p. 9), because most services of this type specialize in a particular subject—for example, art (Ask Joan of Art), education (AskERIC), mathematics (Ask Dr. Math), oceanography (Ask Shamu), and so on. AskA services are to desk reference services what digital libraries are to physical libraries: They more or less recreate the services offered by their physically constrained cousins, but those services are offered primarily electronically.

Since the mid-1990s, a new type of reference service has begun to appear online: so-called real-time reference service. Whereas more "traditional" digital reference makes use of asynchronous methods of communication, real-time reference makes use of synchronous methods of communication, such as chat environments, instant messaging, and graphical co-browsing. Prior to the development of these technologies, synchronous computer-mediated reference had been experimented with in MUD and MOO environments.

The purpose of providing this history is to illustrate the fact that digital reference has many faces (synchronous and asynchronous, affiliated with a library and stand-alone), utilizing a variety of different technologies. The common thread tying these diverse types of services together is that they all employ computer-mediated forms of communication to both receive questions and provide answers. This fact provides the definition of the term "digital reference" that is used in this discussion: Digital reference is a service that provides users with answers to questions in a computer-mediated environment.

The purpose of these opening sections has been to clarify the difference between a digital library and a library with which a digital reference service is affiliated. This can now be accomplished. A digital library, as stated above, is any collection of electronic resources that a patron can access electronically. A digital reference service provides users with answers to questions in a computer-mediated environment. The upshot is that there is no meaningful difference between a digital library and a library with which a digital reference service is affiliated, except insofar as there is a difference between a digital and a physical library. Some physical libraries have affiliated digital reference services, and some of these physical libraries also maintain digital collections. There is no reason why a digital reference service could not be affiliated with an entirely digital library (Buckland's electronic library). Thus, digital libraries and digital reference services are two separate entities, and the existence of one has no necessary impact on the existence on the other. In this way, digital libraries and digital reference services are like physical libraries and desk reference services: Few physical libraries are without a reference desk, but such a library could conceivably exist with no detriment to the library (the detriment would be to the patron). Similarly, although desk reference services are traditionally thought of as being subsumed within physical libraries, reference-like services exist in many other contexts (help desks, information and referral services, and so on) and are therefore not confined to the library environment.

Thus, this discussion, in proposing the integration of digital reference into digital libraries, is making only a small stretch from the history (or histories) of libraries and reference. Physical reference services are integrated into physical libraries, and digital reference services are similarly integrated into physical libraries. Although digital reference services have not been integrated into digital libraries, there is no reason, either technological or historical, why it would not be possible, even logical, to do so. This is entirely in keeping with Levy and Marshall's (1995) suggestion that digital libraries are simply a new form of libraries. Viewed in that light, the integration of digital reference into digital libraries is a logical and natural step in the evolution of both services.

The State of the Art

It is unclear how many digital reference services exist. The Virtual Reference Desk Project maintains a list of AskA services called the AskA+ Locator (http://www.vrd.org/locator/subject.shtml), which, as of this writing, contains more than a hundred services. Bernie Sloan maintains a list on his personal Web site of more than ninety email-based reference services offered by public and academic libraries (http://www.lis.uiuc.edu/~b-sloan/e-mail.html). It is important to note, however, that neither of these lists claims to be comprehensive, and it is impossible to know how many services are *not* listed. White found that 45 percent of libraries at institutions categorized as Master's (Comprehensive) Universities and Colleges I and II by the Carnegie Foundation for the Advancement of Teaching offered either e-mail- or Web-form-based digital reference service (2001, 175). Two years previously, Goetsch, Sowers, and Todd (1999) had found that 96 percent of Association of Research Libraries (ARL) members' libraries offered electronic reference. These two examples surveyed highly constrained populations, and again, it is impossible to know how many services were not surveyed. One's sense, however, is that most libraries in the United States these days—public and academic, with or without digital collections—have an affiliated digital reference service.

Most digital libraries, on the other hand, are not making any effort to incorporate reference service. Some digital libraries have a collection of documentation and other help materials, and some even have a help desk staffed by humans, generally to answer technical questions about the use of the collection. Neither of these, however, rises to the level of a reference service, the purpose of which is to answer users' content-related questions using materials from the collection. Indeed, the Institute of Museum and Library Services' (IMLS) document, "A Framework of Guidance for Building Good Digital Collections," states explicitly that "services have been deliberately excluded as out of scope" (IMLS 2001, Introduction ¶ 4) of the discussion of building good collections.

The IMLS Framework document goes on to state, however, that "it is expected that if quality collections, objects, and metadata are created, it will be possible for any number of higher-level services to make use of these entities" (IMLS 2001, Introduction, ¶ 4). The National Science, Technology, Engineering, and Mathematics Education Digital Library (NSDL) (http://www.ehr.nsf.gov/ehr/DUE/programs/nsdl/) utilizes the IMLS Framework to guide best practices for the NSDL's collections. And, in keeping with the call for "higher-level services," one of three tracks in the NSDL initiative is the services track. The goal of this track is to "increase the impact, reach, efficiency, and value of the digital library" (Directorate for Education and Human Resources Division of Undergraduate Education 2002, 6) through the development of services in support of both users and collection providers.

The author is currently involved in a project at the Information Institute of Syracuse at Syracuse University entitled "Integrating Expertise into the NSDL: Putting a Human Face on the Digital Library," funded under the precursor to this NSDL initiative, NSF grant 01-55. The objective of this project is twofold: to build an operational digital reference service to support the

NSDL, and to conduct research into creating a more effective digital library service through the integration of reference services into digital library collections.

Many of the other projects funded under NSF grant 01-55 are concerned with building collections in specialized subject areas (e.g., biology, earth systems, health education) or with exploring ways to integrate various practices or technologies into collections (e.g., generation of metadata for collection materials, peer review of collection materials). These projects are on the cutting edge of digital libraries. They are integrating various forms of multimedia into collections; developing new ways to create, organize, and access content; and developing innovative practices for managing that content. The work being done as part of the Integrating Expertise into the NSDL project, when the NSDL is launched, will increase the usefulness of these collections and the innovative work that is being done as part of those projects by making use of human intermediation. Indeed, the Integrating Expertise into the NSDL project attempts to emulate the practice of physical libraries, which have historically had the goal of increasing the value of their collection through human intermediation.

Issues Involved in Integrating Digital Reference Service into a Digital Library Environment

In the course of working on the Integrating Expertise into the NSDL project, we have discovered that several issues are involved in integrating digital reference service into a digital library environment. These issues may be divided along two dimensions. The first dimension concerns those issues that are unique to the situation of a digital reference service in a digital library environment and those that are applicable to digital reference service in general. The second dimension along which these issues can be divided concerns those issues that are unique to the situation of a reference service in an electronic environment (though not necessarily a digital library environment) and those that are carryovers of issues from the world of physical reference services.

The first of these "carryover" issues is that of expertise: Who should be allowed to be an "expert" and to answer questions. In the arena of desk reference services, this issue has generally been couched as one of credentials: Should only professionally trained librarians be allowed to provide reference service, or should paraprofessionals be allowed to provide some services? Whitson (1995) presents this distinction as one of differentiated versus undifferentiated service. *Undifferentiated service* assumes that any individual providing reference service can perform any task and answer any question, thus requiring that all reference librarians be highly trained. *Differentiated service*, on the other hand, allows for different individuals to perform different tasks in the reference process, thus allowing professional librarians to perform the more complex tasks and answer the more difficult questions, while paraprofessionals perform those tasks that require less professional training. Although some of the tasks may be different in a digital reference service than in desk reference (McClennen and Memmott 2001), the same issue exists of who is the most appropriate individual to perform any given task.

A closely related issue to that of expertise and credentials is the issue of expertise in what. Ferguson and Bunge state that the "traditional" reference desk is staffed by reference experts as opposed to subject experts (1997, 255–56). This practice probably evolved because of the immediacy of the reference transaction at a reference desk: A patron may approach the desk with any question, and with time constraints to boot, so the librarian at the desk must be able to answer any question relatively quickly. As mentioned above, this requires that all reference librarians be professionally trained reference experts. Particularly in public or academic libraries, it is not feasible that a subject expert routinely staff a reference desk, as it cannot be assumed that patrons will approach the desk with questions within that subject area. In special libraries, such as law or medical libraries, it is more reasonable to assume that patrons' questions will fall within particular subject areas. Still, even in special libraries, the librarians staffing the reference desk are generally professionally trained reference experts with a subject specialization. In an asynchronous digital reference service, on the other hand, it is more feasible to have subject experts answering patrons' questions, not only reference experts with subject specializations, but experts in specific subject areas—physicists, volcanologists, oceanographers, educators, artists, you name it. This is truly Whitson's notion of differentiated service: Who could be more appropriate to answer a question on, say, oceanography than an oceanographer? Sadly, just as not every subject expert is a good teacher, not every subject expert is likely to be a good reference provider. Thus, a balance must be struck between the use of reference experts and subject experts to answer patrons' questions.

A third issue that has carried over from the world of physical reference services is that of referrals: Under what circumstances should one digital reference service forward a question to another? Desk reference services have always received questions that are outside their scope of service. Rather than simply turn a patron away without an answer, reference librarians will often refer the patron to another reference service or organization for which the question is in scope. This situation is no different in an electronic environment: Digital reference services also receive questions that are outside their scope of service, and they may refer a patron to another service or organization. The difference between referrals from a desk reference service and from a digital reference service is who has the responsibility for completing the referral. In desk reference, if a patron is referred from one service to another, the burden is generally on the patron to contact that other service. In digital reference, on the other hand, if a referral is made, it is not the patron who is sent from one service to another, but the patron's question. Thus, the burden is on the service that received the question from the patron to perform the referral and on both services to work out the details of the exchange.

It is in the details of the exchange of a question that the issue of referrals takes on an aspect unique to the situation of a reference service in an electronic environment. In the electronic environment, forwarding a question from one digital reference service to another is technically simple; every e-mail application has a Forward button and an address book. What is more complex is developing policies and standards to govern the making of referrals. Such policies are discussed in depth by Whitlatch in chapter 5 of this book and so is not discussed further here. Lankes (1999) describes the Question Interchange Profile (QuIP), a proposed standard for passing additional information between digital reference services along with a question: information about the patron, about the forwarding service, and so on. Formalization of such a standard is currently being carried out by the National Information Standards Organization (NISO) Networked Reference Services Standards Committee AZ (http://www.niso.org/committees/committee_az.html). The challenge of developing standards for networks on collaborating digital reference services is discussed in depth by McClennen in chapter 4 and so is not discussed further here.

Another issue unique to the situation of a reference service in an electronic environment is that of automation: Which processes involved in providing digital reference service may be—and which ones should be—automated? One of the processes for which automation has been employed is that of forwarding questions between digital reference services, and to the appropriate expert within a service, called triage (Lankes 1998; Pomerantz, Nicholson, and Lankes [forthcoming]). Kresh (2000) describes the Collaborative Digital Reference Service (CDRS, now called QuestionPoint), which utilizes a software algorithm to triage questions to participating digital reference services by matching questions with the most appropriate service based on profiles of the participating services. Another process for which automation has been employed is that of question answering. Bry (2000) describes the Mad Scientist Network (MADSci), which utilizes a CGI script to search the MADSci archives of previously answered questions for potential answers to users' submitted questions. Both QuestionPoint's and MADSci's automation, however, are in the early stages of development. QuestionPoint's profiles of participating services contain only a few criteria, including hours of service, subject strengths and scope of collections, and types of patrons served (Kresh 2000), and so the triage algorithm can only match questions with services based on these few criteria. MADSci's question-answering algorithm matches "approximately 63 percent of questions... with archived files"; however, "only 25 percent of users deem their questions answered by this process (15 percent of all submitted questions)" (Bry 2000, 118). The automation of triage and question answering will require some improvement before it is likely to be widely adopted. Moreover, triage and question answering are only two processes out of the many involved in providing digital reference service. It is possible that other processes may be amenable to automation as well, for which automation has not yet been attempted. Further research and development of algorithms is required to push this automation forward.

The final issue addressed in this section is a carryover from the world of physical reference services, but also from the world of physical libraries in general. This issue is that of serving audiences that are not the primary patron community of a library or reference service. Libraries and reference services have always, to a greater or lesser degree, served nonprimary patron communities. Especially in public libraries, one never knows who will come in and want to use the library's resources. Even academic and special libraries, which may not grant physical access to unaffiliated individuals, may still receive telephone calls or e-mails from individuals outside the organization. This is even more of an issue for digital reference services because users have easy access to services with which they are not affiliated via the Internet. Indeed, it may be no more difficult for a user to access a remote library's digital reference service than it is to access a local service. Silverstein and Lankes (1999) describe four sets of audiences and users that may wish to gain access to a library's resources:

- *Core* users are familiar with a specific resource.
- *Secondary* audiences have great knowledge of an agency's scope but are unfamiliar with a given resource.
- *Topical* users are familiar with an agency's topic on a broad scale.
- *General* users are the general public with minimal understanding of the agency or its resources.

Lankes argues that as Internet adoption has increased, the number of secondary, topical, and general users seeking access to all organizations' resources has correspondingly increased. But these users' increased access to the resources of digital reference services is especially taxing on those resources because one of the primary resources provided by digital reference services is human intermediation. The increase in the number of secondary, topical, and general users seeking access to the resources provided by digital reference services gives new life to the old question faced by physical libraries and reference services: How many resources should be allocated to supporting patrons from nonprimary communities? This is another policy that must be decided on to govern the operation of the digital reference service and/or digital library.

Table 2 presents the issues involved in integrating digital reference service into a digital library environment, along the two dimensions presented above. The issues in the three shaded cells have been discussed in this section. These issues are important to the integration of digital reference service into a digital library environment, as well as to the operation of a digital reference service in general, regardless of its affiliation with a digital library. However, two issues (listed in the unshaded cell) are unique to the intersec-

Table 2. Issues Involved in Integrating Digital Reference Service into a Digital Library Environment		
	Carry-overs from Physical Reference	Unique to an Electronic Environment
Applies to digital reference service in general	• Expertise and credentials • Reference vs. subject expertise • Referrals	• Policies and standards to govern referrals • Automation
Unique to digital reference service in a digital library environment	• Serving non primary patron communities	• Collection development • Creation of resource collections

tion of digital libraries and digital reference service: collection development and the creation of resource collections. Taken in a broad sense, these issues are universal to libraries of all types, digital and physical. However, for the integration of digital reference service into a digital library, these two issues take on unique aspects. The rest of this chapter is a discussion of the unique aspects of these issues.

Collection Development
One of the most important tasks undertaken in any library—physical or digital—is collection development, for without a collection there is no library. As McColvin stated in his classic text on collection development, "book selection is the first task of librarianship... the ultimate value of a library depends upon the way in which the stock has been selected" (1925, 9). Of course, collection development in a digital library is not primarily concerned with book selection but, rather, with the selection of both physical items to digitize and "born-digital" materials in any number of electronic formats. The point remains valid, however, that the value of a library is the value of the materials in its collection. Replace the word "book" with the word "material" or "resource," and McColvin's quote is as accurate today as the day it was written. McColvin might have said that a library's collection is the sum total of that library's book holdings; however, a more modern definition is that a library's collection is the sum total of that library's holdings of materials in any media format.

The value of a library—physical or digital—may take any or all of several forms: economic, moral, philosophical, and so on. In addition, this value may be different for different patron communities and purposes that the library serves. The assignment of value is complex in many ways, but such assignment is not the concern here. Let it simply be acknowledged that libraries have value, in a variety of forms, and that that value (or those values) is both determined and created by the library's patron community.

As McColvin stated, one of the factors that most directly determines the value of a library—value in all its forms—for its patron community is its collection. And the library's collection is directly determined by its collection development policies. Every library develops a collection development policy that guides the selection of materials in its collection. Collection development policies codify (1) the scope and maintenance of the collection, (2) the ways in which the collection should contribute to the mission of the organization of which they are a part, and (3) the scope of the patron community (or communities) of the library and the utility of the collection for the library's patrons.

Collection Development in Digital Libraries
Collection development policies are as important to digital libraries as they are to physical libraries, a fact acknowledged in the IMLS Framework:

> Collections principle 1: A good digital collection is created according to an explicit collection development policy that has been agreed upon and documented before digitization begins (IMLS 2001, collections section, ¶ 2).

Note that this definition assumes that a collection is developed through digitization—that is, through the creation of electronic versions of physical materials. A more inclusive definition of a digital library's collection would include the selection of "born-digital" materials.

That said, the IMLS Framework (IMLS 2001) then goes on to describe how a digital library's collection development policy should address the three purposes, mentioned above, that any collection development policy must fulfill.

In the past, digital libraries ("young" digital libraries, at any rate) have been concerned only with the mission of the organization of which they are a part. Young digital libraries, according to Greenstein and Thorin, experiment with different technologies in an attempt to better support the mission of the organization through technology. As services come to be increasingly of concern to digital libraries, however, there is a correspondingly greater concern with the needs of the library's user community. As a digital library matures, it "seems to rediscover users. ... As the integration of new technologies begins to transform the library and the possibilities for constructing innovative networked services, libraries see a pressing need to engage users and to reassess their interests and needs" (Greenstein and Thorin 2002, 14).

Indeed, a digital library is in many ways like an academic or a special library in that its primary patron community is fairly well defined. Whereas public libraries are by definition public, and therefore serve a heterogeneous patron community, an academic library, for example, serves a reasonably well-defined community of scholars and students in their research and studies. Special libraries also serve a specific user community within an organization and build collections relevant to that community. Similarly, the specific patron community that a digital library is designed to serve is often fairly well defined. For example, the Association for Computing Machinery's Digital Library is available only to ACM members, database subscribers, and individuals affiliated with organizations that maintain a subscription. The Alexandria Digital Library, on the other hand, is freely available to the public but is in fact probably used primarily by those with an interest in the fairly narrow domain of geospatial information. These, like many other digital libraries, have to date concentrated on supporting the mission of the organization through serving their primary user community. As these digital libraries have matured, however, they have begun to more deliberately engage users. The ACM digital library, for example, has introduced, among other things, *The Bookshelf*, a service for creating custom collections, and *DL Pearls*, "a monthly column that will help you get the most out of the vast resources contained in the ACM Digital Library" (http://portal.acm.org/dlpearls/dlpearls.cfm).

Another service that a digital library may offer is to provide reference service. Indeed, Greenstein and Thorin might argue that it took physical libraries many centuries to move from being "young" to being "maturing." Although other user services may have a longer history, it is generally acknowledged, as mentioned above, that reference service as we know it today dates back to 1876 and Samuel Swett Green. It has taken digital libraries far less time to begin to offer reference services.

The Special Collection

In a physical library, the reference department usually has its own special collection, a subset of the collection in the whole library. Reference collections generally consist of two parts: the entire reference collection, and the ready reference collection, which is a subset of the entire reference collection consisting of those information resources most frequently used at the reference desk. The relationship between all of these collections is represented in figure 1.

Digital libraries, like physical libraries, are dependent on their ability to be searched effectively by the patron. Physical libraries organize information resources on the shelves according to some classification scheme and provide a catalog (an OPAC or card catalog) as the interface through which the patron can match his or her information need with the library's organizational scheme. In a digital library, however, the organizational infrastructure is more or less hidden from the user (regardless of whether the user is a patron or a librarian). Thus, there is no need for the two-step process necessary in physical libraries in which the patron must first determine the unique identifier of an information resource (the call number) and then use that identifier to find the

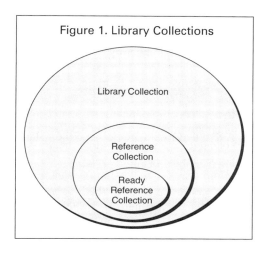

Figure 1. Library Collections

Library Collection

Reference Collection

Ready Reference Collection

resource itself. Instead, a search of a digital library can provide the user with a citation and a link directly to an information resource (as in a search engine) or with the resource itself (as in a full-text database).

In a reference service affiliated with a digital library, therefore, there may not be any need for separate reference or ready reference collections. Desk reference services maintain reference collections because it is unfeasible for a reference librarian to make use of the library's entire collection when performing reference work—and the larger the library, the more this is the case. In a digital library, however, no information resource is any more or less accessible than any other information resource. In effect, the entire collection in a digital library may be considered to be the reference collection. All information resources are equally accessible; it is not necessary to separate out the most frequently used resources. Every information resource is a reference source.

On the other hand, it may be desirable not to separate out but, instead, to gather together in some way frequently used or popular resources from the digital library's collection at large. One of the primary reasons that a physical library's ready reference collection is separated out from the rest of the collection is because it is more convenient for reference librarians to have certain resources at their fingertips. Similarly, some digital libraries maintain collections of related resources for ease of access. The Internet Public Library (IPL), for example, maintains a list of "Subject Collections" on topics presumably commonly asked of the service (http://www.ipl.org/div/subject/). The Perseus Digital Library, for another example, maintains an "exhibit" on Hercules (http://www.perseus.tufts.edu/Herakles/) and another on the ancient Olympics (http://www.perseus.tufts.edu/Olympics/). At the time of this writing, the American Memory Project was featuring a collection on the origins of American animation (http://memory.loc.gov/ammem/oahtml/). In this way, it is possible for a digital library to create a special collection simply by providing easy access to a select subset of the resources in the collection, putting resources at users' fingertips, metaphorically, "nearby." Indeed, any number of such special collections may be created by "slicing" the entire collection in a variety of ways. Moreover, these special collections may change over time based on trends in the resources in the collection that are frequently accessed, current hot topics, or any number of other criteria.

The creation of such special collections is one more service that digital libraries may offer in order to engage users. In a digital library offering reference service, one user population that must be engaged is the population of reference librarians. From a certain point of view, reference collections are simply a special case of special collections: A special collection is a specialized subset of the materials in a library's entire collection, and a reference collection is one such possible subset. The primary user community for a reference collection is reference librarians, and the purpose of a reference collection is to make a certain body of information and set of information resources available. The primary user community and the purpose of a special collection depend on the nature of the materials in the collection and the policies of the library: Some special collections may be in circulation, and some may be in archives and inaccessible to the casual user. In a digital library, however, there is no concern with materials becoming worn or ruined through circulation, and therefore all materials may be made accessible to all users. Because of this difference between physical and digital special collections, the term "resource collections" is used from here on to refer to special collections of materials in a digital library.

In order to provide useful and timely information to the patron, one of the most important tasks of digital reference service (indeed of any reference service, digital or physical) is to provide access to the material in the collection in ways that are appropriate to the patron's particular needs. There are two ways in which this can be done: proactively and responsively. Creating resource collections responsively may be the easier of the two. Trends in the questions received by the digital reference service may be tracked so that frequently asked questions and hot topics may be discovered and resource collections created to meet the information needs that gave rise to those trends.

On the other hand, it is possible, to a certain extent, to anticipate patrons' information needs. For example, it is reasonable to assume that during the modern Olympics, a certain percentage of the Internet-using public would be interested in the ancient Olympic games and would go to the Perseus Digital Library, a digital library that has a particularly strong collection of material on Greek and Roman history, to find information on that topic. And indeed, the Perseus Digital Library made an "exhibit" on the ancient Olympics available around the time of the 1996 games in Atlanta, Georgia. For another example, as I write this, it is September 11, 2002, and the American Memory Project has dedicated its Today in History page (http://memory.loc.gov/ammem/today/), which usually presents events that happened at least twenty-five years in the past, to the events of and commentary on September 11, 2001, a topic on which there is certainly a great deal of interest.

It behooves any digital reference service to get to know its patron community—core through general users—and the information needs of that patron community. Indeed, knowing the community of users of the library and the requirements of that community is one of the first tenets of collection development. And knowing that community, resource collections can be created to meet specific information needs, just as the collection as a whole is developed to support the needs and uses of the community.

The Reference Transaction as Information Resource

There is a long tradition of capturing statistics at desk reference services as a means of evaluating the reference transaction. Often these statistics are nothing more complex than tick marks on a reference transaction slip. A great many forms exist for capturing data about the desk reference transaction, however, and a great many variables and statistics have been utilized in analyzing the reference transaction (Crews 1988; Saxton 1997). Still, even the best reference evaluation form does not capture the actual reference transaction, merely a thin representation of it. And worse still, such forms are generally filled out after the transaction has been completed and are frequently based on the librarian's reconstruction of the transaction.

It took the digital reference community no time at all to realize that this was a problem that simply did not exist any longer: The nature of electronic media allowed the *entire* reference transaction to be captured, verbatim, and completely unobtrusively. The transaction itself, conducted electronically, creates an artifact that may be stored until deliberately deleted. For example, an e-mail-based transaction may create a "thread" of e-mail messages that may be associated through the subject line, while chat-based transactions may create a log containing the entire conversation. This simple fact has two important implications. First, the reference transaction, once captured, may itself be utilized as an information resource. Second, the reference transaction may become in effect an annotation to any information resource that it refers to. This section addresses the first implication; the second implication is addressed below.

In digital reference services affiliated with a physical library, collection development works just the same as in any library. The fact that a physical library offers digital reference service does not necessarily have any effect on the library's collection development policies. The library presumably continues to acquire materials that support the needs and uses of its patron community. These acquisition decisions presumably continue to be made by an acquisitions department, constrained by budgetary limits and other practical considerations.

However, in digital reference services unaffiliated with a physical library (as well as in those affiliated with a physical library above and beyond its physical collection), a collection can be developed directly in response to patrons' questions. A recent study performed by Pomerantz et al. (under review) found that 42 percent of digital reference services surveyed store question–answer pairs in a database or other archive. Thus, a service's experts may have access to an ever-growing pool of previously answered questions when working on an answer to a new question. Some digital reference services even make this archive publicly available, as, for example, does the MadSci Network (http://www.madsci.org), thus in effect treating the archive of previously answered questions as a collection like any other. (Such a collection of patrons' questions raises obvious privacy issues, such as whether or not to strip any information that could potentially identify the patron out of the question-and-answer pair. The issue of privacy as a matter of policy is discussed by Whitlatch in chapter 5 of this book and so is not discussed further here.)

In developing such a collection, digital reference services turn the traditional relationship between collection development and reference service on its head. Physical libraries traditionally have been built around a collection or collections to which reference has been one way of providing an interface. Although reference has been an important component of physical libraries, it is not a component without which the collection would cease to exist or grow. In digital reference services that archive previously answered questions, on the other hand, this collection is itself a result of, and could not exist without, the service. Thus, instead of providing an interface to a collection, the digital reference service becomes the source of the collection.

There are at least two ways in which the digital library's collection can grow as a result of archiving the reference transaction—through deliberate collection development and through incidental "accretion." Deliberate collection development might proceed as follows: One step in the digital reference process, according to Lankes (1998), is the tracking of data about questions that are received by the service, looking for trends and hot topics. By tracking trends, it might become clear that patrons are asking questions about, for example, amphibians, but the digital library's collection does not have many resources on amphibians. It therefore becomes clear (assuming that amphibians are within the digital library's scope) that the digital library must build up its collection of resources on amphibians. This may then be done deliberately by the digital library's collection development staff.

On the other hand, the incidental accretion of materials might proceed as follows: A patron asks a question about, for example, cows. In formulating an answer to this question, the librarian scans, say, some photos of different breeds of cows and a document about animal husbandry (in accordance with fair use, naturally). If they were not previously, these resources now are part of the digital library's collection because the reference transaction is archived and part of the collection. Thus, over time, materials "accrete" due to the fact that they are part of reference transactions. This form of collection development is not the result of a deliberate collection development decision but, rather, the result of demand by patrons for information on specific topics. However, librarians must be careful to ensure that any materials they add to the collection are within the digital library's scope of service. Even for this accretion of materials, which is only an incidental addition of materials to the collection, a collection development policy must be developed. And again, the traditional relationship between collection development and reference service is turned on its head as reference librarians become collection developers.

Collection Development of Previously Answered Questions

As discussed above, every information resource in a digital library is a reference source. And in a digital library in which previously answered questions are archived and made available to librarians and patrons, the reference transaction is itself an information resource. The question is, Is the reference transaction an information resource of the same sort as the main collection? Put differently, should the reference transaction be included in the digital library's collection, or should the archive of previously answered questions be a collection of its own, auxiliary to the main collection?

According to Levy and Marshal (1995), there is nothing privileged about any materials in a digital library's collection (or indeed in any library's collection): Library collections have always contained materials of many different formats, and those materials change over time. This would seem to be an argument for including the reference transaction in the main collection because doing so would be consistent with the multiplicity of formats and life spans of materials in a digital library's collections. On the other hand, including the reference transaction in the main collection runs contrary to the general practice of existing digital reference services, which maintain collections of some sort. Most such services maintain their archive of previously answered questions separate from their main collection. The AskERIC service, for example, provides access to the ERIC database (http://www.askeric.org/Eric/) and maintains a separate archive of questions commonly asked of the service (http://www.askeric.org/Virtual/Qa/archives/). There is a clear distinction between the materials in the ERIC database and the questions that have been answered by AskERIC.

Should the scope of the ERIC database be altered to encompass question-and-answer pairs? Probably not, as the scope of the ERIC database is "abstracts of documents and journal articles on education research and practice" (http://www.askeric.org/Eric/) and not questions and answers about education research and practice. However, this is a deliberate decision made by those responsible for collection development for the ERIC database. This question generalizes to all digital libraries, however: Should the scope of a digital library collection encompass question-and-answer pairs? The answer to this question is a decision that must be made deliberately and as a matter of policy by those responsible for collection development.

One unique feature of collection development decisions in a digital library is that there is no necessary separation between any two "locations" in an electronic environment. This is, in fact, part of the problem that has led to the long debate concerning the copyright issues involved in hyperlinking, started so dramatically by the 1997 case *Shetland Times Ltd. v. Wills* (http://www.jmls.edu/cyber/cases/shetld1.html). In this case, the Scottish newspaper *The Shetland Times* sued another newspaper, *The Shetland News,* to prevent that paper's "deep linking" to its Web site and, according to the *Times,* presenting content created by the *Times* as its own. The fundamental problem represented by this case is that it can be difficult to tell when following a link has caused a user to leave one site and be brought to a different site, thus sometimes making it appear (especially in a framed environment) as if the content from one site belongs to another.

The fact that there is no necessary separation between any two "locations" in an electronic environment means that any separation of a digital library's main collection and a collection of previously answered questions is purely artificial, the result of the presentation of these two collections. The *Shetland Times* case made this point about content on two different sites maintained by two different organizations, but the same is true of content on one site: Any separation of "collections" is purely in the design of the Web site. As mentioned above, AskERIC separates the ERIC database and its list of frequently asked questions, and this is accomplished by locating the links to these two collections under different menus on its Web site. Both collections are searchable, however, and a different design decision could have made both collections searchable via one interface.

Indeed, within the AskERIC Question Archive (http://askeric.org/Virtual/Qa/archives/), there are fourteen top-level categories, with many subcategories on which previously answered questions have been collected. AskERIC has created a set of resource collections on a variety of topics simply by "slicing" its collection of previously answered questions in a variety of ways. And these resource collections may change over time as new trends in the questions received by AskERIC are tracked.

In summary, the scope of the digital library's collection is a decision that must be made by those responsible for development of the collection. Part and parcel of this decision is the issue of whether or not to include previously answered questions in the collection. A subsequent decision, then, is how to present the materials in the collection or collections. Both of these decisions may include those responsible for collection development, the reference staff, and Web site designers.

The Reference Transaction as Annotation

It was mentioned above that in an electronic environment, the entire reference transaction can be captured verbatim. The second important implication of this fact is that the reference transaction may become in effect an annotation to any information resource that it refers to. For example, a user of a digital reference service may ask a question about astronomy, and the reference or subject expert who answers the user's question may provide citations for or links to information resources on astronomy. The reference transaction thus contains "pointers" to those particular information resources. Depending on whether the expert has said good or bad things about those information resources, that pointer may be for better or for worse (though, of course, reference experts generally only provide worthwhile information resources and only rarely provide outstanding negative examples).

This notion of pointers to information resources is, in fact, the principle on which the Google™ search engine works. The principle behind Google is that of "hubs" and "authorities." Authority documents are those that point to other documents, and hub documents are those that are pointed to by authorities. (Of course, in a hypertext environment such as the Web, a document may be both a hub and an authority.) The secret of Google's success is that it ranks authorities so that a pointer to a document from an "A list" authority, as it were, is more heavily weighted than a pointer from a "B list" authority. When a list of retrieved hits is displayed after a search, the hub Web pages with the greatest scores, based on the weights of the authorities that point to them, appear at the top of the list of retrieved hits, thus ensuring that the Web pages most linked to from "A list" authorities appear at the top of the stack (Brin and Page 1998). (For the moment let us ignore the fact that Google, like so many search engines these days, also sells its rankings, so that for a price one can be assured of being listed at the top of the list of retrieved hits [http://www.google.com/ads/overview.html].)

Although information resources in a digital library or a digital reference environment have not, to the author's knowledge, ever been treated as hubs and authorities, it is certainly possible to imagine it being done. It would be possible in this way to build a collection of the most popular information resources in a collection simply by "harvesting" the resources in the collection to which the greatest number of answered reference questions point, even ignoring the additional possibility of weighting these authorities. (Again, it is impossible to know whether an information resource is being referred to positively or negatively. As all academics know, one way to get cited is to be disagreed with.)

Some Web sites do something similar to this already by making available a list of the most heavily accessed Web pages on the site. This is fairly simple to do by analyzing the Web site's logs. However, this practice raises an interesting distinction. There are two ways to determine what the most popular or useful information resources in a digital library or a digital reference environment may be: those resources pointed to by reference or subject experts, and those accessed by users. These may not be at all the same; as any librarian knows, the materials most commonly used by librarians are not the materials with the heaviest circulation among library patrons, and vice versa.

Reference transactions thus may be viewed as annotations to the information resources in the collection to which they point. For example, a patron's question about astronomy is answered using documents A, B, and C in the collection. Another patron's question about the astronomer Edwin Hubble is answered using documents B, D, and E. Clearly, document B contains information useful for answering questions about both astronomy in general and one specific astronomer. Over time, as reference transactions are archived, each information resource in the collection will develop a "profile," as it were, a collection of usage data from which it can be determined what types of questions or information needs a resource may be used to answer. Moreover, this profile will be the result of expert knowledge—what resources subject or reference experts have provided to answer specific questions. This profile contains metadata about the document and, as such, can be used for all of the purposes for which metadata are used—for organizing the materials in the collection, for standardizing the exchange of resources between collections, by information retrieval algorithms to rank a document in a list of retrieved search results, and so on.

Conclusion

Both digital libraries and digital reference services are complex entities with which a number of issues are associated. These issues may be divided along two dimensions:

1. those issues that are unique to the situation of a digital reference service in a digital library environment, and those that are applicable to digital reference service in general; and

2. those issues that are unique to the situation of a reference service in an electronic environment and those that are carryovers of issues from the world of physical reference services.

Out of these issues come a number of decisions (policy, standardization, technical, and so on) that must be made in order to set up and manage them and the services associated with them.

However, two issues are unique to the intersection between digital libraries and digital reference. These issues, although universal to libraries of all types, digital and physical, take on unique aspects for the integration of digital reference service into a digital library environment. These two issues are:

1. collection development of previously answered questions and any supplementary materials that are included in the answers to questions; and

2. presentation of "resource collections," specialized subsets of the materials in the digital library's entire collection.

Underlying the former issue is the process of annotation: As questions are answered using the materials in a digital library's collection, those answers become annotations to those materials. The nature of the electronic medium is such that previously answered questions may become documents and be archived as information resources in their own right. The existence of these annotations as information resources gives rise to the following collection development question: Do these annotations become a collection in their own right? In addition, if in answering a question a reference librarian uses an information resource that was not in the digital library's collection (by scanning it, say), does that resource become part of the collection? These are decisions that affect the nature, content, and growth of the digital library collection and thus must be set by collection development policies for the digital library. If the digital library's collection development policy is to collect these annotations and supplementary materials, another policy question immediately follows: Should these annotations be made available to the digital library-using public or only to the reference staff affiliated with the library?

Underlying the latter issue is the presentation of materials in the digital library's collection to the patron. In an electronic collection, no information resource is any more or less accessible than any other information resource. Digital reference services have taken advantage of this by creating resource collections based on a variety of criteria, including hot topics, frequently asked questions or frequently used materials, and so on. The fundamental issue here is how to create these resource collections. They must be created both responsively and proactively. Trends in the questions received by the digital library must be tracked so that trends and hot topics may be discovered and resource collections created to meet the information needs that gave rise to those trends. In addition, the information needs of the digital library's patron community must be understood so that resource collections can be created to meet those needs ahead of time.

Both of these issues—collection development and presentation of resource collections—involve decisions that must be made on a case-by-case basis by each digital library and its associated digital reference service. As digital libraries increasingly come to have digital reference services affiliated with them, best practices will emerge in collection development and Web site design for different types of digital library collections and different scopes of reference service. Research will be required to determine what factors are relevant to different types of digital libraries in making these decisions. Digital libraries are only recently beginning to realize that they must integrate digital reference into the services they provide. More than a century of research and practice has explored the integration of desk reference into physical libraries, and much more work needs to be done to explore the intricacies of this integration.

References

Association for Library Collections & Technical Services. 2002. *Guidelines for ALCTS Members to Supplement the American Library Association Code of Ethics*. ALA. Available online from http://www.ala.org/alcts/publications/ethics/ethics.html.

Borgman, C. L. 1999. "What Are Digital Libraries? Competing Visions." *Information Processing & Management* 35(3): 227–43.

Brin, S., and L. Page. 1998. "The Anatomy of a Large-scale Hypertextual Web Search Engine." *Computer Networks* 30(1–7): 107–17. Available online from http://citeseer.nj.nec.com/brin98anatomy.html.

Bry, L. 2000. "Simple and Sophisticated Methods for Processing Large Volumes of Question and Answer Information through the World Wide Web." Pp. 111–23 in *Digital Reference Service in the New Millennium: Planning, Management, and Evaluation*, ed. R. D. Lankes, J. W. I. Collins, and A. S. Kasowitz. New York: Neal-Schuman Publishers Inc. Available online from http://www.neal-schuman.com/db/6/226.html.

Buckland, M. 1992. *Redesigning Library Services: A Manifesto*. Chicago: ALA.

Crews, K. D. 1988. "The Accuracy of Reference Service: Variables for Research and Implementation." *LISR* 10(3): 331–55.

Directorate for Education and Human Resources Division of Undergraduate Education. 2002. *National Science, Technology, Engineering, and Mathematics Education Digital Library (NSDL)* (Program Solicitation NSF-02-054). Arlington, Va.: National Science Foundation. Available online from http://www.nsf.gov/pubs/2002/nsf02054/nsf02054.pdf.

Ferguson, C. D., and C. A. Bunge. 1997. "The Shape of Services to Come: Values-based Reference Service for the Largely Digital Library." *College & Research Libraries* 58(3): 252–65.

Goetsch, L., L. Sowers, and C. Todd. 1999. *Electronic Reference Service* (SPEC Kit 251). Washington, D.C.: Association of Research Libraries Office of Leadership and Management Services.

Green, S. S. 1876. Personal Relations between Librarians and Readers. *American Library Journal* 1: 74–81.

Greenstein, D., and S. E. Thorin. 2002. *The Digital Library: A Biography*. Technical report no. 109. Washington, D.C.: Digital Library Federation Council on Library and Information Resources. Available online from http://www.clir.org/pubs/reports/pub109/pub109.pdf.

Institute of Museum and Library Service. 2001. *A Framework of Guidance for Building Good Digital Collections*. Washington D.C.: IMLS. Available online from http://www.imls.gov/pubs/forumframework.htm.

Kresh, D. N. 2000. "Offering High Quality Reference Service on the Web: The Collaborative Digital Reference Service (CDRS)." *D-Lib Magazine* 6(6). Available online from http://www.dlib.org/dlib/june00/kresh/06kresh.html.

Lankes, R. D. 1998. *Building & Maintaining Internet Information Services: K–12 Digital Reference Services*. ERIC Document Reproduction Service no. Ed 427778. Syracuse, N.Y.: ERIC Clearinghouse on Information & Technology.

———. 1999. *Question Interchange Profile*, version 1.01D (white paper). Syracuse, N.Y: ERIC Clearinghouse on Information & Technology. Available online from http://www.vrd.org/Tech/QuIP/1.01/1.01d.htm.

Levy, D. M., and C. C. Marshal. 1995. "Going Digital: A Look at Assumptions Underlying Digital Libraries." *Communications of the ACM* 38(4): 77–84.

McClennen, M., and P. Memmott. 2001. "Roles in Digital Reference." *Information Technology and Libraries* 20(3): 143–48. Available online from http://www.lita.org/ital/2003_mcclennan.html.

McColvin, L. 1925. *The Theory of Book Selection for Public Libraries*. London: Grafton. [Out of Print]

Pomerantz, J., S. Nicholson, and R. D. Lankes. Forthcoming. "Digital Reference Triage: Factors Influencing Question Routing and Assignment." *Library Quarterly*

Pomerantz, J., S. Nicholson, Y. Belanger, and R. D. Lankes. Under review. "The Current State of Digital Reference: Validation of a General Digital Reference Model through a Survey of Digital Reference Services." Forthcoming. *Information Processing & Management.*

Saxton, M. L. 1997. "Reference Service Evaluation and Meta-analysis: Findings and Methodological Issues." *Library Quarterly* 67(3): 267–88.

Silverstein, J. L., and R. D. Lankes. 1999. *Digital Reference Services and Centers at the United States Department of Education: Analysis and Recommendations.* Syracuse, N.Y.: U.S. Department of Education. Available online from http://iis.syr.edu/projects/ed_gov_rpt.html.

White, M. D. 2001. "Diffusion of an Innovation: Digital Reference Service in Carnegie Foundation Master's (Comprehensive) Academic Institution Libraries." *Journal of Academic Librarianship* 27(3): 173–87.

Whitson, W. L. 1995. "Differentiated Service: A New Reference Model." *Journal of Academic Librarianship* 21(2): 103–11.

Chapter 3
Question Negotiation in an Electronic Age

Joseph Janes
The Information School, University of Washington

This chapter briefly frames current digital reference discussion in the history of question negotiation in libraries. The author defines question negotiation beyond the reference interview to include self-searching and informal communications with friends and colleagues. The article then reviews the current state of the art in libraries and identifies issues faced by the digital reference community, including the use of detailed Web forms and the notion of time in digital reference. Finally, a series of research areas are identified, including researching which modes of question negotiation best match user needs, creating success indicators in the reference interview, and determining the possible level of automation for question negotiation.

Definition and Brief History

Although it is generally agreed that reference work in libraries began in the second half of the nineteenth century, what came to be known as the "reference interview" arose somewhat later. The generally acknowledged first article on reference (Green 1876) omits any mention of discussion between patron and librarian (despite mention in the title of "personal relations" between them) in favor of a rapid-fire series of scenarios where the librarian magically produces just the right item or direction in response to each person's request. It is difficult for the modern reader not to speculate on how many of Green's patrons went away happy and whether in fact any discussion or interview went on between them at all.

Many thanks to Lorri Mon, who has provided invaluable assistance and has conducted the research study discussed in the second section of this chapter. The results of that research will be published under her name. The author also expresses thanks to the subscribers to DIG_REF, specifically the people who participated in the reference interview thread last October, in particular, Sara Weissman at the Morris County Library, Camilla Baker at Canisius College Library, Pauline Lynch of AskERIC, and Patricia Memmott of the Internet Public Library.

More than twenty years later, Woodruff (1897) spoke for perhaps the first time of what generations of reference librarians have experienced: "The famous dictum, 'Speech was given to man to conceal thought,' is often forcibly brought to mind by the ingenuity with which visitors of the reference-room succeed in hiding their desires behind their questions." She went on to define the reference interview, without calling it that:

> the ability by skillful questioning, without appearance of curiosity or impertinence, to extract from the vaguest, most general requests, a clear idea of what the inquirer really needs. This faculty—a facility in reducing large, abstract demands to concrete terms ... stands in the equipment of a reference librarian only second in importance to the complete mastery of his tools (p. 67).

Early reference textbooks also stressed the difficulty but necessity of the interview. Wyer (1930) wrote that its two most salient features are mind-reading and cross-examination. He quoted a 1922 article that echoed Woodruff: "You see they will choke to death and die with the secret in them rather than tell you what they want." For one of the first times, he laid out what the necessary components of the interview are—what is desired, format, setting and history, how much is wanted, level of treatment from trivial to scholarly, when it is needed, and so on.

In his 1983 historical review, Charles Bunge believed that Margaret Hutchins, in the next great reference textbook (1944), coined the phrase "reference interview" and indeed Wyer never called it that. Hutchins's discussion of the interview describes the success of a reference encounter as depending on the proper relationship between the questioner, the librarian, the sources, and the question itself. "If any of these relationships is slighted, the work becomes lopsided. If the personal relationships are neglected, although a *correct* answer to the question may be found, it may nevertheless be unsatisfactory to the inquirer" (1944, 21), emphasis in original).

What follows is an era much more concerned with the communication aspects of the reference interview over its functionalism as a method of finding out an information need. The lodestone of much of that thinking is Robert Taylor's seminal 1968 article, "Question-Negotiation and Information Seeking in Libraries." There is much of interest in this paper, and I shall return to it shortly; for the time being, here is Taylor's definition of what he terms "a very subtle problem—how one person tries to find out what another person wants to know, when the latter cannot describe his need precisely" (p. 179). In one of the other significantly influential papers on reference interviewing, Dervin and Dewdney used a similar formulation, saying that "query negotiation [is] determining what the inquirer really wants to know." (1986, 506).

White discussed frameworks for analyzing and evaluating reference interviews in two articles. In the first article, she described four dimensions of the reference interview: structure, coherence, pace, and length. She said that the librarian has two concerns. The first concern is that of "obtaining information useful for carrying out specific tasks" (namely, identifying the information need and developing a search strategy) and the second is that of "using interviewing techniques that have a positive effect on the user's willingness to cooperate and thus an impact on the quality of the information he provides" (1981, 374). This framework is carried forward in her second article on interview evaluation, where she said that a "good" reference interview is "organized to achieve a particular outcome, … coherent, … progresses toward its goals speedily," and has two objectives, "identifying the information the client needs and gathering information to permit a successful search for that information" (1985, 77).

Two research papers of note provide more operational definitions of the reference interview. Lynch said that "[f]or the purpose of this study … dyadic communication units were considered as interviews only if the *librarian asked the patron* one or more questions" (1978, 126), underscoring the communication foundation of her research. Ross and Nilsen (2000) operated as follows:

> We counted a reference interview as having occurred if a clarifying question was asked at any time during the entire transaction by any staff member, including on a second attempt when the user started over with a second librarian. We counted not only well-formed open questions such as "What kind of information do you want on L. M. Montgomery/used computers/pine trees?" or "How much information do you want on this?" but also closed questions such as "Are you writing a paper on this topic?" (but not "Do you know how to use the catalog?"). We also counted responses that were not formally questions but that had the performance function of a question, such as repeating the key words of the user's statement and pausing strategically to encourage further elaboration (p. 150).

It is disheartening to report that Lynch found that only 45 percent of reference transactions included an interview (336 of 751); Ross and Nilsen found that 48 percent did (78 of 161), both based on what must be considered fairly meager and minimal definitions of interviews.

Taylor's article is easily one of the most influential and cited works in the library literature and contains much subtlety, nuance, and depth of thought. His work is well known for the four levels of question formulation (visceral, conscious, formalized, and compromised needs) and the five filters that librarians use to help understand information needs (determination of subject, objective and motivation, personal characteristics of inquirer, relationship of inquiry to file organization, anticipated or acceptable answers). These are, of course, of great importance and have rightly been adopted into thinking about reference work.

There are other aspects of this article, though, that I think too often are overlooked. Taylor (1968) placed the reference process in the broader context of how the user tries to get his or her information need satisfied. His figure on page 181 shows that users have many options rather than—and before—approaching an information professional. They may choose to experiment or observe nature, ask a colleague, or search the literature. If they choose to search first, or if the other approaches fail, they may either search their own information files or may approach a library. And library searching can either be self-help or with a librarian. Thus, a user who asks a reference librarian for help has potentially (and likely, given our knowledge of user behavior) been through several other attempts and approaches and not found satisfactory information. There are certainly some users for whom a reference librarian is a first or early method, but it is likely that for many, the librarian is a last-resort tactic.

Earlier, I quoted Taylor on the central problem of reference interviewing, but, of course, he did not refer to it that way. He preferred the phrase "question negotiation." Many people who have been influenced by his work seem to think that he used this phrase in place of "reference interview" but saw the two as nearly the same. I disagree and would point out that for Taylor, "question negotiation" also includes the self-help use of the library (p. 179). I might even go farther and suggest that the "question negotiation" process incorporates all of the potential paths he described, including searching personal files, asking friends, and so on.

In the current context, this schema can be extended even further. Certainly, searching the free Internet has provided users with another option, and the self-help library search can now take place anywhere a user can authenticate to licensed databases or search his or her library's catalog remotely. It might even be that the Internet has taken on roles similar to those of friends or colleagues in Taylor's original work, as a first-order option. A recent study from the Pew Internet and American Life Project (Kommers 2002), for example, indicates that millions of Americans use the Internet to make major life decisions such as getting more education, changing careers, making a major purchase, helping a loved one through a serious illness, or making a major investment.

It is this broadened sense of "question negotiation" that I shall adopt for this discussion.

Although all of these definitions have served interesting purposes, they all seem to lack specificity, especially as a framework for discussion of a research agenda. It is interesting to note that apart from the White articles discussed above, there is virtually no discussion in the reference literature on what makes reference interviews successful.

Based on the foregoing, I would propose the following as a tentative conceptual definition for question negotiation:

> an interaction between a person with an information need and an information service; its purpose is to refine the information need so that it can be usefully responded to by the information service

State of the Art

One of the great difficulties in researching or studying the reference interview in the past has been its ephemeral nature. Because in the vast majority of cases the interview took place in person or via the telephone, no objective record existed unless it was recorded or transcribed, and even then one is left to wonder whether the recording process had material effects on the nature of the interview.

In the digital environment, such records exist and can be of great use in studying the reference interview. To date, however, very little has appeared in the research literature to describe the nature of these interviews. Abels's (1996) oft-cited article examined purely e-mail interview exchanges, and a number of "how-we-do-it" articles have appeared in the practitioner literature.

To determine what the state of the art is in digital reference interviewing, we turn to a series of studies (Janes, Carter, and Memmott 1999; Janes 2001) that have examined the Web sites of public and academic libraries to determine the nature and characteristics of digital reference services. These studies are being replicated at present, and there are now preliminary data from a new study of the same 352 public library Web sites; more complete results will be presented in the near future.

The salient results of these studies are presented in table 1.

Table 1. Study Results			
	5/1999 150 Academic Libraries	3/2000 352 Public Libraries	5/2002 352 Public Libraries
Libraries with digital reference services	44.7%	12.8%	35.7%
Provide e-mail addresses for question submission	42% (28 of 67)	56% (37 of 64)	56% (82 of 147)
Provide a simple form for question submission	55% (37 of 67)	38% (24 of 64)	5% (7 of 147)
Provide a detailed form for question submission	10% (7 of 67)	25% (16 of 64)	48% (71 of 147)
Use call center software for question submission	0	0	21% (31 of 147)
Use instant messaging for question submission	0	0	0.7% (1 of 147)
Use chat for question submission	0	0	0
Provides an explanation of examples of when/why to choose different types of contact methods	not asked	not asked	20% (29 of 147)

A number of intriguing findings emerge from this table. The proportion of public libraries offering services has risen sharply, almost tripling in a two-year time frame, but is still lower than the proportion of academic libraries in 1999. The methods of question submission also have changed in interesting ways. The percentage of libraries providing e-mail addresses is roughly comparable to what has been observed in the past. However, the percentage of those offering detailed forms (anything more than the simple form questions) has doubled, largely at the expense of the very bare-bones forms. In addition, the number of libraries offering real-time (chat, instant messaging, call center software based) services now exceeds 20 percent, and a similar number provide a page summarizing their services and give guidance as to which might be more appropriate.

A further examination of the Web forms yields a list of the most frequently observed questions asked on Web forms, as shown in table 2. (Nearly all forms asked for name and e-mail address.)

Table 2. Most Frequently Asked Observed Questions Asked on Web Forms	
Phone number	53
Affiliation	22
Street/mailing address	19
Fax number	17
Deadline	14
Sources already consulted	10
Subject area	8
Preferred info delivery method	6
School assignment	6

A number of other questions were asked, but none more than five times. It is interesting to note omissions here. For example, the rationale or motivation behind the query, one of the main reasons for doing a reference interview, was asked on only three forms, as was the preferred answer type (factual, sources, and so on), and the number of items or amount of information desired was asked only once. Most of the frequently asked questions, then, are functional and personal (name, e-mail address, phone number and so on), rather than based on the nature of the query itself. These questions serve more as a profiling activity than an interview aimed specifically at refining the nature of the query.

Only very cursory examination has been made of the Web pages describing and presenting chat-based services. The following are subjective observations, and more substantial analysis of these pages may well yield more sophisticated and trustworthy conclusions. However, I offer these as glimpses into what those pages say and do:

• A handful of the live services provide Web forms to ask the initial set of questions. These are usually very few in number, and the boxes in which users can type their questions are almost always very small, which would tend to encourage people to type relatively little.

• A number of these pages describe technological requirements for using the service but also include restrictions, warnings, and barriers (Macintosh computers cannot be used, what to do if the service freezes, and so on).

- Several of the services described in some detail who (i.e., a librarian) would be responding to the users' question; this is not often seen in other digital reference environments.
- Somewhat more mention is made here about privacy and confidentiality policies than is made in other digital reference environments.
- Almost all specified the hours their services are available, and some also described the process by which the question would be responded to.

Of course, we have no idea what the interviews look like in those services based on this analysis because we looked only at their Web presence and did not ask questions or interview librarians.

Another source of potentially revealing evidence about the reference interview in the digital environment is comments made by librarians. The DIG_REF electronic list, maintained by the Virtual Reference Desk project, is probably the best-known and most widely trafficked discussion list in this area. Although a comprehensive survey of the DIG_REF discussions on the interview is beyond the scope of this discussion (and would be a fascinating and worthwhile venue for further research endeavors), a discussion thread from October of 2001 seemed to encapsulate many of the issues of recent concern to reference librarians about the nature of the reference interview and how it is changing. A posting by Bernie Sloan on October 22, 2001, began the discussion by asking the following: "I'm looking for practitioners' perspectives on how the reference interview is affected by the medium it's conducted in .... From your experience, how does the digital reference interview differ from the traditional face-to-face reference interview in the library?"

A large number of responses were posted over the next several days. Among the points of discussion of interest here are:

On asynchronous (e-mail, Web form–based) interviewing:

- Loss of nonverbal clues (tone of voice, eye contact, and so on)
- The disappearing questioner, someone who never responds when asked for clarification (One person reported receiving more responses when clarifying questions were presented with some information or a guess as to what the original question was about, as opposed simply to questions probing the information need alone.)
- The longer time needed for an interview using repeated e-mail exchanges and the additional strain on staff time that implied
- The creation of a permanent record and ability to track reference performance
- Lack of feedback on whether responses were correct, appropriate, satisfactory
- The opportunity for both user and librarian to think through the question and response, to let the question "percolate" as the librarian works on it
- The importance and role of a form as a simulation of the reference interview, as well as commentary on the perception of reluctance of some users to filling out forms

- The ability to clarify questions received via e-mail or form on the phone

On synchronous (chat, call-center software) interviewing:

- The "probe query," where users ask an initial simple, vague query and on receiving a response then proceed to ask much more detailed questions.
- Ability to make educated guesses based on grammar, syntax, e-mail address, time query was sent, on what an initial vague query might really be.
- People using chat are in a hurry and will not want to fill out a form.
- Chat is better at back-and-forth of an interview, and thus there will be more interaction, but also that little of a traditional reference interview might go on because of perceived time pressures.
- Chat places more of an onus on patrons to make their need clear quickly and to make clear that responses are not what they want.
- Dead time is a problem; perceived need to stay active with user to keep them online and interested.
- Chat can be difficult for users if they are not familiar with the medium.
- Chat can be helpful to estimate the time a response will take to let users know what to expect.
- Chat sessions are not necessarily quick—estimates of average time from 10 to 20 minutes, some as long as 45 minutes or more; also discussion of a "virtual line" that can form if too many chat requests come in simultaneously.
- "You can't chat the way you talk."
- Students may have very different views of the written word than librarians (on punctuation, spelling, etc.), which affects chat behavior.
- Both parties may be somewhat disoriented because of the novelty of the communication mechanism.

Issues and Challenges

Based on the foregoing, several challenges emerge as central to a greater understanding of the development of techniques to efficiently and effectively identify and refine users' information needs.

One of the most heartening results discussed above is the *acceptance of detailed Web forms* to solicit queries. Nearly half of services now use forms that ask nothing more than the most basic questions, and it would appear that the practice is increasing. This has taken place within the context of multiple discussions on listservs and at conferences about the value of using detailed forms and about the frustration over the difficulty of conducting reference interviews via e-mail and synchronous methods. It would seem that using forms that asked for more and more detailed information is being embraced as an option, at least among the public library community in the United States.

At the same time, the past two years have seen the *growth of synchronous services* using chat, instant messaging, and especially call-center software. Much of the discussion around digital reference services has combined the two, probably incorrectly. It seems more likely that synchronous and asynchronous services will use substantially different methods to help users articulate their information needs. (Indeed, this leads to the intriguing conjecture that tele-phone-based and face-to-face library reference services should have been think-ing about using different techniques over the last several decades.) If this contention is correct, although the measures of success are likely the same, services may well require different means to achieve success in the question negotiation process. It appears that, so far, librarians have been attempting to replicate or "automate" the traditional reference interview. This could be counterproductive at the very least, time-consuming to be sure, and impos-sible at worst, leading away from more creative and effective solutions.

Time is often discussed, and concerns are often voiced about keeping chat users occupied while searching and about the often-lengthy time re-quired to conduct an e-mail interview. However, pleasure is expressed about the extra time available to construct a response to a question that comes in from a form with a two- or three-day deadline specified by the questioner. Apparently, trade-offs are at work among speed of response, quality of re-sponse, and other factors such as continuity of interaction, the inclinations and preferences of both user and responder, and so on. To be sure, some users demand immediate responses to complex questions and libraries and librar-ians who require long periods of time to respond to simple, factual questions. Both are likely to be disappointed. However, a greater range of options is emerging for both, which one would presume could lead to greater satisfac-tion and performance.

Among the new challenges to traditional library reference practice is the phenomenon of the *disappearing questioner*, which has manifested itself in both the asynchronous and synchronous domains. Users who do not re-spond to e-mails for clarification and those who prematurely end or evapo-rate from chat-based sessions fall into this category. In the familiar world of reference libraries, if a user hangs up the phone or leaves the library, it is usually not difficult to know what has happened and likely why, based on tone of voice, body language, and a variety of other clues. In the digital world, such clues are gone, and thus in general it is more difficult to know why a response is not forthcoming. Has the user found the response in some other way? Has the user's deadline passed? Is the user simply no longer inter-ested? The librarian is left to wonder and, more to the point, is left in a quandary about what to do next. Should she or he continue to send e-mails asking clarifying questions? Should the librarian send a few suggested sources and hope he or she is on the right track? Should the librarian simply stop, assuming that if the user no longer cares, the librarian's job is finished? This is an unsettling position for a professional to be in, and one that will take careful thought as librarians evolve practice in this area.

On another front is a set of issues generated from *increasing consortial and cooperative efforts*. Our research indicates that somewhat more than one-fifth of public libraries are currently involved in some sort of consortial service, at either a local, statewide, or broader level; and the QuestionPoint service (formerly the

Collaborative Digital Reference Service) continues to grow and add members. Although there is much to be learned in general about cross-institutional services from a question negotiation perspective, it raises the question of the *transportability of the interview*. To save the user's time and effort, it would, of course, be best to engage in a single interview, so any information services working on a query after that might have to rely on the initial interview. But under what circumstances would it be appropriate to reengage the user to obtain further or more detailed information? And if an "interview" is to be passed from one service to another, questions arise concerning confidentiality, privacy, and the standards (technological and professional) by which the interview could be distributed and received.

The information world is a very different place in 2002 than it was even a few years previously in so many ways. In this area in particular, it is possible for people to find information more quickly and easily than ever before using tools that are new to them and drawing on sources of information unavailable, or even nonexistent, not so very long ago. People now have many more and wider options for "question negotiation" in the broadest Tayloresque sense. Consulting an information professional continues to be one of them, and, in fact, such professionals now can be much more accessible via these technologies as well.

At this time of great opportunity, however, there appears to be a vein of skepticism in the library community about the feasibility and practice of doing the work that librarians are accustomed to in this evolving information world. In many ways, they are attempting to fit their familiar practice to this new world and often finding it inadequate or lacking, frustrating, difficult, or unrewarding. There is a great deal to be learned, and important questions to be asked, to assist in developing useful and effective ways to help understand and satisfy individual information needs.

Recommendations for Research

There is much we do not know in this area because of the introduction of new technologies and new uses for those technologies and also because of the relative paucity of research on the reference interview from the literature of library and information science to date. Therefore, the need for a serious and comprehensive research agenda is great, as is the opportunity to use the results of such research to make substantial progress in providing assistance to both the users of information services and those who design and staff them.

Among the important questions for research and development are:

• What is the current state of practice in electronic question negotiation in terms of both synchronous and asynchronous modes?

— What interview questions are typically designed into library electronic reference forms and services?

— Do these questions differ from those that are asked of library patrons at reference desks?

— What new, unique, or interactive features are libraries using in digital reference?

— How are libraries defining to users what they can expect from digital reference services?

• Who is best served by digital reference services, and by which methods of interaction?

— Who is currently using these services?

— What are their information needs?

— Why did they choose the method of interaction (Web, e-mail, chat, and so on) they did?

— What are their expectations of the information service and of the method of interaction?

— What is the nature of the connection between the user and the service, as perceived by the user? by the service provider?

— What factors affect how people select and approach an information service?

• What are the best indicators and measures of success of the reference interview?

• What makes a reference interview successful?

• What is the role of nonverbal information? How important is it and in what situations? What parallels exist or can be created in e-mail, Web form, and chat environments?

• Is there a relationship between the method of interaction and the success of the interaction?

Allow me to digress for a moment. Nearly all of the preceding discussion has come from the traditions of library and information science. Beyond the familiar notions of the reference interview and question negotiation, however, lies another approach that deserves some exploration.

Although technology is obviously an important aspect of this discussion, to this point it has been seen primarily as a communications medium, using networked means to solicit and respond to user queries and so on. However, it might be worthwhile to think about how the process of question negotiation, again broadly understood, might otherwise be supported by technological means. This leads to a new research question:

• In what ways could question negotiation be selectively or even fully automated?

Selective or partial automation has been an area of some discussion within the digital reference world, but without much impact. Several ideas have been raised. A service could take initial queries from a Web form, chat box, or e-mail message and provide the results of quick and dirty automatic preliminary searches using one or more search engines or directories. If those results yield a satisfactory response, the process need go no further; if not, the service could proceed to attempt to satisfy the user's need in its normal way, but with the knowledge of the failed searches. This idea also could be implemented using lists of frequently asked questions or a stored database of previously asked and answered questions to broaden its scope and potential power.

The one area of selective automation that has been implemented is a routing function, one of the centerpieces of the QuestionPoint service. The designers of this service are continuing to develop and refine algorithms for sending a query to a particular service based on its subject matter and the collection and service strengths of members, but also deadline, load, geography, and a variety of other factors. This work is ongoing, and despite some early difficulties, it seems to hold promise as an important and necessary feature of any large-scale cooperative service.

Full automation is an intriguing concept very much in the tradition of artificial intelligence and expert systems work, and, indeed, people have discussed "automating the reference process" for many years (see, for example, Richardson 1995; Alberico and Micco 1990; McCrank 1993). This line of thought seems to have peaked around 1990 and is seldom discussed today. However, a look at work from a different orientation might be instructive.

Kwok, Etzioni, and Weld (2001) discuss MULDER, which they describe as "the first general-purpose, fully-automated question-answering system available on the web." It was designed to answer what they call factual questions, and what librarians would likely call ready reference questions, such as "Who was the first American in space?" or "What is the second-tallest mountain in the world?" Although an extensive discussion of the system is beyond the scope of this chapter, the architecture is briefly described as follows:

An automated QA system based on a document collection typically has three main components. The first is a retrieval engine that sits on top of the document collection and handles retrieval requests. In the context of web, this is a search engine that indexes web pages. The second is a query formulation mechanism that translates natural-language questions into queries for the IR engine in order to retrieve relevant documents from the collection, i.e., documents that can potentially answer the question. The third component, answer extraction, analyses these documents and extracts answers from them.

In testing their system, they used questions from the TREC-8 text retrieval competition and compared their system with the performance of Google™ and AskJeeves,™ finding that MULDER outperformed them both in terms of recall and "user effort" (actually a word distance metric) to achieve given levels of recall, and thus shows promise for implementation and use in a real setting.

Their work draws heavily from linguistics and natural language processing, computing science, and some information retrieval. Sadly, although it was funded by a Digital Library Initiative grant originally entitled "Automatic Reference Librarians for the World Wide Web," no citations to, or recognition of, research or professional literature from librarianship appears in either this paper or the original proposal.

To be sure, the same can be said of the vast majority of library literature as well. One is left to speculate how much the validity—and thus the usefulness—of these research and development strains would increase if they took place with a greater mutual awareness and cooperation. It is difficult to imagine that there would not be ideas and findings of value if they were known, shared, and developed together. Cooperation among these vibrant and complementary communities of research and practice could be among the most important ways to advance our knowledge and activity.

References

Abels, Eileen. 1996. "The E-mail Reference Interview." *RQ* 35: 345–58.

Alberico, Ralph, and Mary Micco. 1990. *Expert Systems for Reference and Information Retrieval*. Westport, Conn.: Meckler.

Bunge, Charles A. 1983. "The Personal Touch: A Brief Overview of the Development of Reference Services in American Libraries." Pp. 1–16 in *Reference Services: A Perspective*, ed. Sul Lee. Ann Arbor, Mich.: Pierian Press.

Dervin, Brenda, and Patricia Dewdney. 1986. "Neutral Questioning: A New Approach to the Reference Interview." *RQ* 25: 506–13.

Green, Samuel S. 1876. "Personal Relations between Librarians and Readers." *Library Journal* 1: 74–81.

Hutchins, Margaret. 1944. *Introduction to Reference Work*. Chicago: ALA.

Janes, Joseph, David S. Carter, and Patricia Memmott. 1999. "Digital Reference Services in Academic Libraries." *Reference and User Services Quarterly* 39: 145–50.

Janes, Joseph. 2001. "Digital Reference Services in Public and Academic Libraries." In *Evaluating Networked Information Services: Techniques, Policy, and Issues*, ed. Charles R. McClure and John Carlo Bertot. Medford, N.J.: Information Today, Inc.

Kommers, Nathan. 2002. *Use of the Internet at Major Life Moments*. Washington D.C.: Pew Internet and American Life Project. Available online from http://www.pewinternet.org/reports/toc.asp?Report=58.

Kwok, Cody, Oren Etzioni, and Daniel S. Weld. 2001. "Scaling Question Answering to the Web." ACM *Transactions on Information Systems* 19: 242–62.

Lynch, Mary Jo. 1978. "Reference Interview in Public Libraries." *Library Quarterly* 48: 119–42.

McCrank, Lawrence J. 1993. "Reference Expertise: Paradigms, Strategies, and Systems." *Reference Librarian* 40: 11–42.

Richardson, John V. 1995. *Knowledge-based Systems for General Reference Work: Applications, Problems, and Progress*. San Diego, Calif.: Academic Press.

Ross, Catherine Sheldrick, and Kirsti Nilsen. 2000. "Has the Internet Changed Anything in Reference? The Library Visit Study, Part 2." *Reference and User Services Quarterly* 40: 147–55.

Taylor, Robert S. 1968. "Question-Negotiation and Information Seeking in Libraries." *College and Research Libraries*, pp. 178–94.

White, Marilyn Domas. 1981. "The Dimensions of the Reference Interview." *RQ* 20: 373–81.

———. 1985. "Evaluation of the Reference Interview." *RQ* 25: 76–84.

Woodruff, Eleanor B. 1897. "Reference Work." *Library Journal* 22 (conference issue): 65–67.

Wyer, James I. 1930. *Reference Work: A Textbook for Students of Library Work and Librarians*. Chicago: ALA.

Chapter 4

Software, Systems, and Standards in Digital Reference: A Research Agenda

Michael McClennen, Ph.D.
Head of Systems, Internet Public Library

There is a close coupling between the practice of digital reference and the shape of the software tools used to enable it. To maximize the effectiveness of these tools, we need to apply analytical methods that bridge the gap between our informal procedural understanding of the digital reference process and the abstract systems that can be modeled in software. We must look at digital reference services, both individually and in cooperative networks, as formal mathematical systems. To tackle the open questions in this field, we must bring together intellectual tools, both quantitative and qualitative, from several disciplines. This chapter presents a model that can be used to analyze and compare digital reference systems. It then identifies four major research challenges and discusses how they may be pursued using methods from library science, computer science, and operations research.

Introduction

The practice of librarianship in the digital age occupies a middle ground between the long-established discipline of library science and the more recent disciplines of computer science and information retrieval. This position has caused no small amount of upheaval in the profession during recent decades, as the primary technology used by the profession changes from paper-based information repositories to digital ones. At the same time, it gives librarians a unique perspective on the evolving process of information seeking. As software-based information technology becomes ever more important to

Thanks are due to Bernie Sloan, whose excellent bibliography I used extensively for my research.

society, it is tempting to imagine that continuing development of this tech-nology will eventually solve all problems of information acquisition. Perhaps the most important lesson we have learned during the past thirty years of the profession is that this is not likely to be true. The abilities of humans and computers are complementary in a number of important ways, and each can greatly augment the other. When well-trained people are given well-designed software tools to use, the combination of human understanding with the speed and precision of digital technology can be far more powerful than either human minds or software alone.

Given an information need and a body of information, the classic prob-lem in librarianship is to resolve the former by means of the latter. A well-trained person can bring to bear a complex and flexible set of rules and processes for knowledge discovery and information retrieval. Equally impor-tant, they can call on their understanding of how to teach, inform, and trans-late among different modes of human perception. Well-designed software can provide fast and accurate searches and correlations, instantaneous electronic communication, and the automation of well-defined sets of tasks. When the processes encoded in the software algorithms mesh well with the processes followed by their human users, each agent is able to take care of those parts of the task that the other agent cannot easily accomplish.

A crucial precondition for this synergy is that the designers of the soft-ware must understand the ways in which the users will be approaching their tasks. For example, if a user naturally divides the overall problem into certain subtasks, the user will be able to use the software most efficiently if it repre-sents the task hierarchy he or she is most comfortable with. Similarly, if the process that is most natural for a user relies on certain information staying constant, he or she will be able to work best with software that represents that information in an unchanging manner. There are many such parameters, and they often vary from user to user. As a result, the task of designing good user interfaces for information tools is often a very challenging one.

Because of this situation, the practice of digital librarianship is closely coupled with the nature of the software tools used to carry it out. This is true of digital reference as much as of any other branch of the field. In designing a service, we are only able to offer those variations that the software allows. Real time? Co-browsing? Forwarding a question to another library? These features are only available to the extent that our software provides them. The converse of this proposition is that the software designers can only include those features that they and their users can envision and specify. If we as a profession are to advance beyond a crude understanding of the field, we will need to learn about two interrelated things: first, the best processes to use for doing reference in various kinds of digital environments, and, second, how to represent them in software. Ultimately, this requires some kind of mapping between our intuitive understanding of how digital reference works and the kind of formally described systems that can be turned into software specifications. And that, in turn, involves research that is informed by the methods of both library science and computer science.

If we are to build a comprehensive research agenda for digital reference, such inquiry must certainly be central to the effort. In pursuit of this goal, this chapter explores the idea of analyzing and modeling digital reference systems using formal models, applying approaches from several disciplines together. By transforming our understanding of digital reference from informally understood *processes* to formally modelable *systems*, we will be able to give our software (and the protocols and standards that enable different software programs to communicate) the best possible correspondence with the way in which we actually practice digital reference. In addition, we can use these same tools to undertake rigorous studies to compare, contrast, and analyze the different procedures and methods of practice.

The next two sections of this chapter provide a rough overview of the current state of knowledge in the field of digital reference and briefly compare reference in the digital domain with more traditional modes. The fourth section presents a paradigm for modeling digital reference systems and provides some examples of how it can be used. The fifth section discusses various research tools that can be useful in this line of study, and the sixth section presents four research challenges that, in the opinion of the author, represent the most useful next steps in digital reference research from a systems point of view.

Overview of the Field

Reference services have been provided over digital channels by libraries and other organizations for at least the past fifteen years. Early efforts were of limited scope, mostly in the nature of demonstration projects, and were carried out by means of existing software tools, primarily e-mail (Weise and Borgendale 1986; Bonham 1987; Lankes 2000). A few sites experimented with multi-user virtual environments such as MUDs and MOOs (Henderson 1994). The first specialized tools for asynchronous digital reference were developed in 1995 (Lagace and McClennen 1998; Bry 2003a), and tools specialized for real-time reference followed soon after. This point can be considered a milestone in the history of digital reference as a field of study inasmuch as it marks the first recorded attempts to model digital reference processes as formal systems. Although digital reference can be practiced and studied using nonspecific tools such as e-mail, the development of special-purpose software necessarily involves a more detailed analysis. A piece of software requires an actual representation of the things being handled and thus a formal model of how those things change over time. Conversely, the existence of such software provides a representation around which to organize a high-level analysis of the processes being captured.

Over the past eight years, digital reference has evolved from an experimental curiosity to a routine, widely accepted service offered by libraries, museums, "Ask-a" Web sites and many other organizations. There is ample evidence that the public is receptive to this kind of service in both its synchronous and asynchronous modes. Moreover, we now know from concrete experience that, given good software tools and appropriate procedures, a well-organized digital reference service can handle dozens or even hundreds of questions per day with great efficiency. Such a service is limited primarily by the number of people available to filter, assign, and answer the questions.

Digital reference has so far been practiced in two modes: real-time and asynchronous. Both modes are widely used, and, as a result, we know a great deal about their characteristics. *Real-time digital reference* is characterized by a synchronous back-and-forth conversation between the question asker and answerer, using channels of communication such as chat, instant messaging, or voiceover IP. This mode has a lot in common with traditional telephone reference and works well in cases where an immediate response is desired and where typical questions can be answered by the first responder within a few minutes. *Asynchronous digital reference* is characterized by communication in one direction at a time, typically by e-mail or Web forms. This mode allows the librarian to take a longer period of time to answer the question and allows questions to be sent in at any time of day, whether or not someone is on duty to answer them. It also imposes fewer technological requirements on the asker; most asynchronous digital reference Web sites can be used by anyone with a Web browser, whereas real-time reference requires more sophisticated software. There has been some limited experimentation with hybrid models, where questions that cannot be answered quickly via real-time interaction are converted to asynchronous mode and the answer is returned to the patron later (Online Computer Library Center 2003; McGlamery 2002).

Purpose-built digital reference software tools currently exist for both synchronous and asynchronous modes of operation. Experience indicates that they do a reasonably good job of modeling particular digital reference processes, although none are general enough to work well for the full range of procedures in current use. The most advanced tools implement a common set of useful features. They manage communication between question asker and answerer, track each question through the various stages of the digital reference process, generate statistical reports, and provide some mechanism for ensuring that every question is answered in a timely manner. Examples include QRC (Lagace and McClennen 1998), Moderator (Bry 2003a), VRD Incubator (Bennett 2000), and QuestionPoint (Online Computer Library Center 2003).

In addition to knowing how individual digital reference services work, we know that networks of services can operate more or less smoothly using a single level of referral. This is a new area of practice and research, and only a few such networks are now operational. Examples include the VRD network (Bennett 2003), 24/7 Reference McGlamery 2003a), and QuestionPoint (Online Computer Library Center 2003). Finally, we know that in certain cases where the domain of discourse is limited, archives of answered questions can be used to automatically answer some patron questions. The MAD Scientist Network (Bry 2003a) provides a good example of how this process works.

Comparison of Digital and Nondigital Modes of Reference

The study of digital reference theory and practice builds on the existing body of work on library reference in general, a field of study more than one hundred years old. In evaluating the applicability of this work, it is instructive to compare the practice of digital reference with more traditional methods of delivering reference services, such as in person, by telephone, and via postal mail. From a systems point of view, the most relevant comparison is in the nature of the procedures used to handle a reference interaction and in the degree to which these procedures are constrained by the particular technologies being used and the situations in which they are used. There are many similarities in this regard between traditional and digital modes of reference, as well as some fundamental differences.

All modes of reference service share basic constraints that have a large influence on the procedures used to handle them. These include availability, timeliness, quality of the answer, quality of the interaction between librarian and patron, and many more. All of these are subject to a greater or lesser degree to limits imposed by technology and circumstance. For example, telephone reference and real-time digital reference both take up the full attention of the librarian for the duration of each call, with unpredictable timing. The librarian can only answer calls if he or she is in the vicinity of the communication device, which may not be in the same physical location as the local collection of reference material. This means that the procedure for handling calls has to take this fundamental limitation into account. The patron will often expect an answer to his or her question before the interaction concludes, which for complex questions may force the librarian to decide between giving an answer that is less than complete and asking the patron to wait for a follow-up at a later time.

Neither of these constraints exists for reference by postal or electronic mail. On the other hand, these modes are subject to limitations of their own. The asynchronous nature of the communication channel makes the traditional reference interview difficult or impossible, forcing the use of strategies to collect as much information as possible from the patron up front. In addition, some kind of follow-up mechanism is often necessary to ensure that each question is answered in a timely fashion. Without a patron waiting on the line, some other form of control may be needed to ensure that questions do not "drop through the cracks."

The similarities between digital reference and traditional modes come about because they are solving essentially the same problem. The differences, on the other hand, spring from the use of different kinds of tools for handling information. In moving from paper-based systems to digital systems, there is a great gain in capacity and efficiency, and a corresponding loss of flexibility.

In traditional processes not mediated by computer software, the question answerers have a free hand in devising procedures and conventions for acknowledging and responding to questions, assigning work among themselves, and keeping records. Tools such as file cards, telephones, notepads, and bookshelves are widely adaptable and place few constraints on the procedures by which they are used. The limits imposed by these tools are generally ones of capacity. Keeping track of 1,000 questions a day would be extremely difficult using pen-and-paper record keeping, and a 100,000-volume ready reference collection would tax the memory and organizational skills of most people unless augmented by electronic indexing. Still, as long as the amount of information flowing through the system is manageable, the people doing the work can arrange that information in whatever form they see fit. A paper ledger for recording the results of reference transactions can include whatever information the question answerers deem necessary, and a shelf filled with reference books can be organized in whatever order the question answerers decide best suits their needs.

Digital reference is different in that all, or substantially all, of the communication, annotation, and record-keeping tasks involved are carried out by means of software. Although digital tools allow for much greater information capacity, they also impose distinct constraints on the procedures to be used. Real-world entities such as people, questions, queues, and documents are represented by digital records, which in turn appear as icons, folders, or items in lists. The software provides for a limited set of actions to be taken on these digital objects and for particular pieces of information to be recorded. Each form or dialog box has a limited set of fields, and each icon or item is linked to a small set of menu items or buttons that can affect it. In most cases, it is difficult or impossible to take actions outside the scope of these elements. Thus, it is crucial that the designers of the software allow for a wide enough variety of actions to encompass the procedures the users wish to execute.

A Paradigm for Modeling Digital Reference Systems

In order to go from the abstract concept of digital reference system to something we can analyze and model, it is useful to consider the different ways we can look at such a thing formally. When we have broken this concept down into components that can be more easily dealt with, we can begin to figure out what questions to ask and enumerate the methods that are available to answer them.

To begin, we need to define what exactly we mean by a "digital reference system." At the most basic level, it could be a service offered by a particular library or other institution. In this case, the system encompasses the people who answer the questions, the software they use to coordinate the process, and the policies and procedures by which they make decisions about how to do the work. We can look closely at individual digital reference services to determine whether there are ways to make the system more efficient, to make sure that the stated policies and procedures are followed consistently, to document the procedures for use in developing software requirements, or to write up a case study or best-practices document to guide others in setting up similar services.

When looked at from a higher level, the institution may be part of a digital reference cooperative, a statewide network, or a large-scale digital reference network such as the *QuestionPoint* or *24/7 Reference* (McGlamery 2003b; Online Computer Library Center 2003). Such networks are digital reference systems in their own right, composed of the software used to manage communication among individual members, the people who use that software, and the policies and procedures that control how it is used. The member organizations can be thought of as subsystems. Possible goals for analysis of these complex systems include the same goals of efficiency, consistency, and documentation that are relevant at the level of a single organization. In addition, a network requires some kind of communication protocol that can be used to convey information among the various parts. Analysis of the system as a whole, including the policies and procedures used within and among the member organizations, is invaluable in developing and refining such a protocol.

How, then, can we formally model digital reference systems in a way that will enable these kinds of analyses? The remainder of this section presents a paradigm that can be used for this purpose, and discusses its elements and the ways in which they interrelate.

Fundamental Elements of the Model

The concept of digital reference can be viewed from at least three different aspects, as summarized in figure 1. Each of these aspects says something different about the process; together they make a unified whole. This section focuses on each aspect in turn, followed by a discussion of the ways in which the different aspects relate to each other and to the other elements of the standard model.

Figure 1. Three aspects of digital reference

- An *activity* which involves question askers and answerers, providing value to the former and employment to the latter
- A *process* whereby questions are received, handled, and disposed of. Questions flow in to the system, are dealt with, and flow out
- An *intermediation* between bodies of information and needs for information. This results in the generation of new pieces of information: questions and answers

These correspond to the three fundamental elements of a digital reference model: *people*, *actions*, and *information*.

People

On one hand, digital reference is an *activity* that involves both the people asking the questions and the people answering them. Correspondingly, *people* are a fundamental element of the digital reference model. From this point of view, one can ask questions such as:

- Who is involved in this activity?
- What roles do they play?
- What results do they expect to get out of it?

The answers to these questions can provide a useful framework for discussing questions of policy and procedure, and can help to guide both general research and the evaluation of specific digital reference services by clearly delineating the actors involved. When this is clear, one can study the way each person is doing his or her job and make sure that the established procedures are in accord with people's expectations and training.

The author has presented a model for asynchronous digital reference [Mcc01a] that recognizes five distinct roles. *Patrons* ask questions by sending them to a digital reference service. *Filterers* check the incoming stream of messages to sort out those that are questions from those that are not and to categorize and/or assign the actual questions. *Answerers* receive the questions and generate answers. *Administrators* are responsible for supervising the day-to-day operation of the service and ensuring the smooth flow of questions, whereas *coordinators* are responsible for setting policy. One person can play more than one role in the system, but they are essentially different jobs.

Actions

From an entirely different point of view, digital reference is a *process* by which questions flow in to the system and are accepted, categorized, and answered, and by which the answers flow back out. Each step in the process is an *action* taken on a question, each action carried out by one of the people involved. Correspondingly, actions are a fundamental element of the model. From this point of view, one can ask questions such as:

- What are the different stages that questions go through during their life span, between being asked and having the patron receive the answer?
- What actions are taken at various stages?
- How long do questions tend to remain in each stage?

The answers to these questions are critical to the design of effective software tools for digital reference. For example, if the procedure followed at your site involves the assignment of questions to individual answerers, implementation of an "assign question" action will be part of your requirements for digital reference software. On the other hand, if your procedure involves having the answerers choose from among the available questions, a "choose question" action will be required instead. Looking at a process in this way also can enable the identification of bottlenecks, with a view toward improving efficiency. This concept of a digital reference process is discussed in more detail below, along with some examples.

Information

Digital reference can be considered as an intellectual construct, an "intermediation" between bodies of information and needs for information. The products of this construct over time include new pieces of information—questions and answers—that add to the corpus available for use in answering subsequent reference questions. These products are themselves most useful if ways can be found to organize them for easy retrieval, leading to such questions as the following:

• How often are questions received that have similar answers to previously received questions?

• What pieces of information about the question and the asker are most useful to record?

• What are the most useful methods of organizing archives of answered questions?

Now that several of the large-scale digital reference networks are beginning to develop archives of answered reference questions, questions such as these are taking on a new importance.

Figure 2. A Three-layer Model for Digital Reference Systems*		
Process *Sequence of steps through which questions flow*		
Procedures *Instructions for carrying out each step*		**Policy** *Guidelines for decision making*
People *Acting in roles*	**Actions** *Carry questions from one step to another*	**Information** *Questions and answers*
The bottom layer consists of the three fundamental components. In the middle layer are the policies and procedures that tie these components together, and at the top is the process defined by these policies and procedures. All of these elements will be discussed in greater detail later in the paper.		

Higher-level Elements (the Three Ps)

Our model, as shown in figure 2, is organized into three layers, each one building on the layer below. At the bottom are the three fundamental components of a digital reference system discussed in the previous section. The next layer up encompasses the rules and guidelines by which the service is operated, and the top layer represents the sequence of steps through which each question travels while being handled by the system. This top-level process sequence is based on the policies and procedures, which are in turn based on the fundamental elements at the bottom. The high-level elements—policy, procedure, and process—and their relationship to the basic three building blocks are discussed in the following sections.

Policies and Procedures

The concepts of policy and procedure are critical in any comprehensive attempt to analyze digital reference systems. These two concepts are thoroughly intertwined both with each other and with the other elements of the model. To be clear about the meaning of these words, we will use the following definitions. A *policy* is a rule or guideline that governs decisions taken in the course of the operation of a system, whether made by a human being or a computer algorithm. For example:

All reference questions are to be answered in the order received, but residents of our library district have priority.

A *procedure*, on the other hand, is a sequence of steps or transformations that are involved in the operation of the system. An example is:

• When a patron connects to our system, send him or her the standard greeting message and wait for a response.

• If the patron does not respond within sixty seconds, close the session and go on to the next patron in the queue.

Procedures typically contain decisions that must be made in the course of following them. Sometimes these decisions are clear and unambiguous, as in "if they do not respond within sixty seconds." Such decisions can often be made automatically by computer software, but other decisions may require judgment, for example, "if a question sent by e-mail does not meet our requirements for service, send the standard rejection message in reply." In this case, the actual requirements, and the criteria for judging whether a message meets them, are matters of policy.

Both policies and procedures are most conveniently defined in relation to the fundamental elements described above. We can describe a procedure by specifying which action it corresponds to, which people (or which roles) are responsible for carrying it out, what parts of the question and associated information must be examined in the course of making any embedded decisions, and, finally, the steps that must be taken to carry it out. Policies can be described in a similar fashion, except that a description should indicate the procedures for which the policy acts as a guideline.

An example of policy and procedure taken from an operational service is shown in figure 3. The examples in the figure are from the Internet Public Library and are excerpts from instructions given to the online reference desk staff. Questions to ask while reading through it include: Who is responsible for carrying this out? What actions are directed to be taken? Which attributes of the question are considered?

Processes

The *process* is the highest-level construct in our model. Every question handled by a digital reference service goes through some sequence of steps, from when the first communication is received until the interaction is declared finished. These steps correspond to actions such as "accepting the question," "assigning

Figure 3. Examples of Policy and Procedure

Procedure for answering a question:
First, read over the IPL's Policy for Answering Reference Questions at… [excerpt below]

You may also find some of our example questions and answers useful, see…

To bring up the input form for answering a question, use the RESPOND button when viewing the question you wish to answer.

Next, click on the radio button next to the ANSWERED status, to make sure that the status of the question will change when you send the answer.

Then, type your answer into the text box provided. Once complete, double-check for typos and that you have included all the mandatory elements listed in the Policy for Answering Reference Questions.

Now, it is okay to go ahead and click on the SEND button. The software will then e-mail your response to the patron, append your answer to the text of the question (along with a note above the text that your response was "sent to the original author"), and change its status to ANSWERED.

Policy:
- Read the entire question and the item's history in QRC (claims, follow-ups, etc.) IPL staff sometimes offer suggestions in the form of follow-ups that can help you answer the question.
- Try to determine the age and the English language comprehension level of the patron you are writing for. Try to find age-appropriate sources if the patron appears to be a child, and try to write in clear, short sentences if the patron appears to be having difficulty writing in English.
- Don't become so caught up in researching the aspect of the question that interests you that you forget what the patron really wants.
- Use the ASK_INFO option to clarify the patron's question. If you can think of at least two ways to answer the question, consider writing to the patron. Try to give the patron at least some sources to start with, though, as we've found that one-third of our patrons never write back to clarify their question.
- Take note of the "needed by" date and what date the question was accepted. IPL policy is to answer every question by its "need by" date or within one week after the question was accepted (whichever is sooner). Don't let the date pass after you've claimed a question.

the question to a librarian," "sending a reply," and so on. Every action moves a question to a new step in its process of being answered. In some situations, more than one different action can be applied to a given question. For example, the procedure used by many digital reference services allows a newly received question to be either accepted or rejected.

The flowchart in figure 4 shows a simple asynchronous digital reference process, with each arrow representing an action that can be taken on a question. Questions can be thought of as starting out in the shaded box at the

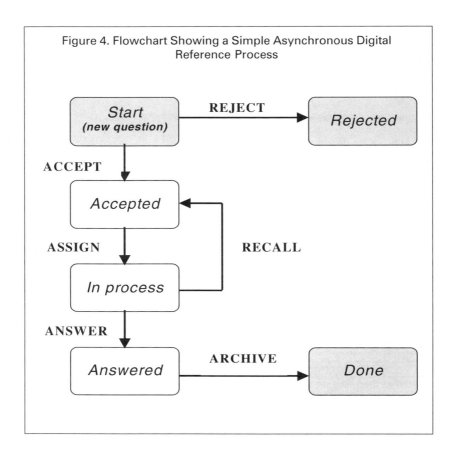

Figure 4. Flowchart Showing a Simple Asynchronous Digital Reference Process

upper left and moving from box to box as they are acted on. When questions reach one of the shaded boxes at right, they are finished as far as this process is concerned.

The flowchart in figure 4 displays only one aspect of the system in that it does not show the people who are working on the questions, the policies and procedures by which they operate, or the questions themselves. These other aspects are necessary to properly interpret the process, and diagrams like this one can be helpful in talking about them. For example, one can see from this diagram that new questions can be either ACCEPTed or REJECTed. In flow-charting terms, this is a "branch point," and a decision must be made for each question about which action is to be taken. Useful questions to ask about this include:

- Which *people* are responsible for making this decision?
- What *policies* are in place to guide the decision?
- What *procedures* are in place to ensure that this decision is made in a timely manner for each question?

    • What *information* from the question itself is relevant to this decision?

We can then define the *process* of a digital reference service to be the set of all the different ways a question can be handled or, equivalently, all the possible sequences of actions that can be taken on a question.

The flowchart is a standard tool for studying dynamic systems such as computer programs and assembly lines, and works quite well for digital reference. Boxes from which more than one arrow emerges are called *decision points*. A question that lands in such a box can go either way, depending on which of the possible actions is actually done to it. Which branch depends on many factors, including decisions based on policies and procedures.

Flowcharts are useful in many ways. They can be used to analyze the efficiency of a system and detect bottlenecks, to compare the processes used by different services, and to develop requirements for software. In addition, they can be of use in the process of redacting reference policies and procedures. By developing a flowchart and going over each step systematically, one can be sure that all of the relevant policies and procedures are accounted for. Finally, flowcharts are useful in identifying points of contact between digital reference systems that are networked together. This, in turn, is relevant to the process of defining interchange standards.

The Model as an Integrated Whole

As the following example illustrates, all six elements in our model are closely interrelated. Consider the initial state of the process shown in figure 4. According to the flowchart, newly arrived questions are subject to one of two actions: A question is either accepted or rejected. For the purpose of illustration, we will assume the following simplified procedure for handling new questions:

    1. Determine whether question is to be accepted or rejected.

    2. If accepted, send standard "accepted" message to user and transfer question to "accepted questions" mailbox.

    3. If rejected, send standard "reject" message to user and transfer question to "rejected questions" mailbox.

Step 1 of this procedure involves making a decision about the question. The guidelines for what kinds of questions to accept constitute a *policy* under the definition given above, whether written or unwritten. For example, the policy of our hypothetical institution might be to accept all questions from patrons residing in the local service area, but from outside patrons only questions relating to the institution's special collections. To make this decision, the *person* who has the job of handling incoming questions must examine the content of the question message (*information*) to determine the subject area of the question and the location of the patron's residence. This same pattern applies to every step of the process: Whenever a decision is to be made, it is made by a person playing a particular role in the system, according to some procedure, based on policy.

Tools for Analysis

In setting a research agenda for digital reference, a number of intellectual tools are available from library science and other areas of research. Some of the latter may seem strange or unfamiliar to a person whose background is in the "soft" sciences. However, when dealing with operational systems, especially software systems, the greatest understanding can be achieved by using methods that have been specifically developed for analyzing such systems.

Library Science

The classic analysis techniques from the field of library science are the *case study* and the *survey*. These techniques elucidate the various policy choices made by different digital reference services so that we can define a common set of parameters by which we can compare and contrast them. In addition, these techniques can provide some indication of what policy choices work well and what choices do not. In designing surveys and doing studies, we can base our work on well-established principles of reference librarianship. Many of the policy parameters for digital reference services are the same as for traditional desk and telephone reference. For example, how many staff members should be on duty at one time, what is the maximum amount of time a staff member should take in answering a question, how should the reference interview be conducted, and so on.

Computer Science

A classic technique from computer science is the *state machine*. This is a formal description of some process, including an enumerated set of states the process can be in at any given time and an enumerated set of transitions between states. If you are unfamiliar with this concept, you can think of a flowchart, which is a way of representing state machines.

It is relatively straightforward to turn a state machine into a set of requirements for a computer program, and then into the program itself. Thus, by developing state machines that model various aspects of the digital reference process, we can provide a sound basis for developing software that will correctly implement the processes we want to use. In the context of the terminology introduced above, the procedures associated with a digital reference process correspond to state transitions. The states correspond to decision points in the reference process, which are in turn defined by policy parameters.

Operations Research

The field of operations research has a useful contribution to make as well, in the form of the techniques of *system dynamics*. Briefly, these techniques involve setting up a series of equations that model flows into and out of various network nodes or states in a system. In the case of digital reference, these could be questions coming in, being assigned, and then answered; or they could be questions being referred from one service to another in a network.

What makes this a difficult problem is that the state of a node can alter the flows into and out of it. For example, a service that accepts questions up to its maximum capacity may then refuse to accept more. Many systems exhibit this kind of feedback, which often makes the equations too complicated to solve mathematically. There are specialized software packages that will take such equations and simulate the flows step by step until the system stabilizes and patterns can be determined. By varying the conditions and the initial values, one can determine, for example, at what point the system will become unstable under steadily increasing traffic. These techniques have been applied to many kinds of dynamic systems, ranging from animal populations to national economies. For simple digital reference systems, this kind of analysis may not be necessary. But as we start to build large-scale referral networks with possible feedback loops, there is a potential for avoidable problems involving bottlenecks and instability under heavy load. These techniques may help us to design these systems to be as robust as possible under a wide range of conditions.

Four Challenges

The field of digital reference is still in a comparatively early stage of development. We have not yet developed a "theory" of digital reference, and we have no way of knowing what is and is not possible except by building systems and seeing how they work. To date, almost all of the published research on digital reference has been observational in nature.

As in any field of inquiry that is closely associated with real-world applications, our research must continue to build on observation of actual systems and actual practice. At the same time, it needs to produce models, correlations, and other abstractions that can guide the continuing development of that practice. As discussed below, these results will help us to refine our understanding of digital reference services and networks as *systems* that follow well-defined patterns of behavior. This understanding, in turn, will help us to develop software, protocols, and practices that can improve the efficiency and efficacy of these real-world operations. Keeping these ideas in mind, I have identified four immediate research challenges facing this field, as shown in figure 5.

Each challenge involves the use of observational data and the generation of formal models, focusing on different aspects of digital reference. These

---

Figure 5. Four Challenges in Digital Reference Research

1. Advancing our understanding of digital reference services as operational systems
2. Learning how to link these services into large-scale networks
3. Figuring out how to mesh the synchronous and asynchronous modes of digital reference
4. Elucidating how to build effective archives of answered reference questions

challenges cover the forefront of current practice, each focusing on one direction in which the state of the art is being extended. They require both qualitative and quantitative analysis, using a variety of tools. By combining intellectual methods from a number of different disciplines, we can overcome the blind spots.

Challenge A: Digital Reference Services as Operational Systems

To determine the most efficient ways of practicing digital reference, we need to understand the range of variation in actual practice and, even more important, the implications of different choices of policy, procedure, and process on the function of a system. This is a huge task, but it can be made easier by generating and comparing process models of the systems being studied. Furthermore, to optimize the design of software systems for digital reference, we need to understand the mapping between the digital reference process as perceived by humans and as reflected in the software. Both these goals can be advanced by learning how to construct process models of digital reference systems.

Figure 6. Examples of Digital Reference Parameter

Patron
- What kinds of software do patrons need in order to use the service?
- What is the privacy policy with regard to user information?

Filterer
- How are questions categorized?
- Are questions assigned to answerers, or do the answerers choose them?
- What kinds of standard response messages are used?
- Is question filtering and assignment done by humans, or will some algorithm be used to do it automatically?

Answerer
- Will answers be reviewed by an administrator before being sent out?
- What happens when the original answerer cannot handle the question?
- What happens when the answerer needs more time?
- Do we allow for dialog between patron and answerer?

Administrator
- What is the target response time?
- Are different kinds of questions prioritized differently?
- Will questions be archived? If so, under what conditions?

As shown in figure 6, the examples of digital reference parameters are, with a few exceptions, applicable to both asynchronous and synchronous digital reference. These are choices made by every organization that offers digital reference services. The particular choices made affect the policies and procedures that define the resulting digital reference system. It is convenient to organize these according to the role they are most closely associated with, as shown in the figure.

The first step in this process is to develop an understanding of the fundamental elements of digital reference: people, actions, and information. Given that most digital reference systems are trying to solve essentially the same problem, there is a lot of overlap in the roles, actions, and question attributes that are important to their processes. What, then, is the best way to take advantage of this situation? By coming up with lists of common elements, we can provide a basis for comparing and contrasting different processes and for determining the extent to which two processes are alike or different. This work also will be useful to software designers, providing guidance in the types of information that will need to be represented in future generations of digital reference software.

After we understand the range of variation in basic elements, the next step is to investigate the various policy choices that influence the design and configuration of digital reference software. Most of these are common to both synchronous and asynchronous digital reference systems. Figure 6 shows a partial list of parameters the author has identified in the course of his own work.

To the extent that we can identify choices that work well and those that do not, we can guide the development of software tools along productive paths. Ultimately, we may be able to generate consensus in the field on a set of best-practice models of digital reference that can be used as starting points for developing new services and new software. Each model would include a set of conditions for which it is targeted. Specific recommendations then could include choices for parameters such as those listed above, even to the level of lists of standard messages and so forth. The various policy choices might be presented in the form of "if you want thus-and-so effect, then choose this policy, otherwise, choose that one," or "policy A has the following implications, while policy B has these others." By basing these models on what is known to have worked well in actual case studies, we should be able to keep the models in rough accord with reality.

Challenge B: Networked Digital Reference Systems

Compared to our understanding of individual digital reference services, our current understanding of networked digital reference systems is quite rudimentary. As noted earlier, several large-scale networks are currently operational. None of these uses more than one level of referral. In other words, when a question cannot be handled by the service that first receives it, the question is forwarded to some central point. Depending on how the network is organized, the central node can either handle the question itself or route it to some other member of the network. This routing can be done on the basis of such factors as subject expertise, availability, and capacity, and it can be handled either manually or automatically.

These current networks are small in scale compared to what will be possible when the relevant software systems and standards are set up. One can envision, for example, a reference network linking all of the libraries in a given country. Such a network might have two or three levels of referral and might handle thousands of questions every day. As one scenario, we may soon see the growth of statewide digital reference networks that can receive and route questions forwarded by member libraries. Questions that cannot be handled in-state then might be forwarded a second time to a national-level routing point or last-resort answerer. Given the necessary standards and agreements, it is even possible to contemplate a worldwide network. Alternatively, a national or international network might be able to identify and route questions on the basis of general topic toward reference services specializing in particular fields, which then would be able to direct specific questions to the most relevant experts. To prepare for these kinds of systems, several research directions are indicated.

Working toward that goal, the NISO committee on Networked Reference Services (National Information Standards Organization 2003) has been meeting since early 2002 to develop a protocol for digital reference interchange. This protocol will allow questions to be sent from one service to another, by either referral or forwarding, and will allow the systems to communicate with each other in order to impose constraints, request the status of a question, ask for clarification and so forth. It will allow both real-time and asynchronous modes of operation. A draft release of the protocol, currently known as Question/Answer Transaction Protocol, or QATP, is scheduled to be ready by early fall of 2003, with plans for a test implementation on at least two different digital reference software tools. The protocol specification will continue to evolve as experience is gained in actually implementing and using it, with a draft version ready to be voted on as early as the first quarter of 2004. Public participation in this process is encouraged. The committee has been releasing early drafts of its documents for public comments and feedback, and welcomes anyone who is interested in implementing the draft protocol on additional platforms.

After a preliminary protocol is in place and tools have been developed or modified to use it, we expect the prevalence of networked digital reference to grow. As networks grow and new ones arise, they will provide more opportunities to study the behavior of such systems on both a large and a small scale. For functional as well as research purposes, we must be sure that the interchange protocol is compatible with the policies used by existing systems and networks, and in order to do that, we must find out what those policies are. Case studies will need to be created for large-scale networks as they develop. Using these case studies, we can begin to determine what policy parameters are most important and to study the effects of various choices. These results will, in turn, inform the design of software tools and refinement of the interchange protocol.

Finally, although we have been discussing digital reference services and networks as static systems, they are in reality dynamic. The flow of questions into and out of the system fluctuates widely over time, and the efficiency of various parts of the system can vary as well. As noted in the fifth section, the well-known techniques of system dynamics can be used to analyze the behavior of these kinds of systems. To apply these techniques, we must develop state machines to model the flow of questions between reference services in a network.

Challenge C: Real-time and Asynchronous Digital Reference

This third research challenge builds on the understanding gained through the first one. To date, all of the established software tools for digital reference focus on either asynchronous or real-time reference, and all of the established services have worked primarily in one or the other mode. However, some services are beginning to experiment with hybrid models.

It may well be the case that the most efficient way to provide digital reference services is to offer both options and allow questions to move from one mode to the other as appropriate. Such a service might answer questions synchronously during staffed hours, and when the patron has the appropriate software available, and when the question requires only a short time to answer. Other questions would be handled asynchronously. Conversely, the synchronous channel could be made available, when needed, in cases of unclear asynchronous questions to allow for conversational interaction between patron and answerer. By making both modes available, we can potentially achieve the benefits of each in a single digital reference service, applying the strengths of each mode where they are most applicable.

The potential for such a hybrid system poses research questions similar to those discussed earlier. To understand the flow of questions between the two modes, it is necessary to have good models of question processing in each mode and then to map out the connections between them. As policy parameters are identified, software tools can be developed or adapted to provide closer integration between these two modes of digital reference operation. Finally, as systems of this sort are developed and put into practice, we can begin to model their dynamic properties in a way analogous to that discussed earlier.

Challenge D: Archives of Answered Questions

Several of the larger digital reference services have been in operation for some years now and have built up extensive collections of answered reference questions. How, then, can they make efficient use of this resource? In theory, many of the questions we receive are quite similar to previous questions whose answers are stored in one of these archives. If we can provide answerers with access to the archives, we can potentially save them from having to duplicate work that has already been done. For even greater efficiency, if we could automatically match up those questions and answers, we could handle a certain fraction of questions without any human intervention at all. Because human labor is the main expense and the most limited resource in all of our operations, such automation would enable a given digital reference service to handle significantly more questions within the limits of its existing resources.

In actual practice, we have begun to have some success in making use of archived questions. At this stage, there seem to be a number of different approaches being taken. A few services provide access to their archives, through either full-text search or categorized under various subject headings. In particular, many of the "AskA" services of the VRD network (Bennett 2003) use this technique. Some services provide relatively small lists of FAQs; others provide extensive archives with sophisticated searching. One service, the MAD Scientist Network (Bry 2003a) automatically matches its patrons' questions against its archive. They report that about one-third of the patrons are satisfied with the found answer and do not proceed to send the question to a human answerer (Bry 2003b).

Although these specialized services have begun to make use of their archives, to the knowledge of the author none of the digital reference services operated by libraries provide access to archives of answered questions. There are many hurdles to doing so, some social and some legal. However, this is also a technical challenge. Two parameters are crucial to understanding this problem. The first is the "domain of discourse," or the range of subject matter covering the questions to be archived. A subject-specific digital reference service can achieve much success by providing direct access to its archive because the set of relevant search terms and keywords is small and easy to understand. The recall and relevance of search results is high, and specialized search techniques are rarely necessary. A service operated by a public or academic library, by contrast, has as its domain of discourse nearly the whole of human knowledge. Professional librarians are taught the specific skills necessary for successful retrieval of information from a large collection of text under such a broad domain of discourse. The very reasons that limit the patrons' ability to find their answers using Google™ will similarly limit their ability to get them from a reference archive. And as for the answerers themselves, the usefulness of their skills is limited as long as full-text search is the only tool available for retrieval from the archives. This is quite a conundrum. To make a useful resource out of general-knowledge question archives, we must figure out some way to make them more accessible than the stores of knowledge from which the answers were drawn.

The second parameter complicating the usefulness of archived answers for library-based digital reference services is the scale of the collections. A small collection of questions and answers can be carefully chosen, edited, and categorized in such a way as to facilitate retrieval from it. A larger collection, although capable of providing many more answers, also requires more skill in order to retrieve information from it successfully. In addition, very large collections preclude intensive manual editing. Whatever techniques of information organization are used with large collections must be uniform and procedural in their application.

In any application of the principles of information retrieval, we have to think in probabilities. What is the likelihood that a given query will find an answer? What is the likelihood that a new question will match something already in the archive? A better way to look at this is to ask: Given an archive whose contents are well distributed across the domain of discourse, how large an archive do we need in order that a given fraction of incoming questions is likely to find matches? This is a quantifiable function, albeit depending on several variables. These variables include the information architecture used to create the archive, the size of the domain of discourse, and the particular algorithm used to find matches.

To determine this function, we can conduct experiments on the existing archives of answered questions. These experiments can be carried out by autocorrelation (matching each question in the archive against the entire archive) and cross-correlation (matching the questions from one archive against another). Both methods simulate a new flow of incoming questions. By experimenting with both automatic and manual retrieval from the archives, we can get an indication of how well these archives will work when automatically matched against incoming questions and when used as a reference resource by patrons and answerers.

Two common methods are currently used to organize question archives for retrieval: classification by subject, and full-text indexing. These are both classic tools of library science. Both are applicable to larger-scale archives, and there is some indication that they complement each other at retrieval time. Full-text indexing can be done automatically, with very little cost. However, by itself it provides only limited usefulness. Full-text retrieval from large collections tends to produce notoriously low relevance. Subject classification can help this but is much more time-consuming and thus expensive. At this point, no one knows how to program an accurate automatic classification algorithm for reference questions.

Conclusion

The four research challenges presented above are linked by two common threads. The first is the creation of *formal models* of what have hitherto been very informally treated systems, and the second is recognition of the importance of different aspects of digital reference, most importantly, *policy* and *procedure*. Each of the four challenges can be summarized as a set of research recommendations, which together make up an agenda for future research in this area.

Challenge A: Digital Reference Services as Operational Systems

   •   Refine the model of *roles* in asynchronous digital reference (McClennen and Memmott 2001) based on studies of many different digital reference services, and extend it to real-time digital reference.

   •   Generate a comprehensive list of *actions* used in digital reference processes. Such a list could be based on case studies and surveys of a variety of different digital reference services. It would include actions such as accept, answer, forward to another service, ask patron for follow-up, and so on.

  • Generate a similar list of *question attributes* (some people call this "metadata") that are used in digital reference processes. This list would include attributes such as date answer is required by, affiliation of patron, level of answer desired, and so on.

  • Analyze case studies of digital reference services, possibly in combination with a survey. Use this information to build a comprehensive list of *policy parameters* that are important for digital reference software design.

  • Develop state machines to describe the *processes* used by a variety of currently operating digital reference services, and compare and contrast them.

Challenge B: Networked Digital Reference Systems

  • Analyze case studies of digital reference networks, possibly in combination with a survey. Use this information to build a comprehensive list of *parameters* that are important for interchange between digital reference systems, especially using different processes and different software.

  • Modify existing digital reference software to use the draft Question/Answer Transaction Protocol as soon as it is released. Develop new special-purpose software for managing networked digital reference.

  • Develop state machines to model the flow of questions among networked digital reference services.

Challenge C: Real-time and Asynchronous Digital Reference

  • Generate state machines describing the two modes of question processing and merge them into a prototype model for a hybrid real-time/asynchronous digital reference service.

  • Experiment with the implementation of such a service in practice.

Challenge D: Archives of Answered Questions

  • Analyze existing databases of answered reference questions to measure the degree to which individual questions overlap enough in subject for a search function to be useful. Plot this measure against the size of the archive and specificity of the domain of discourse.

  • Experiment with different methods of organizing and retrieving from large-scale archives of answered questions.

  • Develop automatic subject classification algorithms for reference questions and answers.

By applying tools that have been tested and proven in other disciplines, we can work toward a solid understanding of the static and dynamic properties of digital reference services and networks, and a new understanding of how to make the best use of large archives of answered reference questions. By studying the variations and commonalities among systems operating under different conditions and different assumptions, we will better understand the ways in which digital reference software and interchange standards must be configurable to meet the needs of different services. Extending our understanding in these two ways will enhance our ability to both manage digital reference services efficiently as operational systems and build software tools and standards that work well with existing practice. As the practice of digital reference continues to spread, and in particular to become networked on an ever-larger scale, this basic understanding will be crucial to the continuing development of the field.

References

Bennett, Blythe. 2000. "Virtual Reference Desk Incubator: A Demo." Paper presented at Facets of Digital Reference Service: The Virtual Reference Desk Second Annual Digital Reference Conference, Oct. 16–17. Available online from http://www.vrd.org/conferences/VRD2000/proceedings/bennett-incubator.shtml.

Bennett, Blythe. 2003. *VRD Network*. Available online from http://www.vrd.org/network.html. Accessed March 2003.

Bonham, Miriam. 1987 (October). "Library Services through Electronic Mail." *College & Research Libraries News* 48(9): 537–38.

Bry, Lyn. 2003a. *About the MAD Scientist Network*. Available online from http://www.madsci.org/info/intro.html. Accessed March 2003.

Bry, Lyn. 2003b. Personal communication.

Henderson, Tonya. 1994. "MOOving towards a Virtual Reference Service." *Reference Librarian* 41/42: 173–84.

Lagace, Nettie, and Michael McClennen. 1998. "Questions and Quirks: Managing an Internet-based Distributed Reference Service." *Computers in Libraries* 18(2): 24–27. Available online from http://www.infotoday.com/cilmag/feb98/story1.htm.

Lankes, R. David. 2000. "The Birth Cries of Digital Reference." *Reference & User Services Quarterly* 39(4): 352–54.

McClennen, Michael, and Patricia Memmott. 2001 (September). "Roles in Digital Reference." *Information Technology & Libraries* 20(3): 143–48. Available online from http://www.lita.org/ital/2003_mcclennan.html/.

McClennen, Michael. 2001. "A Process Model for Digital Reference." Paper presented at the 3rd Annual Digital Reference Conference, November 12–13.

McGlamery, Susan. 2003a. *24/7 Reference—Products*. Available online from http://www.247ref.org/products.htm. Accessed March 2003.

McGlamery, Susan. 2003b. *24/7 Reference—Services*. Available online from http://www.247ref.org/services.htm. Accessed March 2003.

McGlamery, Susan. 2002 (November). Personal communication.

National Information Standards Organization: Networked Reference Services. Available online from http://www.niso.org/committees/committee_az.html. Accessed March 2003.

Online Computer Library Center. *About QuestionPoint*. Available online from http://www.questionpoint.org/web/about/. (Accessed March 2003.)

Weise, Freida O., and Marilyn Borgendale. 1986. "EARS: Electronic Access to Reference Service." *Bulletin of the Medical Library Association* 74 (October): 300–304.

Chapter 5
Policies for Digital Reference

Jo Bell Whitlatch
Associate Dean, San Jose State University

The overall research agenda this paper seeks to address is: What types of policies will promote quality/successful digital reference services? This chapter is organized around policies related to the following topics: scope of service; clientele; privacy issues; partnerships and collaborations; sources; cost; and staffing.

Introduction

This chapter deals with research questions concerning policy issues for digital reference services. From knowledge gained through research, we already know that policies related to user populations served, responsiveness, and type of information provided have an important influence on the quality of services. These findings from traditional reference services suggest that research related to effective service policies should be a high priority for digital reference services.

For the purposes of this paper, digital reference services are defined as Internet-based services that employ human experts or intermediaries to provide information to users. Policy is defined as how an organization sets its rules under which services are offered or as guiding principles and a course of action thought to be advantageous.

Review of the Current State of the Art in Policy

The literature on digital reference policies is buried in articles describing individual case studies of organizations offering digital reference services. Typical of these is a case study of e-mail reference services at the Ohio State University Health Sciences Library by Powell and Bradigan (2001). Their article includes a description of a change in policy. Because of the increased

The author would like to express her appreciation to Donna Dinberg and Franceen Gaudet for their suggestions, which have enriched this paper.

volume of queries, the policy changed from having the head of reference field the questions to having individuals responsible for e-mail questions that arrived during his or her time on the reference desk. The article also contains an analysis of the types of questions (212 questions received between 1995 and 2000) with most being ready reference in nature, but some being more complex.

In late 2000, the Health Sciences Library revised its reference service policy so that equal delivery of services could be provided to all users. Prior to the change in policy, users who were using e-mail as the method of contact were more likely to receive free database searches and free document delivery than people inquiring in person at the reference desk. Under the new policy, only research requests, mostly by lawyers and health professionals not affiliated with Ohio State University (OSU), are referred to the fee-based service. Requests by non-OSU clients requiring use of databases available to OSU only as a subscription service also would be referred to the fee-based service.

The article also advises librarians to think carefully before limiting "remote reference services only to their primary patrons" because, based on the Health Sciences Library experience, the number of questions "does not overburden the librarians" (p. 176). However, the article does not contain sufficient information or analysis to determine the effect of policies related to marketing and identifying the scope of service on the volume of services.

Electronic Mail and Remote Reference Service guidelines are included as an appendix. The guidelines include the following policy topics: population served, division of work, turnaround time, disclaimer for consumer health questions (i.e., material provided is not intended to be medical advice), and types of document delivery and database services provided for OSU and non-OSU patrons.

This article raises interesting policy issues related to method of user request and the possible effect on the quality of service provided because of different service policies. This might be viewed as the reverse of policies that often favor users physically present at the reference desk rather than users phoning into the reference desk.

A case study by Foley, which concerns instant messaging services at the University of Buffalo General Libraries, includes some discussion of staffing policies. Evaluation of instant messaging services revealed that one person could not simultaneously staff the instant messaging chat room and a physical reference desk because "of the many distractions around a reference desk" (2002, 39). In terms of policy, librarians who provided simultaneous reference service via the instant messaging service and the physical reference desk were advised to give preference to patrons within the library. They also were advised to refer difficult questions to a subject specialist or to encourage users to call or visit the library. To ensure patron privacy, session transcripts were not retained, although staff were asked to paraphrase the questions they received (some staff forgot to do this). One of the biggest staffing problems was that librarians (not library school students who worked nights and weekends after receiving training from librarians) frequently forgot their shift or arrived late. Initially, the service was not publicized or promoted through library instruction sessions "to prevent students from sending in a flood of course-specific questions" (p. 40). This case study illustrates the very cautious approach many libraries take to marketing new services.

Kibbee, Ward, and Ma conducted a case study of real-time online reference service at the Reference and Undergraduate Libraries, University of Illinois at Urbana-Champaign. The authors report that "one of the biggest challenges was establishing guidelines and policies for the service" (2002, 26). They believe that virtual service differs from in-person service in significant ways, particularly concerning the extent of user involvement in finding information, defining primary constituency given the difficulty of identifying users, licensing restrictions, and document delivery. The article deals with policy issues related to scope, intended audience, and confidentiality. As with many digital reference services, this service was intended to address short factual answer inquiries, but not the more complex queries related to database searching, extensive research, instructional needs, and so forth. Nonetheless, because the article reports that queries involving extensive instruction were the most problematic, users clearly submitted some out-of-scope questions. However, the digital reference software used did not have co-browsing functionality. Service also was staffed from desks to provide a maximum number of hours for digital reference services, but staff helping digital reference users found the fact that they were helping a virtual reference patron difficult to explain to patrons in the library awaiting service.

The most informative and useful research literature for policy development is related to information seeking. One of the established findings is that for most users, "time is an overriding criterion in the choice of information selection and delivery" (Young and Von Seggern 2001, 164). Young and Von Seggern's study is one of the latest in a series of studies that indicate the frequency with which users will take the most convenient source if it is "good enough" rather than spend additional time to consult a source judged of higher quality.

Focus group participants in Young and Von Seggern's study also noted that the major barrier to finding information in the past was actual physical access to the desired document. However, focus group members reported that the current obstacle was information overload and questionable validity of sources. Bates (2002) confirms this finding in her study. Although the majority of knowledge workers in companies (79%) seek free information on the Internet as first choice, 62 percent say information on the Web is too hard to find. Also, 72 percent say it is difficult to determine the quality, credibility and accuracy of information found. "Knowing where to start" appears to be the most challenging obstacle. Rather than evaluating the sources, "getting to them in the first place" (p.163) appears to create the most problems for users.

Young and Von Seggern's study also echoes findings on the importance of people as a cited source of information. Comments in several groups indicated that a human information source would be preferred for information seeking related to shopping, making travel arrangements, and finding research information. However, Bates (2002) found that, as part of research commissioned for Factiva, 68 percent of company knowledge workers preferred to find information on their own. She notes that in the consulting field the figure is 81 percent and in information systems the figure is 79 percent.

Rieh believes that "alternative reference service models can best be redesigned by looking more closely at how users are dealing with their information problems and how they get help from reference librarians in technological environments" (1999, 185). This observation would certainly also be a good approach for establishing policies for effective digital reference services.

Another research effort of value for establishing digital reference policies is the *Facets of Quality for Digital Reference Services.* The facets were developed based on experiences in managing and coordinating exemplary digital reference services. Several of the facets suggest the type of policies that would be necessary to provide successful digital reference services. For example, Facet 1, Accessible, indicates that successful services must establish a policy that digital reference services meet the requirements of the American with Disabilities Act (ADA). Facet 3, Clear Response Policy, is explicit in recommending that policy be provided: "State question-answering procedures and services clearly in an accessible place on the service's web site or in an acknowledgment message to the user. The statement should indicate question scope, type of answers provided, and expected turnaround time." Facet 4, Interactive, recommends that important user information such as age or grade level be shared. In Facet 6, Authoritative, one of the goals is to indicate on the Web site the qualifications of those who answer questions, and in Facet 7, Trained Experts, a goal is to communicate to users that experts are trained in the service's question–answer policies and procedures. Facet 8, Private, states that privacy policies should be established and made readily accessible on the Web site; that all identifying information should be removed from question answer sets before posting to a public archive; and that consent from users should be obtained before sharing transaction data or identifying information with a third party. Facet 10, Provides Access to Related Information, recommends that digital reference services offer access to supporting resources and information and that selection policies be posted on the Web site to indicate criteria for selecting external resources.

As is true in the more traditional human-mediated services of all kinds, privacy will continue to be an important policy consideration. Doty (2001) has written a major review of privacy in digital environments. He notes that important privacy protections such as the U.S. Constitution limit the actions of government, but not commercial organizations. Doty reviews the major principles included in Fair Information Practices:

1. No secret record-keeping system will exist.
2. People must be able to determine what information about them exists in records and how it is used.
3. Information should be used only for its original purpose; use for other purposes should require explicit permission of the person(s) to whom the information refers.
4. People must be able to correct and amend records of identifiable information about themselves.
5. All organizations that create, maintain, use, or disseminate records of identifiable personal information must ensure that reliability of the information for its intended uses; further, these organizations must ensure that the information is not used for other purposes or is not misused (p.121).

Doty observes that many commercial organizations indicate that principles and policies based on Fair Information Practices restrict their ability to do business, to provide customized services to clients, and to identify potential clients. He also notes that the United States, unlike other countries, has adopted a policy of letting business regulate themselves rather than rely on an omnibus approach implemented by a Privacy Commission with power over both public and private organizations. In the United States, there has been a lack of public policy emphasis on privacy with regard to an individual's relations with large organizations. In the business environment and culture of the United States, this is not surprising given an economic system in which organizations expect to profit from the use or sale of information. Doty notes that privacy concerns include not only information related to individual attributes, but also information about transactions, social and other relationships, access to one's attention, physical location and activity, and freedom to act in politics or in sexual life (i.e., freedom to make certain types of decisions without interference). In a broader sense, privacy can be understood as defined by Agre as "the mechanisms through which people define themselves and conduct their relationships with one another" (Doty 2001, 157). Identification of these relationships may increase threats to freedom and autonomy if people's behavior and demographic characteristics are linked to the digital sources they consult, the online purchases they make, and the words and images they use in messages. Databases maintained by various organizations allow the reconstruction of most of the daily activities of individual. However, the increased commodity value of information and information processes has a dark side: the social exclusion of human beings from adequate food, clothing, education, shelter, health care, and employment that the information society supposedly makes possible for everyone. As information resources and technology become increasingly costly and complex, information is less accessible to less privileged groups in society.

Doty also discusses the concept of privacy in public—people act in public and expect to be observed; however, they might object to others recording, distributing, or otherwise using information about their shopping or other activities performed in public. Digital technologies support and record transactions, are repositories for records, and facilitate secondary uses of transaction information. Because of these capabilities, Doty concludes that reliance on Fair Information Practices is necessary, but not sufficient in a society where private organizations hold, manipulate, and sell information related to everyone.

Empirical Data Regarding Issues and Strategies
Many digital reference services do not meet base standards outlined in the *Facets of Quality for Digital Reference Services*. To obtain a small amount of empirical data, in July 2002, the author performed Web searches using the words "digital reference policies," "digital reference policy," "virtual reference policies," and "virtual reference policy" and then reviewed a few of the first hits in Google.com (a typical user search strategy on the Internet). The author also checked well-known digital reference services, such as QandAcafé, and Webhelp.com, to review statements posted on their pages. Policy statements were compared with policies recommended in the *Facets of Quality for Digital Reference Services*. Results of the comparison are displayed in table 1.

The results of this author's survey provide evidence that digital reference services need to focus on developing and explaining policy to their potential users. Perhaps some of those surveyed have internal policies on some of the topics, but it is certainly not accessible to users. Services were most likely to have some basic information related to clear response policy on question scope, type of answers provided, and expected turnaround time. Privacy policies also were more likely to be provided by digital reference services. Over half the services addressed policy issues related to confidentiality of personal information obtained from users. No site really provided policy information on the expertise of staff who would be answering the questions, given what we know about the public's knowledge of librarian qualifications and training. None of the digital reference services provided policies for users with disabilities, although a few sites addressed policies related to age or grade level. Selection policies for resources were posted on only one of the digital reference service pages.

The findings from the author's informal survey are confirmed by White's (2001) analysis of digital reference services in academic libraries. White found that only half the libraries offering digital reference service specifically mentioned clientele for the service and that half the libraries provided no guidance on the nature of the questions the service was prepared to answer. About three-quarters did provide some information on response time. Although just over 70 percent of libraries used a question form, on average, only six items of information were solicited. She concludes that clients were provided with relatively little guidance on how to formulate questions and provide information that could assist the librarian in putting the question in context and thus provide the most relevant and useful answers for clients.

Clarification of the Policy Issues/Challenges That Need to Be Addressed

This section outlines the major topics for which policy—informed by research—should be developed and prominently displayed to all providers and users of virtual reference services. Many policy issues and concerns about quality of service are equally relevant in the environment of traditional reference service. And much work remains to be done in developing and displaying policies to users in the traditional reference environment. However, devising effective policy becomes more essential because of the digital environment, which fosters the globalization of communication and the storage, manipulation, and communication of extensive amounts of information. Topics are scope, clientele, privacy issues, partnerships and collaborations, sources, cost, and staffing.

Scope

Scope concerns policies such as the type of questions the digital reference service is designed to answer. The most typical categorization of queries is brief factual/ready reference versus research help and instruction. To what extent will the service provide factual information versus research assistance? A related question involves the extent of user involvement in finding the information they seek. To what extent will the service focus on answers to questions, such as searches for the users in databases with results delivered versus referral to sources such as frequently asked questions (FAQs), Web guides, and databases recommended for independent searching by users?

Discussions of scope of service also must consider people's often-strong preferences for self-help and identify the situations in which users expect that human intermediaries significantly add value. Heckart (1998) addresses the larger issue of when human help, as opposed to machine help, is appropriate. He identifies three broad policy alternatives. The first is to postpone policy decisions and launch a research agenda to pinpoint an appropriate dividing line between human and machine help and the second is to make exclusive reliance on machine help a deliberate policy goal. The third alternative is a more effective affirmation of our present beliefs on the importance of human help.

The major research questions for policy development for scope are:
- User preferences and expectations
    — What variables influence user preferences or expectations for consulting digital reference services as opposed to Web search engines or other search methods that do not involve human intermediaries?
    — Do users differentiate among the various types of services?
    — How many people understand that they can ask questions?
    — Are choices of method to use in seeking answers to queries important to users?
    — When users fail to find information on the Web or in other sources by themselves, for what type of questions would they expect digital reference services to be useful?

- In general, what do users expect in terms of an answer from digital reference services, instruction and advice (complete answers)?
- Types of questions and answers
    - Do user satisfaction rates and quality of answers differ for queries that are factual versus those that are primarily related to research help?
    - Do user satisfaction rates and quality of answers differ for queries answered with documents versus those answered by experts who provide advice?
    - For legal and medical queries, when it is clear that users are seeking advice? What type of responses would provide the greatest value to the users?
    - Do users perceive digital reference services in certain subject areas (e.g. health, education) as potentially more valuable than others do?
    - To what extent is scope of service limited by factors outside the control of the institution (e.g., legislation, political requirements, trade agreements, and so forth)? Is this problematic for policy development in institutions serving multiple or overlapping jurisdictions?
- Type of Assistance
    - Under what circumstances does self-help provided by technology supply equivalent quality to help provided by interacting with staff?
    - What categories or types of questions can be answered more cost effectively by automated systems? Can typologies of reference questions and/or answers be developed and classified relative to the required level of interaction?
    - At what point in the process of seeking information should users switch from self-help to human-mediated services, and for what types of questions?

Progress in these areas will best be made by conducting research on the information-seeking patterns of users and the impact that the Web has had on traditional information-seeking patterns. Progress of searches also should be tracked on libraries that are promoting digital reference services. For individual organizations or governments interested in assisting particular population groups, focus group sessions with leaders of that group would assist in developing effective policy related to scope of services.

Clientele

Clientele concerns policies for the primary groups that are the focus of the digital reference service as well as policies on the extent to which groups outside the primary clientele are served. Related to clientele are guidelines on how identity is determined for cyberspace users of digital reference services because affiliation or status of virtual users can be difficult to determine. Another issue under the topic of clientele is the extent to which different user groups in the population are provided with equal access to public services. Legislation may greatly influence the degree to which nations provide access to population groups, such as users with disabilities or speakers of other languages.

The major research questions that will facilitate the development of policy for type of clientele to be served are:

- Nature of primary clientele
  — Do reference services that limit service to their primary clientele provide higher-quality service in terms of responsiveness, quality of answers, and satisfied users?
  — Are there workload effects for institutions that extend digital reference beyond their primary clientele? So often, staff express a fear of becoming overloaded, yet some agencies report that overload did not occur when service was extended beyond the primary clientele.
  — How do participants in a digital reference network or other collaborative reference service resolve issues of clientele (i.e., nonprimary users)?
- Characteristics of clientele
  — Who are the users of digital reference services? What clientele characteristics lead to digital reference use?
  — What clientele characteristics promote effective and successful use of digital reference service?
  — Within the primary clientele, does the audience change in terms of new types of queries and demographics as new digital reference services are offered?
  — From the perspectives of different groups of clientele, what is the value of digital reference service?
  — Is there a distinction in service policies between nations with legislation protecting the access rights of certain population groups (such as users with disabilities) and other nations not having such legislation? Does the quality of service received by these groups differ?
- Trust in digital reference service
  — How do you build up trust in the service? What do we need to know about the social context of the interaction?
  — What factors influence trust in digital reference services? Are user perceptions of trust related to the quality of scripted messages and the personalization of the interaction?
  — How do systems for processing questions, patterns of interaction, and scale of operations influence perceptions of trust?

Progress in this area might best occur by conducting studies of digital reference services and the responsiveness, quality of answers, and satisfied users in relationship to the type of clientele targeted, the extent to which service is limited to clientele, and the volume of queries received.

Privacy

Privacy policies are needed for both users and service providers. For users, a major issue is the extent to which messages possibly containing information traceable to an individual user are stored. Another important user issue is the security of the digital service and the requirements for user identification. How do we protect our users in light of the USA Patriot Act (USAPA)? With the advent of the Children's Internet Protection Act (CIPA) and other similar legislative efforts, privacy rights and protection of children are areas of great public interest and concern. There are expectations that the privacy of minors will be upheld by the institution.

For service providers, the extent and methods the employer uses to monitor performance raises issues related to privacy. Gross, McClure, and Lankes (2001) observe that the presence of electronic transcripts of questions and answers will allow for evaluation of reference service and librarians reference skills in ways that were previously not feasible. Although exciting for evaluating digital reference answers and interactions of client and provider, this enhanced record-storing capability also raises privacy issues related to the monitoring of employee e-mail and other digital records of transactions.

Privacy issues related to policy involve many levels of regulations and laws—international, national, and major jurisdictions within nations. Often regulations and laws that make up overall policies form a network of conflicting and continually changing rules under which digital reference services must operate. This includes balancing between rights of users to privacy and too-restrictive practices on subsequent uses of information by others.

The major research questions in this area are:

- User privacy
  - What do users expect in guarantees to privacy?
  - What is the potential for harm for users who give up privacy rights in exchange for the benefits of service?
  - Is privacy so contextual that there are no general rules?
  - What demographic and other personal user information is essential to provide high-quality digital reference services?
  - What processes and procedures are necessary for protecting the privacy of patron transcripts?
  - What is the balance between protecting patron question–answer transcripts and the group interests and benefits that go beyond individual concerns?
- Privacy protection for children
  - Does offering digital reference service to minors have an effect

on existing child protection policies?
— Are new and/or different policies required for digital reference for children? Do the policies for children differ from those for adults?
- Service provider privacy
  — Will surveillance of the performance of digital reference service providers improve the quality of service?
  — What employee surveillance practices will have positive or negative effects on the performance of digital reference service providers?

Progress concerning privacy issues might best be accomplished by studying models for protecting privacy in other nations and their effectiveness in both safeguarding users of electronic services and providing customer information for business use. Studying and reporting on law and court decisions related to privacy issues also would provide valuable information concerning the impact of electronic information on privacy rights.

Partnerships and Collaborations

Partnerships and collaborations involve policy considerations when questions are referred to more specialized sources. What groups are appropriate for partnerships? Will users and providers form part of a network such as interlibrary loan (ILL) or the telephone system? Who will pay? Who will benefit?

In partnership with the Library of Congress, OCLC is developing a model for virtual reference partnerships that may operate in a manner similar to ILL services. QuestionPoint will offer two levels of virtual reference services to libraries, one setting up local live online reference arrangements and the other setting up participation in the Global Reference Network. Libraries will not only pay subscription fees for the service, but also contribute to the service, which at a basic level includes knowledge-base editing, and, at a higher level, commits staff to answering questions.

Major research questions that will be useful in developing policies concerning partnerships and collaborations are:
- Network structure and organization
  — What types of partnerships and networks provide the highest-quality digital reference service to users?
  — What referral policies are most effective in providing high-quality digital reference services?
  — How should service agreements be formulated and enforced in a collaborative environment?
  — What architecture, specialized and expert versus general, will promote the most effective reference service to users?
- Users of digital reference networks
  — In terms of responsiveness to local clientele, what type of digital reference services is value added?

— How useful is a database of question and answer pairs? Is the cost of creating and maintaining the database worth the benefits to users?

— What are the benefits and costs of networking digital reference services?

Progress in this area might be best made by studying the strengths and weaknesses of a networks, such as ILL, telephone services, and telecommunication networks to determine how successful practices might be best adopted for use in developing and maintaining successful digital reference networks.

Sources

Sources involve policy issues concerning the use of free Web sources versus commercial databases on the Web. In the case of commercial databases, how will licensing restrictions influence the quality of answers provided by the digital reference service? How will service providers advise users of authority of sources and possible bias in sources? To what extent will document delivery be included as part of the service, and how will copyright provisions be met? Problems with access to digital collections and licensing restrictions already have arisen in QuestionPoint. QuestionPoint does not require OCLC membership, but WorldCat and other OCLC reference databases traditionally have been restricted to OCLC members. Will access to these databases be available to all participants in QuestionPoint (Quint 2002)?

Another policy issue under the topic of sources concerns materials created by digital reference staff. How will the accuracy of FAQs and other Web guides be safeguarded? How frequently will information be updated? What criteria will be developed for linking to other Web site sources? By law, the materials created by the user of digital reference services may hold intellectual property rights on their part of the reference interchange. Copyright issues could influence storage, display, and reuse of answers and questions.

Major research questions that will facilitate policy concerning the use of sources for digital reference are:

• In use of sources, how can the benefits be balanced between commercial interests and the educational needs of users?

• To what extent does the use of sources for digital reference services deprive commercial databases of profits?

• How do intellectual property issues affect collaborations and other partnerships? What laws apply when international collaboration takes place?

Collecting uniform data on use of electronic sources is essential for progress in this area. Such data will assist in determining the extent to which electronic journals and other sources are actually used. Advances in technology should make these data easier to collect and analyze than previously; however, standards for use of electronic sources need to be adopted so that use data can be compared across publishers. Research sponsored by the Association of Research Libraries is already under way in this area.

Cost

Policy issues related to cost revolve primarily around how the digital reference service is to be funded. Under what circumstances will fees be charged, if ever? Costs to users also need to be considered, particularly barriers related to disabilities, language, and the level of technology required to access the service.

Major research questions that should be addressed are:

- General costs
  - What is the total system cost of digital reference services?
  - What digital reference service processes minimize costs, while maximizing quality?
- Outsourcing
  - Would it be more efficient to outsource 24/7 reference service?
  - Do digital reference services that have been outsourced provide higher-quality digital reference service than "company" (in-house) digital reference services?
  - Given a potentially global audience, scope issues such as wider audience served and expected languages of the service may push organizations toward outsourcing digital reference services. Under what circumstances might outsourcing become a preferred solution, and is outsourcing, rather than a refusal to serve, the way to go in a broader context?
- Copyright of questions and answers
  - Can a third party claim ownership of and sell questions and answers originally provided freely and collaboratively?

Progress on policy development in this area might best be made by experimenting with outsourcing digital reference services to private firms and then comparing the costs of offering the digital reference service in-house with the cost of having it provided by an external source. Quality comparisons of these services and user satisfaction also would be important.

Staffing

The final policy issues discussed are expertise and training required for staffing the service. Should there be a credentialing process for reference? Can staff who have not been formally trained as librarians answer some portion of the questions more cost effectively than reference experts can? Or are FAQs a better solution than staff for more routine queries? How long should service providers spend answering an individual query?

Other policy issues related to staffing are responsiveness, turnaround times, and delays in service. Policies that determine who answers the questions also may influence the quality of service. The Internet Public Library classifies reference questions by subject, and staff members are encouraged to respond only to questions in their area of expertise. However, in other libraries, digital reference is performed by the reference librarian and may be answered by the librarian on reference duty, regardless of expertise. Location of digital reference away from the desk also may provide better-quality service. Gross, McClure, and Lankes (2002) report that the literature appears to be moving toward a consensus that digital reference should be performed away from the physical reference desk because librarians find the reference service more demanding to provide.

Major research questions on staffing policy that will facilitate providing high-quality digital reference service are:

- Staff skills
  — Are new or different staff skills required for digital reference when compared to traditional reference? If so, what skills associated with successful digital reference service are similar to, and different from, those associated with successful reference service in a face-to-face environment?
  — What staff skills are most important to users and most strongly associated with responses more highly valued by users?
- Answering processes
  — What staff question-answering processes provide higher-quality reference services?
- Expertise of staff
  — What level of staff expertise and training is required to provide high-quality reference services?
  — In which domains of knowledge does subject expertise of staff make a difference, or the most difference, in the quality of digital reference service answers?

To make progress in this area, studies should be conducted on the quality of answers and the user satisfaction with services offered by staff with different levels of expertise and training. In certain areas, sophisticated search engines may provide users with the satisfaction and quality of answers comparable to those of staff. Studies should be conducted to determine under what circumstances self-help provided by technology provides equivalent quality to help provided by staff.

White (2001) noted that, compared to digital reference services in libraries, many AskA services are far more forthcoming about their digital reference policies and procedures, often providing both policies and procedures online to users and making available archives of digital questions and answers. In contrast, digital reference services sponsored by libraries tend to resemble practices used in face-to-face reference services. Automating face-to-face reference policies and practices in libraries may not be the best approach to delivering reference services in a digital environment. Organizations that provide digital reference service would be better served by adopting policies based on the state of current knowledge about effective digital reference practice and continually evaluating the effectiveness of those policies in terms of quality of service to users.

Several of the *Facets of Quality for Digital Reference Services* provide an excellent beginning in establishing policies based on best practices. Digital reference services from all types of organizations need to build on this fine beginning and develop policies that cover scope, clientele, privacy issues, partnerships and collaborations, sources, cost, and staffing. Organizations should post these policies online and begin to measure their impact on the quality of digital reference services.

As research continues in digital reference services, those conducting the research should always discuss the implications of their findings in terms of recommended changes of policies for organizations providing digital reference service. Professional societies should not only support research, but also play a strong role in ensuring that the findings and implications for policies based on best practices are widely disseminated to all organizations providing digital reference services.

References

Bates, Mary Ellen. 2002. "Free, Fee-based and Value-added Information Services." The Factiva 2002 White Paper Series. Available online from http://www.factiva.com.

Doty, Philip. 2001. "Digital Privacy: Toward a New Politics and Discursive Practice." *Annual Review of Information Science and Technology* 35: 115–245.

Facets of Quality for Digital Reference Services. Version 4. (2002.). Developed by the Virtual Reference Desk Project. Available online from http://www.vrd.org/.

Foley, Marianne. 2002. "Instant Messaging Reference in an Academic Library: A Case Study." *College & Research Libraries* 63: 36–45.

Gross, Melissa, Charles R. McClure, and R. David Lankes. 2001. "Assessing Quality in Digital Reference Services: Overview of Key Literature on Digital Reference." School of Information Studies, Florida State University, Information Institute. Available online from http://www.ii.fsu.edu.

Heckart, Ronald J. 1998. "Machine Help and Human Help in the Emerging Digital Library." *College & Research Libraries* 59: 250–59.

Kibbee, Jo, David Ward, and Wei Ma. 2002. "Virtual Service, Real Data: Results of a Pilot Study." *Reference Services Review* 30: 25–36.

Powell, Carol A., and Paula S. Bradigan. 2001. "E-mail Reference Services: Characteristics and Effects on Overall Reference Services at an Academic Health Sciences Library." *Reference & User Services Quarterly* 41: 170–78.

Quint, Barbara. 2002. "Question Point Marks New Era in Virtual Reference." *Information Today: News Breaks & Conference Reports*. Available online from http://www.infotoday.com/.

Rieh, Soo Young. 1999. "Changing Reference Service Environment: A Review of Perspectives from Managers, Librarians, and Users." *Journal of Academic Librarianship* 25: 178–86.

White, Marilyn Domas. 2001. "Diffusion of Innovation: Digital Reference Service in Carnegie Foundation Master's (Comprehensive) Academic Institution Libraries." *Journal of Academic Librarianship* 27: 173–87.

Young, Nancy J., and Marilyn Von Seggern. 2001. "General Information Seeking in Changing Times: A Focus Group Study." *Reference & User Services Quarterly* 41: 159–69.

Table 1. Policies & Digital Reference Quality			
Policies Excerpted from *Facets of Quality*	[1] Toronto Public Library	[2] Vanderbilt	[3] Ryerson University Library
Meet ADA Requirements	No information provided	No information provided	No information provided
Clear response policy on question scope, type of answers provided, expected turn-around time	Brief factual answers on a wide variety of topics. No info on turnaround. For in-depth answers, try fee-based reference service.	Scope: Showed attempt to answer all questions. No info on turnaround.	Scope: Any questions related to teaching and learning needs of the Ryerson community. Most sessions last 15–20 minutes.
Important user information such as age or grade level be shared	No information provided	No information provided	No information provided
Indicate to users the qualifications of those who answer the questions	No information provided	No information provided	No information provided other than librarian
Privacy policies should be established and made available to the user and include removing all identifying information from public question–answer sets, obtaining consent from users before sharing with third party	No information provided	No information provided	Detailed privacy policy addressing confidentiality and obtaining consent
Postselection policies for selection of external resources	No information provided	No information provided	No information provided

1.   Toronto Public Library Ask a Librarian—http://www.tpl.toronto.on.ca/ask_index.jsp
2.   Vanderbilt Ask a Librarian LIVE/Policies and Procedures
     http://staffweb.library.vanderbilt.edu/liveref/aall%20policies%20brief.htm
3.   Ask a Librarian LIVE @ Ryerson—http://www.ryerson.ca/library/ask/asknew.html

Table 1. Policies & Digital Reference Quality (continued)			
Policies Excerpted from *Facets of Quality*	[4] University of Guelph	[5] Drexel University Hagerty Library	[6] Internet Public Library
Meet ADA Requirements	No information provided	No information provided	No information provided
Clear response policy on question scope, type of answers provided, expected turn-around time	Scope: Questions related to teaching and learning needs of the Guelph community. Most sessions last 15–20 minutes.	No info on scope or type of answers. Turnaround time not specific—"as soon as possible"	Scope — help get started but not lengthy research – turnaround time average 3 days.
Important user information such as age or grade level be shared	No information provided	No information provided	Some information, special form if under 13
Indicate to users the qualifications of those who answer the questions	Mixture of library assistants and librarians	Reference librarians are information specialists/ limited information.	Librarians are volunteers. Limited information.
Privacy policies should be established and made available to the user and include removing all identifying information from public question–answer sets, obtaining consent from users before sharing with third party	Privacy policy addressing confidentiality of personal data and reasons for requesting	No information provided	Detailed privacy statement on confidentiality and use
Postselection policies for selection of external resources	No information provided	No information provided	References to resources but no explicit criteria on policies

4.   Virtual Reference @ University of Guelph Service Model
      http://www.lib.uoguelph.ca/reference/VRD/vrdpolicies.html
5.   W.W.W. Hagerty Library Reference Services
      http://www.library.drexel.edu/services/ref.html
6.   Internet Public Library: Ask a Question—http://www.ipl.org/div/askus/

Table 1. Policies & Digital Reference Quality (continued)			
Policies Excerpted from *Facets of Quality*	[7] Q & A Cafe	[8] Chat with a Librarian (LC)	[9] Web help
Meet ADA Requirements	No information provided	No information provided	No information provided
Clear response policy on question scope, type of answers provided, expected turn-around time	Scope: Answer brief factual questions or suggest sources where user might find answer. Average transaction 7–35 minutes. Check with client after 10.	Scope: Historical collections chat service turnaround answer within 5 business days	No scope information provided; faster service if you pay
Important user information such as age or grade level be shared	No information provided	No information provided	No information provided
Indicate to users the qualifications of those who answer the questions	A reference librarian	A librarian	Real live expert
Privacy policies should be established and made available to the user and include removing all identifying information from public question-answer sets, obtaining consent from users before sharing with third party	Detailed privacy statement on personal information for both librarians and clients secured reasons for collecting info and use of personal information	All personal information removed before archiving detailed privacy statement	Detailed privacy policy statement
Postselection policies for selection of external resources	No information provided	No selection policy, only a disclaimer that links do not constitute an endorsement	Disclaimer that cannot be responsible for content of other sites; no selection policy

7.   Q and A Café
     What to Expect—http://qandacafe.com/whattoexpect.html
     Privacy—http://qandacafe.com/privacy.html; Handbook—Q and A café
     Policies and Guidelines—http://www.goldengateway.org/services/qandacafetraining.htm
8.   Chat with a Librarian: An online reference service from the Library of Congress
     http://www.loc.gov/rr/askalib/chat-memory.html
9.   Webhelp—http://webhelp.com/

Table 1. Policies & Digital Reference Quality (continued)			
Policies Excerpted from *Facets of Quality*	[10] Ask Jeeves	[11] Prior Health Sciences Library	[12] Ask Dr. Math
Meet ADA Requirements	No information provided	No information provided	No information provided
Clear response policy on question scope, type of answers provided, expected turn-around time	Answers to everyday questions	Health-related questions; no info on turnaround	K–12 Math students and then teachers usually 24 hours; does not guarantee to answer all questions
Important user information such as age or grade level be shared	Has Ask Jeeves for kids	No information provided	Mentions archive by level and topic
Indicate to users the qualifications of those who answer the questions	Human editors; state-of-the-art search technology	Health science librarians	Volunteer "doctors"
Privacy policies should be established and made available to the user and include removing all identifying information from public question-answer sets, obtaining consent from users before sharing with third party	Detailed privacy statement	No privacy policy	Accept only questions if agree to publish; privacy statement detailed
Postselection policies for selection of external resources	Editorially selected answers, includes criteria	No information provided	No criteria for link

10. Ask Jeeves—http://www.ask.com/
11. Prior Health Sciences Library—http://bones.med.ohio-state.edu/ref/refdeskform.html
12. Ask Dr. Math—http://mathforum.org/dr.math/

Chapter 6

Impact and Opportunity of Digital Reference in Primary and Secondary Education

R. David Lankes, Ph.D.
School of Information Studies, Syracuse University

This chapter examines the domain of digital reference services for and by the primary and secondary education community. It begins by placing education digital reference services (later divided into library-based digital reference services and AskAs) into the larger context of digital libraries and digital reference services in general. It presents a wide range of models for examining digital reference services and providing exemplary services in the education domain. Data are provided to demonstrate the current understanding of education question types and education users in digital reference. Finally, issues and future research areas are discussed.

Introduction

This chapter seeks to frame the research discussion in digital reference in primary and secondary education. As a general note to the reader, primary and secondary education refers to formal education of youth, normally in the age range of five to eighteen years of age. In the U.S. education system, this is often referred to as K–12 education because it covers kindergarten through twelfth grade. These grade levels vary internationally and also are called elementary and secondary education. The point of reference is the basic, and mostly mandatory, education of youth before they enter the workforce or optional postsecondary education in universities and colleges.

This chapter also seeks to explore this discussion at the intersection of digital reference and digital libraries because digital reference is a particu-

The author would like to acknowledge Blythe Bennett, former KidsConnect coordinator; Mary Ann Weiglhofer; and Wendy Juniper for their work in compiling the KidsConnect data. The author would also like to acknowledge Pauline Shostack and the AskERIC Service for their assistance in compiling the AskERIC data.

larly powerful tool for the building and maintaining of digital libraries, particularly in the field of primary and secondary education where a great deal of this work has been done. The chapter generally follows the outline proposed in the Digital Reference Research Symposium overview (http://quartz/symposium/Overview.htm) and is organized as follows:

- *Scope:* This section defines the issue and area under investigation, in this case, digital reference in primary and secondary education. This will be accomplished by using the Lankes–Sutton model of Education Information Infrastructure (EII) to place digital reference in the context of digital libraries and then using the General Digital Reference Model to present a clear picture of digital reference and finally a new scheme of the primary and secondary stakeholders and their needs in a digital library environment.

- *Current state of the art:* This section provides a picture of key projects in digital reference and education. These projects will provide not only the current thinking and work in education digital reference, but also invaluable research environments for ongoing research based on the expected research agenda.

- *Issues and challenges that need to be addressed:* This section specifies generally unique issues that research will need to either focus on or take into account when studying digital reference in education. These issues are drawn from a wide range of inputs, not simply within the current digital reference literature and development work. They take into account general policy and legal issues, primarily within the United States, that have been encountered by education information researchers.

- *Recommendations for future research:* This section proposes specific items for a digital reference research agenda. It builds on the previous section and attempts to delineate specific research questions, environments, and methods.

The goal of this chapter is to present what is known and what needs to be known in order to prompt future research in this area. Certainly, some work has been missed in the writing of this material. My intention was not to be comprehensive but, rather, to present a broad survey with special attention to the large scale and the high impact. Certainly, this chapter draws heavily on my own work and background. Once again, this is not to downplay others' contributions but, instead, is a reflection of the lack of wide-scale scholarship in digital reference for education.

Primary and secondary education is clearly a crucial environment for examination in digital reference, not only because of the high-priority service that students and young learners have in our cultures, but also because of the advanced nature of their work. Digital reference, and digital library work in general, has seen great advances in the education domain. Projects such as the National STEM Education Digital Library (NSDL) and AskERIC have garnered large resource bases, and have either generated a great deal of generalizable knowledge or synthesized digital library work from a wide range of efforts. Put simply, the education domain presents a revelatory case rich with experimentation and development.

Scope

This chapter addresses the general topic of digital reference as a specialized digital library service targeted to the primary and secondary education domain. This statement of scope has three components: digital libraries, digital reference, and primary and secondary education. There are two ways to present the relationship among these concepts. The first is to see the components as separate with areas of overlap. Each has a body of literature, colleagues, practice, and history; however, all have common aspects of use and implementation. For example, although digital reference has its history clearly in the domains of library practice and AskA services as opposed to the large computing science influence in the digital library community, both seek to serve users' information needs via digital networks. Both embrace the concepts of services and collections, and both often use common terminology and metaphors. Certainly primary and secondary education has a rich and long-standing research tradition and a preponderance of nondigital issues. Yet, education, too, overlaps with digital libraries and digital reference in accessing digital information and the ongoing efforts to incorporate information technologies into the classroom (and to use information technology to extend education far beyond the traditional classroom). Figure 1 offers a thumbnail representation of these sets of relationships.

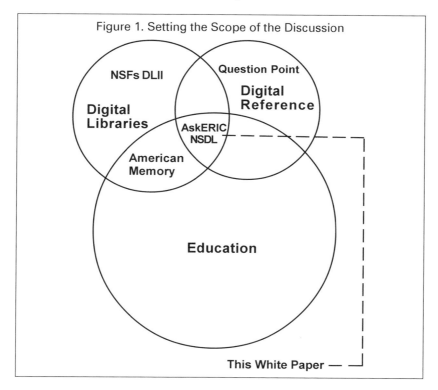

Figure 1. Setting the Scope of the Discussion

For the purposes of this discussion, and to coincide with the overall purpose of the symposium, I will present these three components—digital libraries, digital reference, and education—in a second way, as a hierarchy. Digital library is the largest concept encompassing services, collections, and interfaces. Nested within digital libraries is digital reference as a specific type of service offered by the digital library. At the most concrete and highly resolved level is digital reference for education, where not only is the service type defined, but so is the audience. This hierarchical view is seen in figure 2.

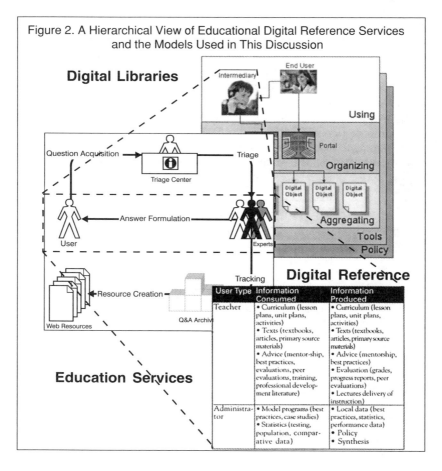

Figure 2. A Hierarchical View of Educational Digital Reference Services and the Models Used in This Discussion

A hierarchical approach will make it easier to familiarize diverse audiences with the relevant issues in digital libraries, digital reference, and education in all three fields. This is simply a rhetorical tool and not intended to dismiss work in any of the three areas as unimportant.

Defining Digital Libraries

The National Science Foundation cites Collier's (1997) in defining a digital library as:

> A managed environment of multimedia materials in digital form, designed for the benefit of its user population, structured to facilitate access to its contents, and equipped with aids to navigate the global network … with users and holdings totally distributed, but managed as a coherent whole.

Although this definition emphasizes materials and collections, it also calls for a variety of services as "aids to navigate." This definition is also intentionally broad. To provide greater specificity for the reader, and to better orient the reader in the hierarchical approach used in this chapter, a more specific framework of a digital libraries is adapted from Lankes and Sutton's discussion of an emerging Education Information Infrastructure (Lankes and Sutton 1999). The framework consists of five distinct core functions of the EII (analogous to a digital library): (1) aggregating, (2) organizing, (3) using, (4) tool building, and (5) policymaking. The first three functions represent the core of the digital library infrastructure that connects users with needed resources. The last two functions may be viewed as enabling functions without which a fully operable digital library is not possible. The remainder of this section describes the parts of this framework.

Aggregating

Aggregating is defined as a "bit bucket," or digital repository, that is agnostic toward file format, document purpose, or organizational scheme. The digital repository simply stores digital objects for use by some third-party agent. One could use the analogy of a computer hard drive that stores hundreds of different files (word-processing documents, music, programs) as a set of 1's and 0's.

Organizing

Organizing is the creation of context, or creating a higher-level, abstract view of the information stored in a repository. Where the repository is simply a collection of digital objects with no inherent structure, an organizer imposes some structure or, broadly, a point of view, on the objects. As Lankes and Sutton state, "the organizing function can be likened to the organizational functions of the traditional library—albeit a library that contains only metadata (data about data) and no primary resources" (1999, 174).

Using

Using is the application of some digital information or object, as housed in a repository and organized by some service or agent, to a given situation. Lankes and Sutton (1999) describe two aspects of information use:

(1) direct end-user information discovery and retrieval of educational materials through one or more of the mechanisms of organization, and (2) indirect information discover and retrieval performed for the end-user through digital agency (pp. 175–76).

Digital agency is a form of intermediation by an automated agent or information consultant, such as a reference librarian or topical expert.

Tool Building and Policymaking

The enabling factors in the framework are tool building and policymaking. Tool building is "the design, development, and deployment of the enabling technologies for aggregating, organizing and using" (Lankes and Sutton 1999, 177). These tools can be "soft," such as metadata and organizational schema, or "hard," such as code or hardware access devices. Policymaking is a human process for developing rules and guidance for building, maintaining, and using the digital library. This framework is represented in figure 3.

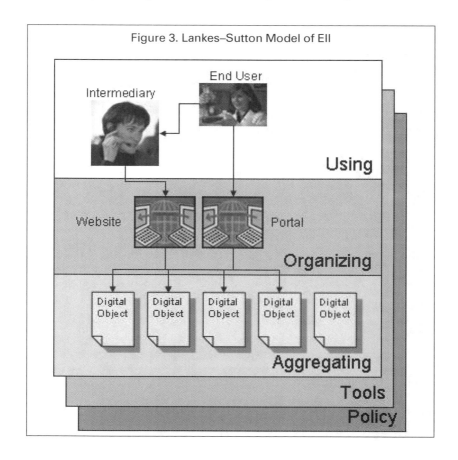

Figure 3. Lankes–Sutton Model of EII

Although the Lankes–Sutton framework acknowledges the existence of digital agency, little more than examples are presented to define the method of digital agency or the interplay between digital agency and other components of the framework, such as aggregation and organization. The next section explores one means of digital agency —digital reference.

Digital Reference as Digital Agency within the Framework

There will no doubt be many means of "indirect information discover and retrieval" in digital libraries. A great deal of work has been done on the research and development in agent technologies. These "intelligent agents" are seen as software programs that can scour a digital library's resources searching for material of interest to a given end user or situation. Of particular interest in this context is the use of human intermediation. The use of human agents in a digital library is digital reference.

Digital reference refers to a network of expertise, intermediation, and resources put at the disposal of a person seeking answers in an online environment. The field of digital reference touches on metadata issues, human intermediation in a networked environment, and quality determinations of networked resources. Some of these issues are shared with the field of digital libraries, yet little work has been done to bridge these two areas of investigation. Digital reference has remained primarily the province of practicing librarians and educators, whereas the digital library community has maintained strong roots in computer science and information retrieval.

It is important for the digital library community to work closely with the digital reference community. The use of human intermediaries within an information system is more than simply a tradition in the library world. Reference, particularly the ability to talk with information professionals, is seen as a core function of a library. Years of practice have shown the need for human-to-human communication to help a user identify an information need and the most appropriate resources to answer it (Mardikian and Kesselman 1995). According to the Library and Information Technology Association (LITA), a division of the ALA, putting a human face on the virtual (digital) library is a key need (LITA 1999).

> It's time to put a human face on the virtual library. What's the crucial factor in the success of the nonvirtual library? The people who work there and serve the user! What do libraries emphasize on their Web sites? Resources, collections, facts with no human guidance or presence! On many library Web sites, the user is hard-pressed to identify the staff, whose names, if they're there, are five levels down. The human factor is still important.

The question in the LIS community is no longer whether to provide reference services in a digital environment or human intermediation services on the Internet, but, rather, how to best provide such services.

Digital Reference Background

The digital reference field has two progenitors. The first is in traditional library and information science (LIS), particularly LIS practice. The second major contributor to digital reference is the category of Internet services known as AskA services, or expert question–answer sites.

Library Reference

Digital reference as an examination of the librarian's role in a digital environment began with e-mail reference efforts. These efforts extended the traditional core reference function of the library past the reference desk to the desktop. Users were able to ask reference questions and consult with trained librarians via e-mail. Still and Campbell (1993) provide an excellent example of early e-mail reference studies. This thread of digital reference concerns issues such as the role of the librarian in cyberspace, the impact of distance service on the traditional reference interview, evaluation (McClure and Lankes 2001), and new skills needed by the information professional (Mardikian and Kesselman 1995).

AskA Services

The second progenitor to the current digital reference arena is that of AskA services (Lankes 1999c). AskA services (so-called because services tend to take on names such as Ask-A-Scientist, Ask-A-Teacher, and so on) are expert-based, question-and-answer services. They use networked communities of experts to answer questions via the Internet. AskA services have been extremely popular on the Internet and have given rise to a separate set of issues concerning system development and scalability.

Current Issues in Digital Reference

As previously stated, some issues are common to both the digital library community and the digital reference community. For example, in the area of metadata and standards for interoperability, both fields share related approaches to the issues of joint services and information reuse. (For a discussion of metadata in digital reference, see Lankes 1999a). Certainly, questions of intellectual property and reuse of digital products are common to both digital libraries and digital reference. Technology approaches, repositories, and all manner of networking resources also are common concerns. Some aspects of digital reference, however, are unique. These aspects center on the inclusion of human expertise (be it process expertise typified by the librarian or subject expertise typified by the AskA expert) into information systems.

Two issues that are specific to digital reference are identified in *Digital Reference Service in the New Millennium: Planning, Management, and Evaluation* (Lankes, Collins, and Kasowitz 2000). They are:

- *Scalability:* How can a digital reference service grow (scale) to handle a large number of questions given that traditional scaling mechanisms such as service hours and geographical constraints run counter to users' expectations of the Internet?

- *Ambiguity:* How can digital reference services identify a priori the amount of context and human intermediation needed to meet a user's needs?

These issues are related (e.g., by better identifying low-context questions, fewer human resources need be applied and more users can be served). These two issues are addressed in systems built and discussed by Janes (2000) and Kresh (2000).

Other issues being explored in the digital reference community relate to the transition from traditional in-person services to at-a-distance processes. These issues include quality measures for digital reference, the nature of the reference interview, real-time versus asynchronous intermediation, media selection in digital reference, and economics of human intermediation.

The General Digital Reference Model

Once again, the previous sections present a broad definition of digital reference. In an attempt to provide more specificity for this discussion's hierarchical approach, a more specific model of digital reference is presented.

The Digital Reference Model, pictured in figure 4, is a general-process model developed through an empirical study of high-capacity digital reference services, primarily in the math/science area (Lankes 1999b).

The model consists of five steps:

1. *Question acquisition* is a means of taking a user's questions from e-mail, Web forms, chat, or embedded applications. This area of the model concerns best practice in "online reference interviews" and user interface issues.

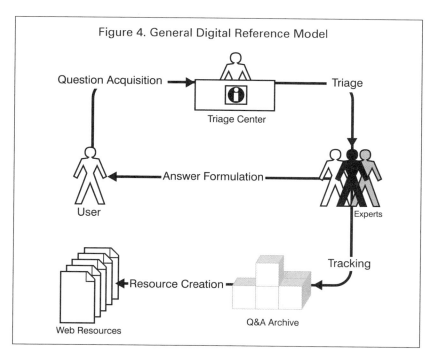

Figure 4. General Digital Reference Model

2. *Triage* is the assignment of a question to a process or topic expert. This step may be automated or conducted via human decision support. Triage also includes the filtering of repeat questions or out-of-scope questions.

3. *Experts answer formulation* details factors for creating "good" answers, such as age and cultural appropriateness. Answers also are sent to the user at this point.

4. *Tracking* is the quantitative and qualitative monitoring of repeat questions for trends. This step allows the creation of "hot topics" and may indicate where gaps exist in the collection(s).

5. *Resource creation* concerns the use of tracking data to build or expand collections and better meet users' information needs within and outside the digital reference process.

Every digital reference system uses this simple model. The important question, however, is how efficiently and effectively can the model be automated to deal with ambiguity and scalability in a distributed environment? The concern in this discussion is when the user represented in this model is a member of the primary and secondary education community (a teacher, student, and so on) or is interested in access to expertise about primary and/or secondary education (represented by either the "experts" or the "Web resources" in the model).

Digital Reference for Primary and Secondary Education

There are several ways to represent the education community: topically, by education level, role, or even geography. In an attempt to include the entire community and to maintain a focus on digital reference, I have adopted concepts presented as part of the "sharium" put forth by Marchionini (1999) in which he states that populations will not simply be users of digital libraries, but consumers as well. In this view, any given community would give information as well as take resources. This creates the basis of a matrix to model the education community: members of the community, what they consume (take from a digital library for application in their particular context), and what they produce (move from their given context to the larger digital library and community).

In table 1, users are matched to the information they either consume or produce. The user types are a simple taxonomy broken into:

- *Professional population:* This class includes the paid staff of an educational institution whose purpose is to deliver education content or the equivalent (such as a parent who home-schools).
- *Student population:* This class covers members of the education community who are primarily receiving education information.
- *Affiliated population:* These are stakeholders who are indirect users and beneficiaries of the primary and secondary education system. They include parents/guardians who are tasked with ensuring that youth learn and education researchers who study the education system. Also included is the higher education community that draws from the primary and secondary student population as well as prepares the education professional population.

Table 1. Information Consumed or Produced		
User Type	**Information Consumed**	**Information Produced**
Professional Population		
Teacher	• Curriculum (lesson plans, unit plans, activities) • Texts (textbooks, articles, primary source materials) • Advice (mentorship, best practices, evaluations, peer evaluations, training, professional development literature)	• Curriculum (lesson plans, unit plans, activities) • Texts (textbooks, articles, primary source materials) • Advice (mentorship, best practices) • Evaluation (grades, progress reports, peer evaluations) • Lectures (delivery of instruction)
Administrator	• Model programs (best practices, case studies) • Statistics (testing, population, comparative data) • Performance data (evaluations) • Policy (standards, legislation, regulation)	• Local data (best practices, statistics, performance data) • Policy
School Library Media Specialist	• Curriculum • Source documents • Research literature (journal articles, ERIC publications) • Multimedia data	• Synthesis (pathfinders, list of links, Webliographies) • Assessments (Web assessments, peer evaluations)
Counselor	• Career data (job availability, career trends) • Higher education data (entrance requirements, school rankings) • Research literature	• Synthesis • Trend Data (student performance, career choice, alumni data)
Specialist Educator	• Training (topical education for technology, special education, etc.) • Best practices	• Best practices • Assessments

Table 1. Information Consumed or Produced (continued)		
User Type	Information Consumed	Information Produced
Student Population		
Primary Student	• Lessons (activities, online activities, simulations) • Fiction (storybooks, educational television) • Primary source material • Texts	• Projects (multimedia materials) • Fiction
Secondary Student	• Lessons • Nonfiction (biographies, histories) • Higher education Information (college brochures, school rankings) • Primary source materials • Texts	• Projects • Papers • Fiction • Field data • Synthesis
Gifted Student	• Evaluations (tests, assignments) • Enrichments (further readings, college courses) • Lessons • Nonfiction (biographies, histories) • Higher education information (college brochures, school rankings) • Primary source materials • Texts • Evaluations (tests, assignments)	• Projects • Papers • Fiction • Field data • Synthesis • Advice
Special Education Student	• Added assistance (tutoring) • Lessons • Nonfiction (biographies, histories) • Primary source materials • Texts • Evaluations (tests, assignments)	• Projects • Papers • Fiction • Field data • Synthesis

Table 1. Information Consumed or Produced (continued)		
User Type	**Information Consumed**	**Information Produced**
Affiliated Population		
Education Researcher	• Statistics • Case studies • Research • Professional produced materials (curriculum resources) • Student-produced resources • Evaluations • Peer assessments	• Research results (articles, data sets, lectures) • Research tools (methodologies, apparatus) • Assessments • Advice
Parent/Guardian	• Assessments (school performance data, teacher performance data, student performance data) • Curriculum (assignments, topics) • Texts	• Advice • Assessments
Pre-Service Educator	• Curricula • Texts • Assignments • Research	• Assignments
Higher Education Teacher	• Case studies • Curriculum	• Case studies • Curriculum • Statistics • Research
Policy Maker/Government	• Statistics • Research • Statistics • Best practices • Assessments	• Policies (law, regulation, rules)
Public Librarian	• Source material	• Synthesis
Business Community	• Assessments • Statistics	• Assessments
Media	• Best practices • Statistics • Research • Synthesis	• Synthesis

This list is not meant to be exhaustive but, rather, to demonstrate major information types and a manner of modeling the education community. It also demonstrates that the members of the education community can be not only users of digital reference services (such as users of AskERIC discussed below), but also providers (as evidenced by KidsConnect, also discussed below). Issues examined in this chapter and later research must take this dual role of consumer and producer into account.

Current State of the Art

To present a picture of digital reference for education, two major types of service in the education domain are discussed in this section. Each type is also illustrated with an exemplar service.

Types of Digital Reference Services in Education

Taken from the previous discussion of digital reference progenitors, there are two obvious, though often overlapping, categories of digital reference services in education: library-based services and AskA services. The AskA services may be divided into general services that may be of use to the education community as part of a more general mission (such as Ask Joan of Art, which answers questions concerning American art for anyone who asks, but is particularly useful in art education) and services targeted squarely at the education community (such as AskERIC, though it covers all levels of education including higher and continuing education). The discussion in this chapter concentrates on the AskA services.

Library Reference

For purposes of this discussion, the term "library reference" refers to digital reference services centered in either a public, academic, school, or special library or with primary reliance on library programs. With the advent of digital reference, a great number of libraries now offer reference service to remote patrons (Janes 2000). These services take a variety of forms—from e-mail systems to real-time chat systems. In the library context, digital reference is referred to as virtual reference, e-reference, networked reference, live reference, online reference, and even chat reference. Although some in the community make a distinction in the mode of delivery and the synchronous nature of the service offered, most agree that these are all part of a single, larger concept of digital reference.

The library reference community also provides the most in-depth discussion of policy evaluation (McClure and Lankes 2001) and the largest set of documented digital reference services (as opposed to the body of systems and development work out of the AskA community discussed later). Much of this work is encapsulated in the proceedings of the annual Virtual Reference Desk Conferences (Virtual Reference Desk 2002) and has a strong library emphasis. In fact, this chapter and the larger symposium were an outgrowth of this conference and work.

As a result of this intense interest in digital reference by the library community, several large-scale digital reference projects are available to the research and scholarly community for examination. The Collaborative Digital Reference Service (CDRS) spearheaded by the Library of Congress (LOC), which has evolved into the QuestionPoint service run by OCLC in cooperation with the LOC, certainly demonstrates the breadth of library-based digital reference services spanning public, academic, and international libraries. The National Library of Canada's recent introduction of Virtual Reference Canada to work with Canadian digital reference services also promises to be a major source of digital reference activity and development. Other prominent digital reference efforts in the library world include KnowItNow from the Cleveland Public Library; the 24/7 Reference service, which acts as a statewide digital reference network for the State of California; and the recent efforts of the State Library of Washington. Also of interest to researchers in digital reference are digital reference vendors in the library domain, including LSSI's Virtual Reference Service. One special case that should not be overlooked is the Internet Public Library (IPL), for although it is not based in a library setting (it is part of the School of Information at the University of Michigan), it has its roots and traditions firmly planted in the library community.

Library Reference Exemplar: KidsConnect

Although many library services that serve the education community (of course, academic libraries serve a higher education population and public libraries answer questions of students), few target primary and secondary education exclusively. One exception is the KidsConnect service. KidsConnect is a question-answering, help, and referral service on the Internet for K–12 students (KidsConnect 2002; see also Bennett 1998). A project of the ALA's American Association of School Librarians (AASL), it has three missions. The first is to educate school library media specialists in the use of the Internet and digital reference as part of the larger ICONnect project. The second is to promote information literacy in students through digital reference (Mancall, Stafford, and Zanger 1999). The third is to promote local school libraries (and school library media specialists) as valuable sources of information and instruction.

The KidsConnect model uses a large number of volunteer school library media specialists (primarily in the United States). Each volunteer is trained using an in-depth mentoring process and then answers questions (ranging from one a day to one a week). The service is targeted at the primary and secondary student population. The digital reference transaction is conducted via e-mail and Web forms.

Data from the KidsConnect service provides valuable insight into the types of students using digital reference services and the types of questions they ask. The service has been widely advertised to schools and teachers as well as to school library media specialists. This advertising has been done through the professional association for school library media specialists (AASL), as well as via the Internet. It is generally available.

The data presented is from 1996–1998; however, recent data (following) will be used to estimate the current validity of these numbers.

Figure 5 shows the number of questions answered by KidsConnect for the years 1996–1998:

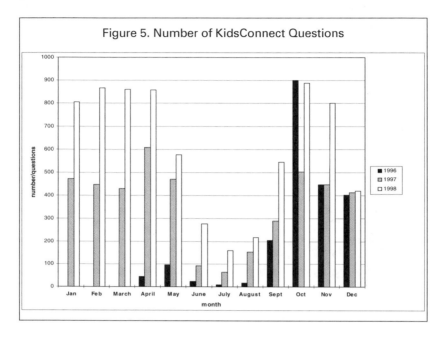

Figure 5. Number of KidsConnect Questions

These numbers are very much in line with, though on the high end of, current numbers of library-based digital reference services as reported at recent library meetings, including the annual ALA conference.

Figure 6 shows how these questions were distributed across different student and adult populations.

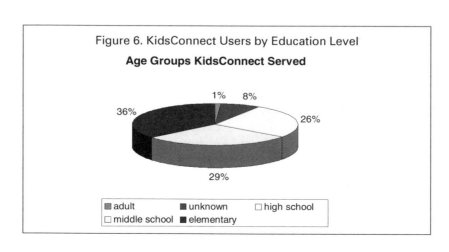

Figure 6. KidsConnect Users by Education Level

These figures demonstrate a rough equivalence between primary (elementary and middle school) and secondary education (high school). The low numbers in "adult" are easily explained by not only the focus of the service, but also the knowledge that at the time of these statistics, teacher questions and questions on the process of education were routed to the AskERIC service.

A more interesting finding, however, was the gender distribution of the questions as seen in figure 7.

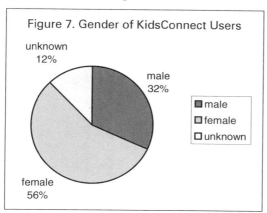

One interesting finding of the KidsConnect staff was the prominence of girls asking questions. Although many hypotheses were put forward to explain this situation (e-mail providing a "safer" environment to ask questions than the well-documented male-dominated classroom, for example), no formal research was conducted to follow up on this finding.

The other interesting finding from the KidsConnect data related to the topics, or subjects, of the questions asked of KidsConnect. The KidsConnect team utilized a Subject Line Analysis technique, whereby the subject lines of a random sample of questions were examined and classified inductively into a subject scheme. If the subject lines were felt to be uninformative (they did not indicate topicality such as "Hello" or "Please help"), the underlying question was examined. The results of this analysis are shown in figure 8.

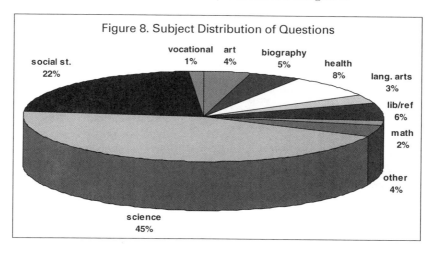

It is clear from figure 8 that science constituted the bulk of questions received. To provide a clearer picture of this category, it was further refined by "type of science questions" shown in figure 9.

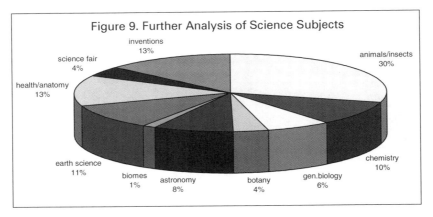

Figure 9. Further Analysis of Science Subjects

inventions 13%
animals/insects 30%
science fair 4%
health/anatomy 13%
chemistry 10%
earth science 11%
biomes 1%
astronomy 8%
botany 4%
gen.biology 6%

Data such as these should prove of great use to new digital reference services geared toward education, most notably, the NSF's National STEME Digital Library (NSDL 2002).

As mentioned earlier, these statistics represent somewhat dated analysis (four years old). In 1999, operation of the KidsConnect service moved from Syracuse University to Drexel University (the previous statistics are based on Syracuse data). Syracuse then transferred much of the staff and processes of KidsConnect into the Virtual Reference Desk Learning Center. This project had a slightly different aim (it had a broader focus and also worked in a network of AskA services with general foci). However, the main concentration of the service was still school library media specialists answering the questions of the education community.

Statistics from the VRD service show a strong correlation between older KidsConect statistics and more recent VRD usage. For example, figure 10 shows the user populations of the VRD service.

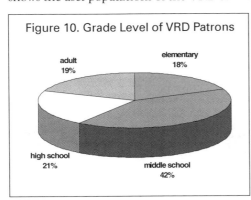

Figure 10. Grade Level of VRD Patrons

adult 19%
elementary 18%
high school 21%
middle school 42%

Note the higher "adult" population reflecting the broader focus of the VRD Network members. However, with this result removed, the distribution in primary and secondary education remains roughly equivalent, with a greater number of "middle school" questions. Also note in figure 11 that science questions still dominate the service.

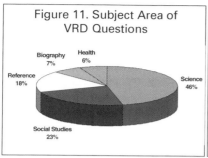

Figure 11. Subject Area of VRD Questions

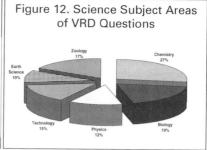

Figure 12. Science Subject Areas of VRD Questions

Once again figure 12 provides a more fine-grained analysis of science questions. This distribution seems to hold over the three most recent years of the service, as seen in figure 13.

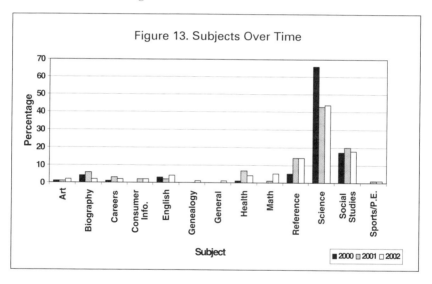

Figure 13. Subjects Over Time

From these more recent statistics, it seems difficult to argue that there has been a massive shift in the types of education users asking questions or the types of questions they ask.

What also is clear from these two services is that the library community has many contributions to make to the digital reference research agenda with respect to education and in general. Moreover, it is clear that the library community contains large-scale digital reference efforts that make excellent research environments that can be utilized in the search for generalizable knowledge.

Education AskA Services

The second progenitor of current digital reference systems is AskA services.

AskA services take their name from expert question-and-answer services that tend to adopt names such as Ask-A-Scientist and Ask-A-Volcanologist (Lankes 1999b). These services tended to originate without interaction with formal library systems and emphasized topical expertise (as opposed to process expertise, such as a librarian's ability to search for information).

A fuller picture of AskA services can be drawn from two studies conducted by Lankes (Lankes 1999b and 1999c; White 1999). Lankes presents an in-depth analysis of the structure and commonalities of "exemplary K–12 digital reference services." Specifically, this study sought to:

•   build and apply a conceptual framework based on complexity research, literature, and the researcher's experience;

•   use this conceptual framework to empirically describe how organizations, specifically K–12 digital reference services, build and maintain services in the dynamic Internet environment; and

•   seek commonalties across these descriptions.

The outcome of this study included detailed "blueprints" and a tuned framework of AskA services grounded in complexity theory as seen in figure 14.

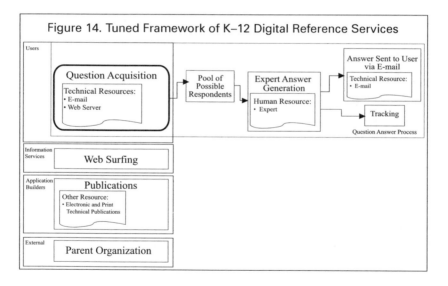

Figure 14. Tuned Framework of K–12 Digital Reference Services

White developed an analytical framework based on systems for evaluating AskA services. This framework was then applied to eleven services in a variety of services (including library-based services).

Unlike library digital reference services that have seen to this point modest usage, AskA services in general have begun with large usage and seen dramatic increases. The most recent Virtual Reference Desk survey of AskA services done in 1999 demonstrates this situation. Table 2 shows an average 44 percent in-

Table 2. Virtual Reference Desk Survey of AskA Service Usage					
GEM Subject	Service Name	Questions Received per Week in 1997	Questions Received per Week in 1998	Percent Difference in Questions Received	Percent of Questions Answered in 1998
Multiple Subject	ScienceNet	500	1200	+140%	100%
The Arts	National Museum of American Art Reference Desk	60	108	+80%	75%
General Education	AskERIC	800	833	+4%	100%
General Reference	KidsConnect	125	225	+80%	100%
	The Internet Public Library	150	150	0%	62%
Health	Ask the Dentist	50	85	+70%	1%
	Ask the Diabetes Team	48	70	+46%	100%
	Dr. Greene's HouseCalls	300	250	-17%	10%
Language Arts	The ESL Help Center	75	150	+100%	100%
Mathematics	Ask Dr. Math	270	867	+221%	35%
	Ask The Math Tutor	35	50	+43%	75%
Religion	Ask an Amish Expert	50	30	-40%	100%
Science					
Astronomy	Ask an Astronomer	10	20	100%	50%
	Ask a NASA Scientist	20	70	+250%	60%
	Ask the Space Scientist	150	190	+26%	70%
Engineering	Ask Professor Construction	5	10	+100%	90%
General Science	The MAD Scientist Network	250	450	+80%	88%
Geology	Ask-An-Earth-Scientist	50	125	+150%	65%
	Ask-a-Geologist (Geological Survey of Canada)	100	10	-90%	100%
	Ask a Hydrologist	5	12	+140%	100%
	Ask a Volcanologist	125	150	+20%	100%
Natural History	Dino Russ's Lair	27.5	15	-45%	95%
Oceanography	Ask Jake, The Sea Dog	200	200	0%	100%
	Ask Shamu	300	55	-82%	100%
Social Studies	Ask The Harkster (Canada)	10	15	+50%	50%
Total Questions		**3,715.5**	**5,340**	**44%**	
Averages		148.62	213.6	44%	77%

crease in use of these asynchronous services from 1997 to 1998, with an average answer rate of 77 percent in 1998 (Lankes and Shostack [forthcoming]).

Compare these statistics to the libraries studied as part of McClure and Lankes's quality study, "In all cases the volume of digital reference question is low, ranging from three to 33 per day" (Gross et al. 2001, 5). This study covered a range of libraries in terms of size and scope (academic, public, federal, and state).

One result of the large volume encountered by AskA services has been an emphasis on process, software development, and automation. Whereas many library services have quickly adopted real-time technologies in which one-to-one interactions require full human intervention, AskA services have looked to asynchronous technologies, at least at their onset. See figure 15 for the distribution of questions received by AskERIC by mode of digital reference as an example of the predominance of asynchronous means (note that "Web" and "e-mail" are both asynchronous modes) and means of shunting users to resources (see Lankes 1999b for a richer discussion of AskA services and their architectures). These techniques run the gambit from sophisticated techniques, such as automated searching of previously asked questions (as in the MAD Scientist service), to forcing users through a list of frequently asked questions before they are able to submit a question (as in the AskA Volcanologist service).

AskA services have tended to also develop more in terms of software and

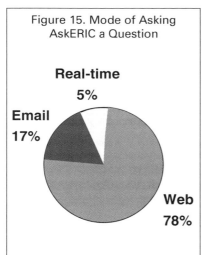

Figure 15. Mode of Asking AskERIC a Question

Real-time
5%

Email
17%

Web
78%

systems. Early examples include Ask Dr. Math, the MADScientist Network, and How Things Work. Though there are excellent examples of software development in the library arena (Meola and Starmont 2002), library services have by and large adopted software from the help desk and e-commerce community, such as LSSI and 24/7 Reference's use of eGain and the common use of LivePerson and NetAgent. Although this may be changing, such as the use of Remedy in CDRS being replaced by original software development in QuestionPoint, AskA services still remain a hot bed of systems development.

Another common attribute with AskA services is their attention to the primary and secondary education community. In the case of some services, this attention is part of a larger view of the general Internet population; but in many cases, it is a special attention where education is foremost and the general population is welcome as well. This can be seen in Dr. Math and MAD Scientist network's attention to students. It also can be seen in services such as AskERIC and their focus on education professionals.

Education AskA Service Exemplar: AskERIC

Whereas the KidsConnect discussion shed light on digital reference use by primary and secondary education students, AskERIC can shed light on use of digital reference by education professionals.

AskERIC is a project of the U.S. Department of Education's ERIC program. It began, and is still operated by, the ERIC Clearinghouse on Information and Technology, although nearly all ERIC components (Clearinghouses, AC-CESS ERIC, the ERIC Processing Facility, and even the parent institution of ERIC, the National Library of Education) are involved in answering questions. AskERIC has two primary components: a question-answering service staffed by ERIC, library, and education professionals (see figure 16 for the volume of questions); and a virtual library of lesson plans, pointers to reviewed sites on the Internet, and an archive of previously asked questions. A more in-depth description, though slightly dated, can be found in Lankes (1999b).

The purpose of AskERIC is to answer questions related to all areas of the process of education. The emphasis on education professionals can be seen in AskERIC's mission as well, as seen in figure 17, by AskERIC's users.

This distribution of users, with the majority being K–12 teachers followed by graduate students (with preservice educators being traditionally heavy users of any ERIC service), is in line with AskERIC's stated mission:

> AskERIC is a personalized Internet-based service providing education information to teachers, librarians, counselors, administrators, parents, and anyone interested in education throughout the United States and the world (AskERIC 2002a).

In fact, AskERIC explicitly does not answer:

> Thank you for visiting the AskERIC Web site! If you are a K–12 student with a homework question, AskERIC may not have the resources to respond to your question.

> AskERIC is designed to provide education information to teachers, librarians, counselors, administrators, parents, students, and others throughout the United States and the world. Our focus is not on the specific things you are learning in school; instead, we specialize in research and ideas about how students of all ages learn best. As an example, we can respond to a question such as "What is the best time of day to teach math?" but not "What is the formula to determine the radius of a circle?"

> If you are looking for information in other specific subject areas or need homework help, you probably won't find AskERIC very helpful. Instead, you may want to investigate the following sites which are designed specifically for students (AskERIC 2002b).

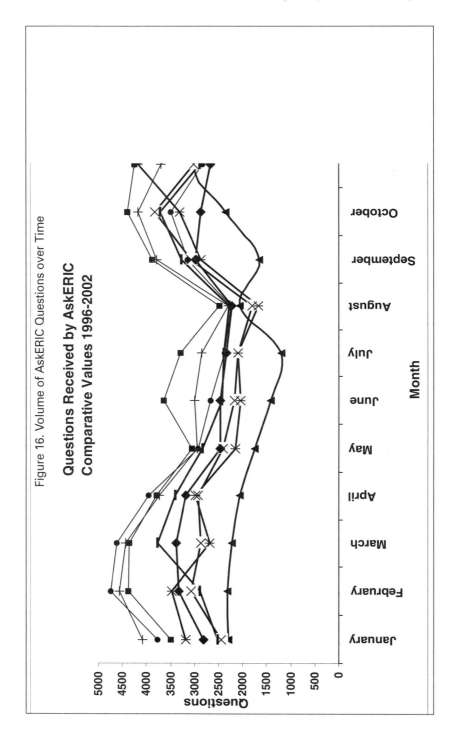

Figure 16. Volume of AskERIC Questions over Time

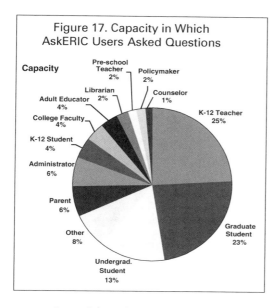

Figure 17. Capacity in Which AskERIC Users Asked Questions

Capacity

- Pre-school Teacher 2%
- Policymaker 2%
- Librarian 2%
- Counselor 1%
- Adult Educator 4%
- College Faculty 4%
- K-12 Student 4%
- Administrator 6%
- Parent 6%
- Other 8%
- Undergrad. Student 13%
- Graduate Student 23%
- K-12 Teacher 25%

Any student questions received by AskERIC are forwarded to other services, such as the Virtual Reference Desk.

What can one determine about AskERIC users beside their educational roles? First, one can determine the education level users were asking about (a K–12 teacher was asking a question about high school, for example), as seen in figure 18.

One also can analyze the nature of the questions being asked by the professional community. AskERIC user surveys provide the anticipated use of the information gained as seen in figure 19.

Using subject line analysis once again, figure 20 shows question types identified in AskERIC questions.

Figure 21 shows the relative stability of this question distribution over time.

In figures 20 and 21, "subjects" refers to particular topics or academic disciplines taught in the classroom (note information from AskERIC responses may be used in higher and continuing education contexts, as seen in figure 18 where 18% of answers were intended for higher or adult education).

Figure 23 shows the relative stability of these subjects over time.

Of particular interest is the predominance of language arts as a topic for educators versus science for students, as seen in figure 8 of the KidsConnect sample. One possible reason for this difference may be the abundance of science material, particularly education-related science material, on the Internet versus instructional resources in language and English instruction.

Aside from the information AskERIC provides

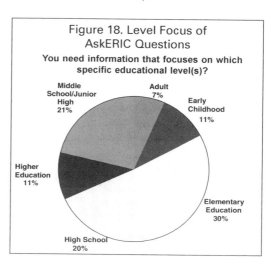

Figure 18. Level Focus of AskERIC Questions

You need information that focuses on which specific educational level(s)?

- Middle School/Junior High 21%
- Adult 7%
- Early Childhood 11%
- Higher Education 11%
- Elementary Education 30%
- High School 20%

on digital reference use by the education professionals, it also provides an exemplar of reference authoring (Lankes 2001). Reference authoring refers to the capture of information in the reference process and its transformation into resources that can be used outside the reference process as part of a larger digital library context. This authoring process can be from the simple, say, the creation of frequently asked questions on a Web site, to the complex, say, the creation on the

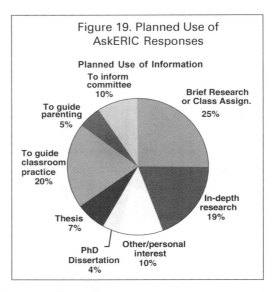

Figure 19. Planned Use of AskERIC Responses

MAD Scientist Knowledge Base (http://www.madsci.org/circumnav/circumnav.html) to the central, as in the AskERIC Resource Collection.

The heart of the AskERIC Web site consists of a resource collection:

> In response to questions we've received at AskERIC, our network information specialists have compiled over 3,000 resources on a variety of educational issues. This collection includes Internet sites, educational organizations, and electronic discussion groups (AskERIC 2002c).

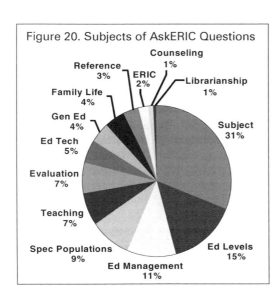

Figure 20. Subjects of AskERIC Questions

This resource collection acts not only as a set of Internet links for end users, but also for AskERIC digital reference specialists. As digital reference specialists constantly comb over this collection of Internet resources, ERIC citations, discussion groups, and more, they also find new resources to add and old resources to delete. This means that the digital reference process itself is used as collection development, annotation, and expert review.

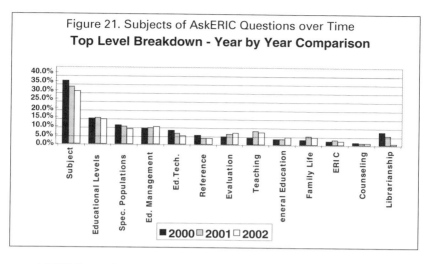

Figure 21. Subjects of AskERIC Questions over Time
Top Level Breakdown - Year by Year Comparison

AskERIC is only one example of AskA services geared specifically to the education community. It does, however, serve as a revelatory case. In the AskERIC exemplar, we see the predominance on asynchronous technologies, the high-volume usage, and the interconnection of the reference process with systems and digital libraries. With these two exemplars and the larger concepts raised in the operation of both services, the discussion now moves to outlining issues and challenges facing digital reference services in primary and secondary education.

Issues/Challenges That Need to Be Addressed

Many of the issues and needed research in the education domain exist in other contexts as well. For example, issues of scalability and ambiguity (Lankes, Collins, and Kasowitz 2000) seem universal to digital reference. Certainly, issues of copyright, authority, and evaluation are crucial in education as well as government, business, and the general population. I do not intend to duplicate these issues here. Instead, I will concentrate on issues unique to primary and secondary education or on aspects of more general topics of special concern to the education community.

The first and foremost challenge facing the education digital reference community can be encapsulated under the broad header information literacy.

Information Literacy

Although alternate definitions for information literacy have been developed by educational institutions, professional organizations, and individuals, all are likely to stem from the definition offered in the *Final Report* of the American Library Association (ALA) Presidential Committee on Information Literacy: "To be information literate, a person must be able to recognize when information is needed and have the ability to locate, evaluate and use effectively the needed information" (1989, 1). In the primary and secondary contests, information literacy has become the primary curricular focus of the school library media specialists and, in general, can be summed up as "helping people find answers, not simply giving them the answer." Following this model, services such as KidsConnect and AskA services such as Dr. Math seek not simply to answer the questions of students with straightforward answers (e.g., "Mount

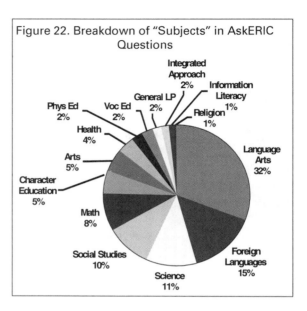

Figure 22. Breakdown of "Subjects" in AskERIC Questions

Everest rises 8.9 kilometers above sea level") but, rather, seek to impart information skills to find the answer (e.g., "try looking this up in the encyclopedia"). The idea is not homework help in the classical sense but, rather, an educational endeavor.

This concept can be complicated by the ahistorical nature of the Internet itself. Simply put, it may be impossible to tell who is asking a question. This factor is important in that AskA services, though not seeking to be "answer" machines used to answer homework questions, do tend to serve the education professional community in a slightly different manner. Services such as AskERIC want to give answers to teachers. This can create a conflict when a digital reference service does not know who is asking the question. It is much like selling a teacher's copy of a textbook with the answers included to students by mistake. The issue is, how do digital reference services teach effective research skills to students while best serving the education professional population? In many cases, this is a problem shared with academic libraries that seek to teach information literacy skills to undergraduates and graduate students while providing more direct answers to faculty and researchers.

The debate, although in a higher education context, can be seen in internal ERIC discussions concerning preservice educators. Several ERIC clearinghouses commented that they were receiving AskERIC questions that, at least on first inspection, were assignment questions from graduate students (e.g., "please discusses the relative merits of the inclusion of computers in the classroom and cite any detractors in the research literature"). To provide an answer (though AskERIC responses are not quite so in-depth) may well alleviate a student's need to do his or her own research. However, how can ERIC be sure that this user is not, in fact, a school superintendent asking this question or a school board member? With only a question and an e-mail address, how can any service determine the intention or eventual use of an answer and therefore differentiate answer types? The final result of the ERIC debate, by the way, was to provide the same service to all users regardless of perceived use. The argument, beyond the practical one of not knowing who a user is, was simply that preservice educators should get to know what ERIC has to offer for when they become teachers.

With the advent of better forms of identity representation in cyberspace and the implementation of user profiles in certain systems, perhaps response differentiation may be possible and, indeed, preferable. This remains an open question. Of course, with greater identity information comes a whole host of new issues that relate to privacy.

Privacy

Privacy certainly has general application across digital reference environments and digital library applications, but it takes on a keen sense of importance when discussing youth (in an education context or not). Certainly, the recent spate of legislation in the United States (e.g., the Children's Internet Protection Act, and the Children's Online Protection Act, or COPA) has caused a serious discussion of children's identity information on the Internet. The heart of digital reference is an information exchange. The end user must disclose information (a question) in order to use the service. Although this information may not be of a personal nature (a general interest question or a class assignment), it may well be very personal (e.g., "Where can I find information on effective drug treatment programs?"). The problem with questions

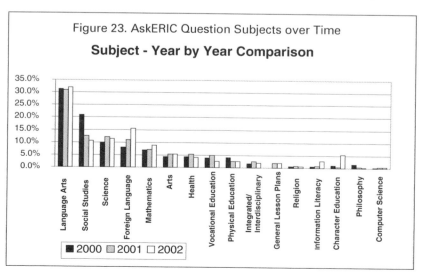

Figure 23. AskERIC Question Subjects over Time

is that they often require personal information in order to provide an effective answer. Although a service may not seek to gain personal information through a deliberate form or set of database fields, this information may be embedded in the text of the question itself (e.g., "Where can I find effective drug treatment programs for 15-year-olds in the Syracuse area?").

Many digital reference services rely on old norms of library and research to preserve the privacy of end users. They may not make archives publicly available. They may destroy reference transaction at their close. Some services even enter into a prolonged editing process to weed out personal information in public archives (though to this point, no automated means of doing so have been readily available). Other services have opted for end-user choice over a blanket privacy policy (e.g., "by clicking here you acknowledge this information will be made public" or "anything entered into the following box will be made public"). This has worked mostly due to the nonprofit nature of digital reference services (COPA currently applies to for-profit organizations in the United States).

However, another force complicates the privacy situation further; that is, the advent of digital reference networks. Education digital reference networks such as the Virtual Reference Desk project link diverse digital reference services together. Questions from users flow freely from service to service crossing a variety of contexts (not for profit to for profit, university to public library, and so on). Currently, no systems or standards are in place to enforce the original policies across the network. In many cases, end users are not even informed that questions asked at a service may be routed to other services. Although, to date, there have been no problems in this type of open exchange, this is a new environment with little precedent. The education community has always operated under a sort of open information doctrine that information can be freely exchanged as long as it has education merit. Will this doctrine survive in a more examined and structured Internet environment?

Privacy is only one of a panoply of difficult issues related to identity in cyberspace. Another key identity issue in education concerns expertise and credentials.

Credentials and Expertise
The story of Marcus Arnold has become something of a legend in digital reference circles. The *New York Times* ran an article (Lewis 2001) revealing that the top-rated legal expert on the commercial AskA service AskMe.com had little legal expertise. In fact, he was a fifteen-year-old with no legal background who relied heavily on common sense and legal television shows for his advice. Arnold is often used as a cautionary tale for digital reference services.

The issue of origin or authorship, so-called provenance, is by no means unique to digital reference. However, expertise in the classroom has special meaning. The problem lies in students' ability to evaluate expertise and education professionals' ability to vet sources of information. Although linked to the information literacy discussion above, evaluation of expertise is certainly a special case. Many services prominently feature the credentials of expertise whether it is organizational association, such as AskERIC's association with the ERIC system and U.S. Department of Education, or individual's background and credentials, such as Louis A. Bloomfield of the "How Things work" service where he highlights his Ph.D. from Stanford and his professorship at the University of Virginia. However, many services have no such credentialing. In fact, other than a University of Virginia URL, there is nothing that actually certifies that Bloomfield is a professor or where his Ph.D. is from.

Related to provenance is the question of bias. Libraries have a long-standing tradition of nonbias information. Where there are multiple views on a given topic, libraries and many AskA services seek to provide information on all or many of these views. However, much of what defines expertise is a specialized form of bias. The *World Book Dictionary* defines expertise as "expert opinion or knowledge, often expressed on some matter submitted to consideration by experts." Much of what one seeks from an expert is his or her opinion. What makes one expert is often not the breadth of one's knowledge, but the depth. A case in point is the Ask Shamu service offered by SeaWorld/Busch Gardens (http://www.seaworld.org/AskShamu/asintro.html). Ask Shamu answers questions concerning marine biology and wildlife. The service employs recognized experts on the topic. However, it demonstrates a clear bias or opinion on the value of marine animals in captivity and preservation of species through marine parks.

Rhetorical Levels

Aside from issues concerning "what" to tell education users, the issue of "how" to communicate information also is large in education. Issues relating to the rhetoric used in digital reference interchanges include:

- *Sophistication of language and terminology:* When providing a factual answer, the level (grade or knowledge level) of the intended receiver is crucial. Explaining why the sky is blue to a first grader is a markedly different experience than explaining it to a secondary school physics student. This is related to issues of identity in knowing who asked a question, but it also is very much related to the experts providing the answer. University professors are simply not used to (in most cases) explaining topics to primary school students. How answers are generalized or made simpler is not a common skill.

- *Sophistication of procedures:* Particularly in the math and science domain, often the most efficient and effective answer is either a formula or equation. Aside from the limitation of current digital reference systems (and indeed Web browsers) on presenting complex formulae, the original end user must be able to understand and process this information. This is a special case of the preceding bullet.

- *Primary language affiliation:* Although language (in this context spoken and written languages such as English, French, and Spanish) is a general issue in digital reference services, it can be of particular concern in an education setting. Even in the United States, where there is almost a presumption of English proficiency, this is far from a guarantee:

> State Education Agencies in the United States and Outlying Areas respond to an annual survey regarding limited English proficient (LEP) student enrollment and services. Based on the most recent survey results, it is estimated that 4,416,580 LEP students were enrolled in public schools (Pre-K through Grade 12) for the 1999–2000 school year. This number represents approximately 9.3% of total public school student enrollment, and a 27.3% increase over the reported 1997–98 public school LEP enrollment (Kindler 2002).

- *Motivational aspects of communication:* The answer is only one part of the information communicated in a digital reference transaction. Aside from terminology and procedures, a related issue in communication might be called the "style" of communication. These often "softer" portions of an answer relate to how the presentation motivates a student (or any user) to pursue the topic further or how satisfied the student feels with the transaction. A simple statement such as "look it up in a basic text" may provide the best reference, but does it support the learning efforts of the student who asked the question?

Clearly, many of the issues in primary and secondary education concern identity and attributes of the users. However, these are not the only areas in need of research and further investigation. The next section outlines further items for a research agenda in digital reference as it concerns primary and secondary education.

Recommendations for Future Research

In many ways, digital reference in primary and secondary education is a well-researched topic. The presence of large and relatively stable funding for education, at least in the United States, has lead to in-depth empirical study of education users' interactions with digital libraries and digital reference in the form of AskERIC, the National STEM Education Digital library, the Virtual Reference Desk, Ask Dr. Math, and the LOC's American Memory Collection, among others. This work has resulted in systems, technical standards, quality standards, and even forums for the continued discussion of digital reference activities. However, much of this work has been of a general nature, applying to all of digital reference, with little attention paid to the direct impact of services in the primary and secondary education field.

In addition to the questions and issues raised above, three areas of needed investigation are uniquely applicable to the education community (primary and secondary first and foremost, but possibly higher and continuing education as well).

Motivation

A key area of research in education is in motivation and shaping instruction for maximum effectiveness. The questions center on what gets and keeps a student's interest. Certainly, it has been hypothesized that talking to experts, and indeed simply other people on the Internet, is motivational (What student would not want to talk to an astronaut?), but no work has been done to assess just how motivational it is. Does the presence of human intermediaries motivate students to ask more and/or better questions? In what way does the presence of intermediaries motivate students to continue investigations outside the traditional classroom or within the confines of the curriculum? Is the information transferred within an answer motivational, or is the interaction itself?

Impact on Assessment

There is a current emphasis placed on assessment of student performance in the United States. Testing initiatives have seen widespread adoption at the national, state, and local levels. Although there is a great deal of controversy over how to assess student performance and the effectiveness of standardized testing, there is little question that determining the benefits of any educational activity is important. As discussed here, the impact of digital reference on student performance might be assessed in both direct and indirect ways. A direct way might be to ask whether the inclusion of digital reference services as part of an educational agenda has an impact on student performance. An indirect way might be to ask whether giving education professionals access to digital reference services such as AskERIC improves their ability to deliver or assess educational material.

Classroom Integration

Related to assessment are questions related to the means of integrating digital reference services into the curriculum. Currently, digital reference, as with most digital library initiatives, is seen as enriching standing curriculum. How can digital reference services be more directly tied to what is taught in the classroom? Two possible avenues for exploration can be labeled as reference authoring and what I will call transactional education.

As previously discussed, *reference authoring* would generate new resources as part of a digital library that could be used in classroom instruction and enrichment. *Transactional education* refers to the concept of learning a topic through a series of digital reference transactions as opposed to a directed delivery of instruction such as a lesson plan or unit plan. Imagine a student learning a new concept in science not by sitting through a formal presentation of materials but, instead, by asking questions, reading suggested readings from the answers, asking more questions, and self- experimentation. This is linked to education concepts such as guided education or discovery learning, but where expertise was always present to the self-learner. Would this mode be effective?

Resource Type Delivery to Education Professionals

Another research area relates solely to the education professionals served by digital reference. The question centers on the types of information that should be used in answering professionals' questions. Should teachers, for example, only receive information (articles, lesson plans, and so on) that has been peer reviewed? Should administrators only be made aware of Web sites and education interventions that have been fully vetted by some official source? Who, in essence, provides quality assurance in education information?

This is not a complete list but seems to capture the main concerns of the education community in terms of digital reference. Certainly, education-oriented digital reference services also will benefit from the results of other, more general digital reference and digital library research.

Conclusion

Digital reference for primary and secondary education has a rich and well-documented tradition. It serves as a revelatory case for other digital reference research and can provide valuable insight into digital libraries serving the education community as well as other digital reference services.

What is apparent from this small examination of the education context is that all levels of education use digital reference services and that their questions, although covering the gambit of topics, concentrate on science (in the case of students) and language arts (in the case of education professionals). Also apparent is the usefulness of education digital reference services as research environments. AskA services and library reference services alike hold large data sets of question-and-answer transactions. These data sets can be used in evaluating how questions are asked, topics of interest to the education community, language use by the education community, and myriad other facts that can be examined. Some of these data sets are publicly available on the Internet; others remain locked in services because of privacy concerns.

From this examination of digital reference services, some methodological techniques can be added to the digital reference research discussion. First among these is the concept of subject line analysis. This technique seems to provide excellent exploratory power and may provide a rapid way to compare question types across services.

Lastly, digital reference services targeted to the primary and secondary education community (or at least the study of these services) provide a wealth of models, theories, and frameworks that can be brought to bear in future research. From the Lankes–Sutton Framework and the General Digital Reference Model (a result of Lankes's complexity framework) to White's evaluative framework, there are rich analytic tools that can be used in the broader digital reference and digital library domain.

References

American Library Association. 1989. *Final Report*. ED 315 028. Chicago: ALA Presidential Committee on Information Literacy.

AskERIC. 2002a. "About AskERIC." Available online from http://www.askeric.org/About/

AskERIC. 2002b. "AskERIC Student Information Page." Available online from http://www.askeric.org/Qa/students.shtml

AskERIC. 2002c. "Welcome to AskERIC." Available online from http://www.askeric.org

Bennett, B. 1998. "Pilot Testing the KidsConnect Service." Pp. 147–50 in *AskERIC Starter Kit: How to Build and Maintain Digital Reference Services*, ed. R. Lankes and A. Kasowitz. Syracuse, N.Y.: ERIC Clearinghouse on Information and Technology, Syracuse University.

Collier, M. 1997. International Symposium on Research, Development, and Practice in Digital Libraries. Tsukuba Science City, Japan.

Gross, M., C. McClure, R. Hodges, A. Graham, and R. Lankes. 2002. "Phase II: Site Visit Summary Report." http://quartz.syr.edu/quality/VRDSiteVisitsummary.pdf

Janes, J. 2000. "Current Research in Digital Reference VRD Proceedings." Available online from http://www.vrd.org/conferences/VRD2000/proceedings/janes-intro.shtml

KidsConnect. 2002. "ICONnect – KidsConnect." Available online from http://www.ala.org/ICONN/kidsconn.html.

Kindler, A. 2002. "How Many School-aged Limited English Proficient Students Are There in the U.S.?" Available online from http://www.ncbe.gwu.edu/askncela/01leps.htm.

Kresh, D. 2000. "Offering High Quality Reference Service on the Web." Available online from http://www.dlib.org/dlib/june00/kresh/06kresh.html.

Lankes, R. D. 1999a. "The Virtual Reference Desk: Question Interchange Profile." White Paper for the Virtual Reference Desk. Syracuse, N.Y.: ERIC Clearinghouse on Information & Technology. Available online from http://www.vrd.org/Tech/QuIP/1.01/QuIP1.01d.PDF

———. 1999b. "Building & Maintaining Internet Information Services." Dissertation, Syracuse University.

———. 1999c. "AskA's: Lesson Learned from K–12 Digital Reference Services." *Reference & User Services Quarterly* 38(1).

———. 2001. "Creating a New Reference Librarianship." VRD Proceedings. Available online from http://www.vrd.org/conferences/VRD2001/proceedings/reinventing.shtml

Lankes, R., and P. Shostack. Forthcoming. "The Necessity of Real-time: Fact and Fiction in Digital Reference Systems."

Lankes, R. David, and Stuart A. Sutton. 1999. "Developing a Mission for the National Education Network: The Challenge of Seamless Access." *Government Information Quarterly* 16(2).

Lankes, R. David, J. Collins, and A. S. Kasowitz, eds. 2000. *Digital Reference: Models for the New Millennium: Planning, Management, and Evaluation*. New York: Neal-Schuman.

Lewis, M. 2001. "Faking it." *New York Times Magazine*, 15 July.

LITA. 1999. "Top Tech Trends." Available online from http://www.lita.org/committe/toptech/trendsmw99.htm

Mancall, J., B. Stafford, and C. Zanger. 1999. "ICONnect: A Snapshot of the First Three Years." *Knowledge Quest* 28(1): 24–37.

Marchionini, G. 1999. "Augmenting Library Services: Toward the Sharium." Pp. 40–47 in *Proceedings of the International Symposium on Digital Libraries 1999, Tsukuba, Japan, September 28–29*. Available online from http://ils.unc.edu/~march/sharium/ISDL.pdf

Mardikian, J., and M. Kesselman. 1995. "Beyond the Desk: Enhanced Reference Staffing for the Electronic Library." *Reference Services Review* 23 (1): 21–28

McClure, C., and R. D. Lankes. 2001. "Assessing Quality in Digital Reference Services, OCLC. Research Project (WWW Document)." Available online from http://quartz.syr.edu/quality

Meola, M., and S. Starmont. 2002. *Starting and Operating Live Virtual Reference Services: A How-to-Do-It Manual for Librarians*. New York: Neal-Schuman.

NSDL. 2002. "National Science, Technology, Engineering, and Mathematics Education Digital Library." Available online from http://www.ehr.nsf.gov/ehr/due/programs/nsdl/

Still, J., and F. Campbell. 1993. "Librarian in a Box: The Use of Electronic Mail for Reference." *Reference Services Review* 21(1): 15–18.

White, M. D., ed. 1999. *Analyzing Electronic Question/Answer Services: Framework and Evaluations of Selected Services*. ERIC Clearinghouse on Information and Technology; Syracuse, NY (ERIC Document ED Reproduction Service No. 433019)

Virtual Reference Desk 2002. "VRD Conferences." Available online from http://www.vrd.org/conf-train.shtml

Chapter 7

Image Intermediation: Visual Resource Reference Services for Digital Libraries

Abby A. Goodrum
School of Information Studies, Syracuse University

In mediating between image collections and image information needs, librarians have traditionally helped users to define and express their image needs and to match those needs to appropriate images from a variety of sources. This chapter describes the challenges to providing digital image intermediation and presents a research framework for addressing them in digital libraries.

Introduction

Many libraries, museums, and other educational and cultural heritage institutions have developed digital collections of nontextual objects with the goal of making these materials accessible to the widest possible audience via the Web. However, this has not always been done in a consistent way, as evidenced by the plethora of metadata, thesauri, and file formats exhibited within the University of Arizona's online directory of image collections, The Clearinghouse of Image Databases (http://www.library.arizona.edu/clearinghouse/). The sheer amount of pictorial information available, as well as rapidly advancing technologies for wide-scale storage and distribution, has made image description and retrieval a central focus of research in library and information science (Goodrum 2000; Goodrum and Spink 2001; Rasmussen 1997).

At the same time, digital libraries now serve larger, more diverse groups of people, and this presents a challenge to emerging digital library reference services in their provision of image intermedaition. A study by Janes (2000) estimated that nearly 44.7 percent of academic libraries were providing digital reference service by 1999, and a number of large-scale digital reference

The author wishes to thank Dave Lankes and the Information Institute of Syracuse for supporting her research and providing access to their archive of digital questions and answers.

projects are currently under way (QuestionPoint, 24-7, VRD, and so on). Unexplored altogether in these projects is the set of problems associated with providing digital reference for which the desired answer is an image or video rather than a text document. Yet, preliminary studies conducted by Goodrum, Lankes, and Annabi (in progress) demonstrate that online requests for assistance in locating appropriate educational images are problematic.

Among the many challenges encountered by visual resource reference providers are those associated with helping users to translate visual information needs into appropriate terminology for input into information systems designed to retrieve textual information. An additional challenge in this setting is the difficulty users often have in translating their image needs into verbal or written expressions, as exemplified by the patron who states: "I can't tell you what I want, but I'll know it when I see it."

Experts who provide visual resource reference assistance within the digital library environment may require additional tools and training to handle questions and provide solutions to users with nontextual information needs. Patrons in this environment are diverse and demonstrate a wide range of skills and online tools to seek out and evaluate appropriate image resources. For example, the following are actual requests for images received by the Virtual Reference Desk Project at Syracuse University:

- "I have a project in identifying the attached picture. The only clue I have is that it's 'astronomical.'"
- "I need to locate pictures on the Web depicting religious persecution (i.e., inquisition, etc.)."
- "I need resources that show common farm animals and their homes. For example, a dog lives in a kennel, a horse lives in a stable, etc. I need pictures for this."
- "I am searching for a graphic depicting the rates of development in adolescents—physical, cognitive, and social development graphed versus time."
- "I need educational cartoons concerning the alphabet."

For many patrons, online tools and resources for locating images and other nontextual materials may be unfamiliar, difficult to learn, or insufficient to answer their information needs. Finding and selecting appropriate images on the Web is problematic because of user difficulty in expressing information needs, in general, and image needs, in particular. Moreover, finding nontextual information using textual access mechanisms presents challenges even to highly skilled intermediaries.

The limitation of text-based access to images has prompted increased interest in the development of access mechanisms that exploit the inherent visual content of an image. This is most often referred to as content-based image retrieval (CBIR). CBIR relies on image processing to define images in terms of primitive features such as shape, color, and texture that can be automatically extracted from the images themselves. However, these methods appear to be somewhat limited in their ability to assist users with higher-level forms of image description and retrieval. For example, there is a considerable gap between primitive image features and the higher-level cognition necessary to equate these features with terms that occur to human beings in the course of a search. Until automated systems can resolve these issues, expert human intermediation is necessary.

An examination of the reference practice literature offers little information on image intermediation in a digital environment, and there is no cohesive body of research to inform this practice. Therefore, in this chapter, I propose a research framework that draws on three areas of related research:

- studies exploring users' image needs and their descriptions or depictions of those needs;
- studies exploring image content classification and representation; and
- studies exploring users' interactions with images and with image search tools in the digital environment.

The following section overviews the research in these three areas and discusses its implications for informing a framework for image intermediation in the digital environment.

Image Description, Representation, and Use

Image-seeking behavior is essentially an act of translation. Cognitive image needs must be translated into external descriptions or depictions in order to communicate those needs to other humans and to systems. The primary difficulty stems from translating a visual information need into a verbal expression. An additional challenge lies in the diversity with which both users and organizers of collections may describe images. To add to the dilemma, many digitized images available via the Web are not accompanied by any textual descriptions of their content, and the practice in some institutions has been to describe images at the collection level rather than the individual image level.

The role of the librarian is thus one of translation, or intermediation, between the user's image needs and the access mechanisms that can connect the user to an appropriate image or image collection. For the most part, the reference practice literature either ignores image intermediation altogether or treats it as a special case of textual reference. The research literature examining the role of human intermediation in supporting image seeking also is sparse. Existing studies on users' image needs and image access have focused primarily on three areas: image needs, image content, and image search. It seems useful, therefore, to review the research in these three areas with an eye toward developing a framework for researching image intermediation in the digital environment.

Image Needs
Much of the research in visual information-seeking behavior and use has been conducted with nondigitized collections and has examined written or verbal queries for images in specific visual resource collections. Early work in this area focused primarily on the needs of students and faculty in art history

(Pacey 1982), art historians (Brilliant 1988; Stam 1984), and artists (Layne 1994; Hastings 1995; Stam 1995). These studies reinforce the importance of visual information to specific populations that rely heavily on visual collections but do little to address the everyday image needs of the general public.

Studies examining image seeking within a wider context have focused primarily on the analysis of queries. The seminal work in this area was done by Enser (1993), who analyzed nearly three thousand written requests to the Hulton Deutsch archive. The results indicated that queries for visual materials exhibited a greater level of specificity than requests for textual materials and that the majority of requests were for specific instances of a general category (for example, "London Bridge" rather than the generic "bridges"). Although not the majority, Enser also identified a significant number of requests for images modified by visual attributes such as time, movement, color, shape, or age (couples dancing the Charleston). Similarly, Keister's (1994) analysis of queries from advertising and marketing professionals, medical professionals, and the general public at the National Library of Medicine demonstrated that most were structured using both generic categories and specific visual elements.

Research examining users' image queries in the digital environment are still quite sparse. Goodrum and Spink (1999) analyzed 33,149 image queries made to EXCITE, a general-purpose search engine on the Web. The study demonstrated that users input very few terms per query and that most query terms occurred only once. The terms that occurred most frequently appeared in less than 10 percent of all queries. Also noted was the presence of terms that modified a general request, such as "rock stars," into a specific request with visual attributes, such as "fat, aging rock stars in spandex."

But queries are not necessarily accurate reflections of information needs. Users tend to formulate queries based on system constraints and their knowledge of systems and collections; but freed from a retrieval task, users describe images using richer, more narrative and emotional terms that go well beyond a description of the objects depicted within the frame (Jorgensen 1995, 1996; O'Connor, O'Connor, and Abbas 1999).

The challenge for image intermediaries is to assist users in expressing image information needs in all their richness and to provide tools that bridge the gap between image needs and systems for retrieving images. This challenge extends beyond traditional reference interviews and question negotiation. What is needed are tools and practices that can elicit and translate users' needs for visual, semantic, and emotive image content.

Image Content

It is one thing to get users to describe the content of images sought, but quite another to match that expression to an existing image. Most IR systems are text based, but images frequently have little or no accompanying textual information. Historically, the solution has been to develop ontologies and thesauri that reflect the unique characteristics of a particular collection or clientele and to assign terms from the controlled vocabulary to describe the subject matter of an image, the objects depicted within an image, or both. As a result, image cataloging and classification varies widely across collections. Moreover, studies examining the consistency by which images are indexed indicate very low levels of agreement and consistency within the same collections (Markey 1988).

These issues, as well as the costs associated with manually assigning terms to images, have prompted interest in using natural language, user-generated descriptors, and automatic image-based approaches to representing image content. Although natural language approaches have performed very well for retrieval of textual information, there still are large numbers of images without accompanying text of any kind. This approach is well suited to the retrieval of news photos and videos with accompanying audio track or textual transcript but does little to retrieve images that have not been formally produced with accompanying text or audio.

O'Connor, O'Connor, and Abbas's proposal that we elicit natural language terms and image descriptions from users seems promising, but we lack a central repository from which to capture and build a searchable archive of user-generated image terms and the images to which they refer. Recent proposals to mine digital reference question-and-answer pairs as a means of generating profiles of users and objects (Lankes 1999) may well provide user-generated image terms, rich natural language, and explicit connections between descriptions of images sought and their image solutions.

Image-based solutions, often referred to as CBIR, rely on image-processing and recognition programs that match on primitive features such as color, texture, and shape that can be automatically extracted from the images themselves. In these systems, user queries may take the form of submitting a sketch and clicking on an exemplar image, texture, or color palette or using a combination of drawing and querying tools. Although promising, these approaches are still in an early phase of development and little is known about their utility for general-purpose image retrieval by untrained users.

There are many challenges in representing images effectively to enable users to find what they seek. The primary challenges for visual resource reference provision are to (1) become familiar with the wide variety of approaches to image content description in order to assist users in matching image needs to images and (2) work collaboratively with other visual resource collections to develop and implement image metadata consistently.

Image Search

In art and art history collections, the traditional image-searching pattern has been one of browsing through slides arranged by period, culture, or artist and then selecting potentially relevant images for viewing on a light box. The limiting factor in finding appropriate images in this manner is the time and attention required to sort through numerous images in search of the most relevant one. The Web equivalent for this may be found in search engines and directories such as Google™ and Yahoo™ that allow users to browse "shot sheets" of thumbnail images retrieved in response to a query or organized according to broad generic classes such as "celebrities." General-purpose Web search engines match terms in user queries to terms appearing anywhere on the Web site where an image file appears and present either lists of Web-site surrogates or pages of thumbnail images for browsing. Although there appears to be some weighting for terms that appear in the image's file name, in many cases the search retrieves a staggering number of images that are simply not relevant to the query (Goodrum and Spink 2002). As a result, users spend a great of time browsing for relevance.

A recent study of image search moves on the Web (Goodrum 2002) indicates that approximately 60 percent of search moves are devoted to browsing and image inspection and approximately 20 percent are devoted to queries and query reformulation. In this study, users of search tools that provide thumbnails viewed many more retrieved images before making a relevance judgment then users who scanned lists of textual descriptions of Web sites with potentially relevant images. The subjects in this study spent an average of twenty minutes to locate an image and expressed frustration at the amount of time spent browsing nonrelevant, but retrieved, hits.

Although browsing is an important and necessary activity in image seeking, it is clear that we have done little to "Save the time of the reader" (Ranganathan 1963). The challenge for intermediaries here is to develop tools that will aid in the presentation of image information and make the users' search easier and more effective. We need to understand how users seek out images in the digital environment and how they make relevance judgments for digital images. Finally, we need to translate our knowledge of users' seeking behavior, image description, and available search tools into useful training and tools for user instruction.

Digital image intermediation links aspects of image metadata, image-seeking behavior, and the provision of visual resource reference services in a networked environment. These are the components of digital reference that must inform procedures and mechanisms for the exchange of questions and answers that support the intermediation of image requests on the Web.

Research Framework

This research framework is built on a digital reference model developed by Lankes, Collins, and Kasowitz (2000) and used in the design and development of digital reference services and software by the Virtual Reference Desk Project. It is a general-process model consisting of the following steps:

1. question acquisition;
2. triage;
3. answer formulation;
4. tracking; and
5. resource creation.

Currently, every text-based digital reference system uses this model. The important question is whether the model can be extended to enable digital libraries to provide reference assistance in the retrieval of images.

The central focus of this framework is to explore how human expertise mediates between image needs and image resources in the digital library environment. As a first step in this research, it is important to develop a model and metrics for examining image needs, the sufficiency of image resource description, triage, and intermediation. From this, it is hoped that recommendations for ways to improve both image resource description and image intermediation in the digital library environment can be made.

A related goal of this framework is to build support for image intermediation into software and processes that can allow for "one-stop, any-stop" input of image requests so that any digital reference service can provide access to appropriate image resources, regardless of where they are located. To extend the General Digital Reference Model to support image intermediation, two aspects of the model will be closely examined: question acquisition (how users enter questions), and expert answer formulation (how experts answer the users' questions). Specific research questions addressed in this framework include:

- Are elements related to image intermediation missing from the existing digital reference model?
- What support do users need to express image information needs in this environment?
- How is triage affected by expanding the existing model to include image reference services? What does "out of scope" mean in this environment?
- What tools do experts need to provide image answers?

Question Acquisition

To develop knowledge about the characteristics of image-related questions, we need to study the characteristics of image-based reference questions, including the presence or absence of visual modifiers (Enser 1993). This analysis may be conceptualized within a framework of existing studies of image queries on the Web (Jansen et al. 2000; Goodrum and Spink 2001) as a way of identifying gaps in our understanding of image intermediation.

Experts Answer Formulation

We need to examine the assignment of image questions to subject and collection experts. Specifically, we need to explore image reference triage and identify variables that appear to drive the assignment of image requests to different types of experts, institutions, or collections. In examining the assignment of questions to experts at different institutions, we also should explore the metadata descriptions of resources provided by these collections. Of interest is the presence or absence of image metadata at the collection level.

We need to model factors for creating "good" answers to image requests, such as format description, and discussion of bandwidth and viewing constraints. We also need to examine the actual image "result(s)" provided in response to questions. Specifically, we should explore the metadata description of answers at the image object level. Of interest is the presence or absence of image metadata and overlap between terms used by patrons and terms used to describe image objects.

Expected Outcome

The expected outcome is a model for providing image intermediation among digital library reference organizations that had not previously existed. Such a model will be useful not only in building software and systems to support image intermediation, but also beneficial in the training and education of reference librarians and visual resource providers overall.

Conclusion

"Just as today's library requires systems and records management expertise on the staff, so must they acquire or grow visual management skills" (Marcum 2002). This research has the potential to make several significant contributions to the digital library and digital reference communities. Research in this area will extend the general understanding of image intermediation so that we can develop effective and appropriate tools and processes to aid in the provision of visual resources reference, to inform the creation of image metadata, and to design interfaces to support image seeking and use. This research will add to our basic understanding of users' image-seeking behavior specifically and information-seeking behavior overall. By building on an existing model of digital reference, we also have the opportunity extend our understanding of digital reference and to identify gaps in the model. This will, in turn, help to inform our daily practice and user instruction in the digital image environment.

References

Brilliant, R. 1988. "How an Art Historian Connects Art Objects and Information." *Library Trends* 37: 120–29.

Cobbledick, S. 1996. "The Information-seeking Behavior of Artists: Exploratory Interviews." *Library Quarterly* 66: 343–72.

Enser, P. G. B. 1993. "Query Analysis in a Visual Information Retrieval Context." *Journal of Document and Text Management* 1(1): 25–52.

Goodrum, A. 2002. "Image Search Moves on the Web: An Exploratory Study." *Proceedings of the Annual Meeting of the American Society for Information Science & Technology, November, 2002.* Vol. 39: 537–538.

————. 2000. "Image Information Retrieval: An Overview of Current Research." *Journal of Informing Science* 3(2).

Goodrum, A., R. D. Lankes, and H. Annabi. In progress. "Media Mediation in the Digital Library."

Goodrum, A., M. Rorvig, K. Jeong, and C. Suresh. 2001. "An Open Source Agenda for Research Linking Text and Image Content Features." *Journal of the American Society for Information Science* 52(11): 948.

Goodrum, A., and A. Spink. 2001. "Image Searching on the World Wide Web: Analysis of Visual Information Retrieval Queries." *Information Processing and Management* 37(2): 295–311.

Hastings, S. K. 1995. "Query Categories in a Study of Intellectual Access to Digitized Art Images." In *Proceedings of the 58th ASIS Annual Meeting, Chicago, October 9–12, 1995*, ed. Tom Kinney. Medford, N.J.: Information Today, Inc., 3–8.

Janes, J. 2000. "Current Research in Digital Reference." *Proceedings of the Virtual Reference Desk Conference*. Available online from http://www.vrd.org/conferences/VRD2000/proceedings/janes-intro.html.

Jansen, B. J., A. Goodrum, A. Spink, and U. Pooch. 2000 "Searching for Multimedia: An Analysis of Audio, Video, and Image Web Queries." *World Wide Web Journal* 3(4).

Jorgensen C. 1995. "Classifying Images: Criteria for Grouping as Revealed in a Sorting Task. In: Schwartz R.P., Beghtol C., Jacob E.K., Kwasnik B.H., Smith P.J. (ed) ." *Proceedings of the 6th ASIS SIG/CR Classification Research Workshop, American Society for Information Science, 1995*. pp. 65–78.

———. 1996. "Indexing Images: Testing an Image Description Template." *Proceedings of the 59th Annual Meeting of the American Society for Information Science, Baltimore, MD Oct. 21–24*. Pp. 209–213

Keister, L. H. 1994. "User Types and Queries: Impact on Image Access Systems." In R. Fidel, T. B. Hahn, E. M. Rasmussen, and P. J. Smith, *Challenges in Indexing Electronic Text and Images*. Medford, N. J.: Learned Information.

Lankes, R. D. 1998. *Building and Maintaining Internet Information Services: K–12 Digital Reference Services*. ERIC Document Reproduction Service no. ED 427778.

Syracuse, N.Y.: ERIC Clearinghouse on Information & Technology at Syracuse University.

———. 1999. *The Question Interchange Profile Metadata for Digital Reference*. Syracuse, N.Y.: ERIC Clearinghouse on Information & Technology at Syracuse University.

Lankes, R. D., J. Collins, and A. Kasowitz. 2000. *Digital Reference: Models for the New Millennium*. New York: Neal-Schuman.

Layne, S. S. 1994. "Artists, Art Historians, and Visual Art Information." *Reference Librarian* 47: 23–36.

Marcum, J. W. 2002. "Beyond Visual Culture: The Challenge of Visual Ecology." *Portal: Librarians and the Academy*, Vol. 2(2): April 2002. pp. 189–206.

Markey, K. 1988. "Access to Iconographical Research Collections." *Library Trends* 37: 154–74.

O'Connor, B. C., M. O'Connor, and J. Abbas. 1999. "User Reactions as Access Mechanism: An Exploration Based on Captions for Images." *Journal of the American Society for Information Science* 50(8): 681–97.

Pacey, P. 1982. "How Art Students Use Libraries—If They Do." *Art Libraries Journal* 7: 33–38.

Ranganathan, S. R. 1963, 1931. *The Five Laws of Library Science*. 2nd ed. Bombay: Asia Publishing House.

Rasmussen, E. M. 1997. "Indexing Images." *Annual Review of Information Science and Technology* 32: 169–96.

Stam, D. 1995. "Artists and Art Libraries." *Art Libraries Journal* 20(2): 21–24.

———. 1984. "How Art Historians Look for Information." *Art Documentation* 3: 117–19.

Chapter 8
Education for Digital Reference Services

Linda C. Smith
Graduate School of Library and Information Science, University of Illinois at Urbana-Champaign

Digital reference services encompass any reference services provided via the Internet and can involve the use of both print and digital resources. Education for digital reference services includes: (1) courses taken in a library and information science degree program; (2) on-the-job training; (3) continuing education; (4) evaluation; and (5) acquisition of substantive, multidisciplinary knowledge. This chapter explores the topic of education for digital reference services by providing a brief history of education for reference services; results of a survey of reference instructors in the U.S. and Canada; a case study of education provided to students in Web-based reference courses at the University of Illinois at Urbana-Champaign; a discussion of the issues and challenges that need to be addressed; and recommendations on how to make progress in this area.

Introduction and Definitions

With the emergence of digital reference services, defined by the symposium organizers as "human intermediation services over the Internet," attention has naturally been focused on the education needed by those individuals who are to provide such services. What knowledge, skills, and values will digital reference librarians need? How can these best be taught? What are the educational needs of novices (students enrolled in library and information science [LIS] programs) versus the needs of experienced providers of "traditional" reference services? To indicate the needed scope of investigation of education for digital reference services, it is helpful to begin with an elaboration of the component terms.

Education

Although a discussion of education may naturally focus on preparation provided by the first professional (master's) degree, Hauptman (1989) reminds us that education for reference services actually encompasses five types of activity:

1. formal sequence of courses as part of the master's degree;
2. on-the-job training;
3. continuing education (conferences, seminars, workshops, professional association programs, formal university courses, professional reading);
4. evaluation (self, peer, supervisor); and
5. acquisition of substantive, multidisciplinary knowledge.

On-the-job training includes both orientation to an organization at the beginning of employment and the ongoing learning that comes with the experience of doing reference work and consultation with more experienced reference librarians. Continuing education can come from a variety of providers, which may result in a lack of coordination or logical sequencing of content.

Reference Services

Although the focus of discussion of reference services is often on question answering, it is important to recognize the full scope of activities that can be undertaken by reference librarians. Katz's classification of "direct" and "indirect" reference is helpful in this regard (1969, 35). *Direct reference* is a person-to-person relationship, usually one in which the librarian answers a patron's question or provides instruction. *Indirect reference* comprises behind-the-scenes activities: preparation and development of catalogs, bibliographies, and all other reference aids that help in providing access to the library's collection; selection and organization of reference materials; evaluation of the reference collection and reference services; and interlibrary loan (ILL). Such activities no longer need be centered on a physical library. For example, Heilig (2001) notes that services provided by Jones e-global library include bibliographic instruction, research assistance, a core collection of research materials, access to electronic databases, reference assistance, and document delivery management.

Digital Reference Services

Arms defines a digital library as "a managed collection of information with associated services, where the information is stored in digital formats and accessible over a network" (2000, 2). He observes that "by *intelligently* combining searching and browsing, *motivated* users can *usually* find the information they seek" [emphasis added] (p. 223). Digital reference services seek to enhance the ability of users to locate needed information through the work of reference librarians providing both direct and indirect services. However, this is just one aspect of digital reference services. Indeed, digital reference services encompass any reference services provided over the Internet and can involve the use of both print and digital resources.

Digital reference allows individuals to submit questions to library staff using synchronous (real-time) or asynchronous technology. Because the transaction takes place through written communication (e.g., often text chat or e-mail), it is possible to record and store questions and answers in a searchable database ("knowledgebase"). Library Web pages and "Webliographies" are new forms of delivery for the products of indirect reference service. *Collaborative* digital reference involves multiple institutions and requires additional software support in order to route questions to the most appropriate participant. QuestionPoint (http://www.questionpoint.org), a joint service of OCLC and the Library of Congress, is an example of such a service.

The remaining sections of this chapter explore the topic of education for digital reference services by providing a brief history of education for reference services; results of a survey of reference instructors in the U.S. and Canada; a case study of education provided to students in my Web-based courses at the University of Illinois at Urbana-Champaign; a discussion of the issues and challenges that need to be addressed; and recommendations on how to make progress in this area.

History of Education for Reference Services

"The functions of the librarian have always been to select the material that his constituents will require; to catalog it so that those who would use it can know what is available and where it is kept; and to preserve it so that both contemporary readers and those who will follow will be able to use it. With the opening of libraries to a wider public, another task fell to the librarian, that of helping the patron to choose the library materials most appropriate to his needs" (Lerner 1998, 211).

Reference service has been a recognized aspect of library work for only about 125 years. Green's (1876) paper, "Personal Relations between Librarians and Readers," is often cited as an early statement of the scope of reference work. Rothstein (1955) provides more details on the development of reference services in different types of libraries. The computer is, of course, not the first technology to affect the provision of reference services. Ryan (1996) notes that a consideration of three technologies to which librarians have had to adapt—mail, the teletype, and the telephone—was useful to the designers of reference service for the Internet Public Library (IPL) Reference Division.

Databases—accessed online, on CD-ROM, and now via the Internet—have been a part of reference services for more than thirty years. Tenopir and Ennis (2002) remark on the changing role of these resources over the past ten years. They suggest that the expectations of both reference staff and patrons changed profoundly during the 1990s as both groups came to believe that information related to almost every question can be found if the right combination of resources and search strategies is chosen.

Education for reference services has likewise evolved over more than one hundred years. Library schools throughout the U.S. have treated reference work as one of the core courses in their curricula since 1890, when the New York State Library School at Albany offered an advanced, senior course entitled "Reference Work" (Richardson 1992). The original courses emphasized what today would be termed "ready reference." The generally prevailing method that library schools have employed in teaching the basic reference course has been to present the special characteristics of a number of reference books in a number of fields and to assign questions that would test the ability of students in their solution. This procedure has depended largely on memory of facts about specific reference books and the ability to use the reference collection in answering questions. Sixty years ago, Boyd (1943) noted the limitations of this approach: Emphasis on the formal reference book useful in answering the ready reference type of questions gives undue importance to ready reference service at the expense of other types of service.

By the 1960s, coverage of the basic reference course included a description of the nature and kinds of reference service as a library function; study of a core set of reference materials arranged according to type (encyclopedia, dictionary, biographical source, and so on); study of reference techniques with emphasis on search strategy and the reference interview; and selection and evaluation of reference materials (Rothstein 1983). Summers (1982) reported additional changes in the 1970s: first, a major shift away from a focus on specific tools to a broader focus involving search strategies and a much wider context of information service; second, a much greater emphasis on the technological aspects of reference, especially computerized databases; and third, increased emphasis on the behavioral aspects of information seeking and the processes of human communication. He expressed concern that "education for reference service in library schools lags somewhat behind the practice of reference service in libraries" (1982, 167). Treatment of technology has been uneven: Although the use of computerized databases has received considerable attention, use of the telephone for reference service has received little attention from library schools (Yates 1986). This is the case despite the fact that use of the telephone is not identical to good face-to-face reference work because of the lack of visual exchange.

Harter and Fenichel (1982) reported the results of a survey of educational practices in the teaching of online searching in LIS schools. They identified three educational patterns: single online course, large component, and integrated approach (into all general reference and subject bibliography courses). Although many instructors felt that integration was the ideal, most had a separate course. Reasons given included lack of adequately trained faculty. Although learning a system's (e.g., Dialog) command language was part of such a course, many other types of knowledge were covered. Topics included file-loading practices and their effect on retrieval; the effects of specificity, exhaustivity, stoplists, and other indexing practices on retrieval; Boolean logic; ability to read and interpret database documentation; ability to conduct a good reference interview; selection of appropriate databases and fields for searching; design of a search strategy likely to produce relevant output; and evaluation of search strategies. None of these are purely technical skills, such as typing, for example. Rather, they involve intelligence, judgment, and knowledge of principles. Practice in using a particular online system can help students learn principles.

Finally, Powell and Raber (1994) conducted a survey to investigate how LIS students were being educated for careers in a changing reference/information environment. The authors observed a gradual shift in focus from consideration of titles and questions to broader concerns of information service. Educators indicated that basic reference courses in the future must provide students with the ability to fully grasp the implications of information technology. Foreshadowing the impact of the Internet, Powell and Raber concluded that: "Educators recognize that information refuses to stay within traditional formats and institutional arrangements, and librarians must learn how to find, retrieve, and deliver traditionally inaccessible information by means of technology" (1994, 165).

In summary, education for reference work has evolved as the practice of reference has changed. There is still considerable emphasis on the tools, but less emphasis on specific titles and more on search strategy. In addition, greater emphasis is being placed on the reference interview and the range of reference services. Treatment of technology has varied: Telephone reference has received little special attention, whereas online searching has been part of curricula for twenty-five years. Although digital services are increasingly being integrated into the basic reference course, for an extended period of time online searching was the focus of a separate course at many schools. The next section reports the results of a survey to gauge the extent to which digital reference services, the latest innovation in technology affecting reference, are being integrated into basic reference courses.

Survey Results

To date, little has been written about education and training for digital reference services. To gauge current practice in master's degree programs, in June 2002, I distributed a brief e-mail survey to full-time faculty who teach reference at one of the ALA-accredited LIS schools. Individuals were identified from school Web pages and located by using the Directory of Accredited LIS Master's Programs on the ALA Web site (http://www.ala.org/alaorg/oa/lisdir.html). Sixty individuals were contacted, and thirty-three responded, representing faculty from twenty-five schools (21 U.S. and 4 Canadian). Although limited to full-time faculty (and thus excluding adjunct faculty who also may be involved in teaching reference) and representing 45 percent of the accredited schools, the responses are at least indicative of the current state of the art.

The survey consisted of four main questions:

1. *Have you incorporated "digital reference services" as a topic in one or more of your courses?* Respondents who answered yes were asked to indicate

which course(s) and through what means (lectures, guest speakers, readings, and/or assignments). If assignments were used, respondents were asked to briefly describe them.

2. *Have you taught a Web-based version of one or more reference courses?* Respondents who answered yes were asked to indicate which course(s) and how the course(s) was adapted for delivery via the Web. Respondents also were asked to comment on whether they felt students in a Web-based course were gaining experience that would be useful to them as digital reference librarians, and in what way.

3. *Has your department/school sponsored any continuing education programs related to digital reference services?* Respondents who answered yes were asked to indicate the scope of such programs and to identify the intended audience.

4. What topics and issues do you feel I should address in a white paper on education for digital reference services?

Responses to these questions are summarized in the following paragraphs.

Treatment of Digital Reference Services

Respondents indicated that some attention is given to digital reference services in almost all the basic reference course offerings, primarily through lectures and readings and occasionally through guest speakers involved in digital reference. Other courses cited as including coverage of digital reference topics are government documents, social science reference, humanities reference, health sciences reference, library instruction and information literacy, information searching, advanced information searching, academic library administration, and special libraries. One respondent noted that a number of her students explore selected topics related to digital reference services in depth through independent studies.

A number of faculty members attempt to give their students practice in digital reference, with e-mail reference being the most common focus of these assignments. Through the generous support of Patricia Memmott from the IPL (http://www.ipl.org/ref) staff, students from several schools in addition to the University of Michigan gain practice responding to patron questions via e-mail. Other schools use the Virtual Reference Desk and AskA services for this purpose. Students typically answer questions for the service and write a paper based on their experience. Giving students practice in real-time digital reference via chat has proved more challenging. Although students can experience such services as users, software commonly used to support the service in libraries (such as that from LSSI) has not been readily available until recently for students to gain practice as a provider.

Other assignments seek to hone students' skills in comparative evaluation (traditional sources versus AskJeeves; AskA services versus search engines; critiquing one's experience using digital reference services offered by academic or public libraries, similar to traditional "observation" assignments used in reference courses with particular attention on the reference interview and sources used in responses); analysis (studying a corpus of e-mail queries to determine topical emphasis and implications for collection development, subject reference expertise, and staffing levels); Web-site design; service design using a team approach; assessing online information literacy tutorials; and discussing distance education support service options.

Web-based Course Offerings

Although several respondents indicated that the Web is being used increasingly as an adjunct to their face-to-face reference instruction, only eleven of the respondents currently offer Web-based courses. No specific evidence that learning in this mode enhances expertise in digital reference was given. Potential benefits noted included that students use electronic reference sources extensively (because the instructor cannot assume all students have access to the same print collection), are more comfortable with technology, and become aware of the advantages and disadvantages of technology as they use it. Chandler (2001) describes how she adapted the reference course at the University of North Texas for delivery via the Web.

Continuing Education Programs

Relatively few respondents indicated sponsorship of any continuing education programs related to digital reference services. Some schools provided access to videoconferences on the topic produced by other organizations. The University of Michigan, Kent State University, Syracuse University, and the University of Maryland are examples of institutions that have offered short courses for practitioners. For example, the University of Maryland's Virtual Reference Workshop 1.0 focuses on sharpening reference skills for the live, online environment. Lynn Westbrook of Texas Woman's University secured grant funding from the Institute of Museum and Library Services to develop an educational program in digital reference for librarians from small academic libraries in Texas.

Issues in Teaching Digital Reference Services

Several respondents pointed out digital reference services issues that need further research. (These issues are addressed later in this chapter.) Challenges specific to teaching master's students about digital reference services were twofold: (1) the sense that basic reference courses are already "swamped" and it is difficult to integrate additional topics; and (2) the need to give students practice in being digital reference librarians, but not having support materials and access to appropriate software. Moreover, there are conceptual/philosophical challenges. For example, to what extent is digital reference fundamentally new rather than a logical extension of content already covered? The next section addresses these challenges by focusing on the experience of a reference instructor at one school where reference has been taught for six years via the Web.

Case Study: University of Illinois at Urbana-Champaign

Library (and information) science courses have been offered in Urbana-Champaign since 1897. Five years later, Isadore Gilbert Mudge, reference librarian and assistant professor, published a brief article on instruction in reference work at the Illinois State Library School in which she identified multiple goals for the reference courses:

> The purpose of the courses in elementary and advanced reference work at the University of Illinois, stated briefly, is to familiarize students with the general aims and methods of reference work, to give them a working knowledge of the principal reference books, to develop the power of research and the ability to follow a clue quickly from book to book for more difficult questions, to cultivate rapid thought and quick answers for simpler questions and to test and increase general information. The purpose is accomplished in two ways, by class instruction and recitation and by independent practical work not directly connected with any class exercise (Mudge 1902, 334).

Assignments included questions that had actually been asked at the reference desk in the university library. "A statement of the amount of time spent upon these problems is required, and, as work is graded for both accuracy and speed, rapid work is encouraged" (p. 334). Work experience in the university library included practice in maintaining various indexes and records, including "a card index for all difficult or frequently repeated questions" (p. 334). Students also developed lists of reference sources for the programs of various women's clubs of Champaign and Urbana and for university classes, debates, and so on. Moreover, emphasis was placed on the ongoing need to learn broadly: "To help the students to acquire this information and to impress upon them the necessity of keeping abreast of the times, work in current events is combined with the course in advanced reference" (p. 335). Mudge's description of the course concludes with a sample quiz in which students had to identify sources where they would expect to find information on questions such as: Where might one find a good biographical sketch of Cardinal Wolsey? What was the Ostend manifesto? Who is president of Ohio State University? What is the national debt of Russia? Who is editor of the *Atlantic Monthly*?

The goals of my course, LIS 404LE Reference and Information Services, though expressed in somewhat different language compared to those of Mudge, are still quite similar (but without the emphasis on testing and increasing general information). (Recent research by Dilevko and Dolan [1999] leads them to conclude that LIS schools might wish to stress the value of keeping up with current events in the syllabi of any reference courses they offer.) The scope of the course includes reference services in all types of libraries and information centers; examination of widely used print and online sources; and development of question negotiation skills and search strategies. At the end of the course, the student will be familiar with reference services for different user communities, basic types and representative samples of general reference sources, and basic search strategies for print and online sources.

I have taught reference-related courses (basic reference, science reference, online searching) since 1977. For the first twenty years, these courses were taught face-to-face to on-campus students, with a computer laboratory component for online searching. To reflect the continuing changes in the world of practice, these courses have been revised and updated on a regular basis. Beginning in fall 1997, I have offered the basic reference course in a Web-based format to distance students and, more recently, adapted the science reference course to this format as well. A previously published paper (Smith, Lastra, and Robins 2001) describes in some detail the structure of the LEEP (online M.S.) program and the changing roles of instructors and students in LEEP. The LEEP technology includes bulletin boards for asynchronous communication; a virtual classroom environment for "live," real-time sessions (streaming audio for lectures by the faculty member, text chat for discussion by the students, pushing of Web pages for viewing by the students under the control of the faculty member); and an archive of all parts of each live session (audio, text chat, URLs for Web pages displayed). For the purposes of this chapter, the focus of discussion is on how learning in this mode may contribute to enhancing students' knowledge, skills, and attitudes as future digital reference librarians, as well as some parallels between the experiences of online instructors and digital reference librarians.

In a recent presentation, Chris Dede (2002) of the Harvard Graduate School of Education used the expression "learning in chords" to characterize some experiences in Web-based learning. I find this a useful metaphor for describing the experience of students in a Web-based reference course. By virtue of learning via the Internet, they gain facility in using the technology and at the same time develop expertise in the subject matter of the course. Because I see a number of parallels between online teaching and digital reference services, I will first explore the changes in roles that we have observed in a study of LEEP faculty (additional details can be found in Smith, Lastra, and Robins 2001).

Web-based courses such as those offered in LEEP alter familiar patterns of time and place, and new roles emerge. Parallels with digital reference librarians include:

- *Teaching as collaboration:* Unlike the autonomous classroom teacher, the online teacher collaborates with technology support staff in delivering instruction. The online environment also allows collaboration at a distance, drawing on guest speakers in any location. Digital reference librarians must collaborate with technical support staff to maintain the medium through which they communicate with patrons. They also can collaborate with reference librarians in other sites to answer questions through referral. For example, Penka (2003) identifies several types of cooperation in digital reference and illustrates how different levels of cooperation are used in answering questions through QuestionPoint.

• *Teaching as public (and permanent) performance:* Through electronic bulletin boards and archives of the audio, slides, and text chat of live sessions, LEEP technology creates a much more complete (and potentially permanent and publicly accessible) trace of the act of teaching. There are definitely potential benefits to such a complete record: Students, peers, and the faculty member him- or herself can review "performances" that would otherwise be ephemeral. But this permanence also may be somewhat intimidating, especially to anyone teaching in this environment for the first time and for whom each aspect of the course is an experiment. In digital reference services, the transcripts of chat sessions and archived question-and-answer pairs are similarly more complete traces of the act of question answering than we have for face-to-face or telephone reference.

• *Teaching as creating a learning environment:* The content and organization of the virtual classroom space are planned to support the learning objectives of a given course. The teaching strategy may shift from "sage on the stage" to "guide on the side" as students explore aspects of the course both independently and under the guidance of the instructor. Similarly, in digital reference we may seek to make the "information landscape" more understandable to our patrons through design of digital reference collections and instructional materials.

• *Teaching as media management:* Media management involves deciding which activities to allocate to synchronous, asynchronous, and face-to-face communication channels, taking advantage of the strengths of each medium. Similarly, digital reference librarians must learn which types of questions can be handled synchronously via chat versus asynchronously via e-mail, and when computer-mediated communication needs to be supplemented with telephone or face-to-face discussions.

• *Teaching 24/7 and time management:* No teacher can be available 24 hours a day, seven days a week, but one can no longer treat teaching as a one-day-per-week responsibility. Similarly, digital reference librarians must be more open to service provision at times that are convenient for the patron.

• *Teaching as computer-mediated communication:* Faculty must learn to compensate for limitations of the available digital communications media. In LEEP live sessions, faculty can speak but must translate words the students type as indications of understanding, puzzlement, or frustration that might otherwise be expressed nonverbally. Asynchronous communication using bulletin boards and synchronous communication using text chat are completely text based and, thus, writing and reading intensive. Faculty members must be skillful writers as well as interpreters of others' written communication (and it certainly helps to be a touch typist). Likewise, the digital reference librarian who has refined oral interviewing skills must now adapt to text-based communication.

- *Teaching assistantships—new forms of partnerships:* The archive of live sessions also facilitates a more in-depth dialogue about the process of teaching between faculty member and teaching assistant. Together, they can review the archive and discuss what worked and what could be improved in a particular class session. Transcripts of digital reference interview and question-answering sessions should be similarly helpful in training reference staff.

The themes identified above can serve as a framework for communicating to faculty and students new to LEEP how it may differ from their prior experience in teaching and learning. To the extent that these same themes highlight particular characteristics of the digital reference environment, they may be useful in the education and training of digital reference librarians as well. The online environment is significantly different from that of a traditional classroom and thus requires considerable self-reflection on the part of the faculty member. A common theme in interviews with LEEP faculty is the observation that faculty who teach in LEEP become much more self-reflective, not only about their teaching in the online environment, but also about what they do (almost intuitively) in the face-to-face classroom. The extent to which this contributes to increased quality in teaching—in whatever setting—deserves further investigation. Do digital reference librarians likewise become more self-reflective about the conduct of their work in face-to-face as well as computer-mediated encounters?

A brief description of the basic reference course I have taught online can be used to illustrate the "learning in chords" aspect of learning online—the students gain facility in using the technology while also developing knowledge and skills that are likely to be directly relevant to digital reference services. The basic text used is *Reference and Information Services: An Introduction* (Bopp and Smith 2001), and additional readings are made available through electronic reserves. Students have participated in the class from many of the fifty states, including Alaska, as well as countries such as France, Italy, Argentina, and Japan. Live sessions are scheduled approximately every other week; in alternate weeks, there are "live" office hours during which students can connect to the course Web site and ask questions via text chat, with the instructor responding via text chat. Text chat also is the medium for asking questions during lectures in regular class sessions as well as for collaborating in real time on group projects (in which group members are often distributed across multiple time zones). Lectures are intended to give the students a framework for navigating the digital information landscape, with links provided to many sites they are encouraged to explore in more depth on their own. Instruction in online searching involves real-time demonstrations of searching Dialog, with students viewing the commands as they are typed by the instructor and the system responses as they appear on the instructor's screen.

Assignments are of four types:

- sources (locating answers to sets of reference questions and a final exercise focusing on assessment of the strengths and weaknesses of Internet resources);

- services (examination of issues in digital reference services—instruction, organization of reference services, and services to specific populations; participation in an electronic journal club, a small group discussion of recent journal articles in a specific topic area);
- online (basic commands and features associated with online retrieval systems often used in reference work); and
- IPL AskA Question Service (volunteering as a digital reference librarian, answering at least five questions).

The syllabus for the most recent offering of LIS 404LE Reference and Information Services can be found at http://leep.lis.uiuc.edu/fall02/LIS404LEA/index.html. The syllabus for LIS 412LE Science Information Sources and Reference Services may be found at http://leep.lis.uiuc.edu/spring03/LIS412LE/index.html. Discussion here focuses on aspects of these courses related to digital reference services:

- *Experience in text chat:* Students have repeated opportunities to use chat in dialogues with other students and with the instructor.
- *Experience in e-mail reference:* The IPL assignment illustrates best practices for e-mail reference work; virtual training (Patricia Memmott conducts a live training session from Ann Arbor illustrating IPL policies and procedures); development of a knowledgebase (students post their IPL questions and answers on a shared class bulletin board, providing many exemplars of digital reference questions); and practice in using free digital sources to answer reference questions (because IPL discourages use of licensed databases).
- *Exposure to librarians with real-world experience:* Invited guest speakers participating in live sessions include Sarah Wenzel discussing implementation of chat reference service at MIT using LSSI software and Janette Shaffer discussing distance education and virtual reference at the McGoogan Library of Medicine, University of Nebraska Medical Center.
- *Experience in using digital resources:* Because students have access to diverse print reference collections, varying in size and composition, they use a wide range of sources in answering the questions in the sources assignments. Although they are encouraged to use print sources, where available, they often explore digital resources and come to appreciate their strengths and weaknesses. Multiple strategies for the same question are shared via the bulletin boards, demonstrating the relative value of print and purchased or licensed digital reference sources versus freely available Web-based sources in answering questions. Consideration of the various categories of reference tools (e.g., geographical sources, biographical sources) reveals that coverage is uneven. Some questions are readily answered using freely available digital resources; others require access to a good library reference collection.
- *Experience creating digital resources:* The science reference course includes the assignment of creating a Webliography, a topical guide to selected Web sites. Topics selected by the students have ranged from science fair project resources to biodiversity in Illinois and bioethics.

- *Electronic journal club as a form of continuing education:* Discussion of recent articles is modeled on Medical Library Association guidelines for electronic journal clubs (see http://www.mlanet.org/education/telecon/jcguide.html). Students are free to use text chat or a group bulletin board as the medium for small group discussion.
- *Confronting the issues in provision of digital reference services:* Students investigate and write short papers on topics such as assessment of Web-based instructional materials; issues in developing policies and procedures for supporting Web-based reference service delivery; and how Web-based systems hinder or help information access by specific populations (e.g., low-literate adults, children, seniors).

So how does this compare to what students learned in Miss Mudge's courses a hundred years ago? Apart from the obvious difference of using technology, there is the marked difference in the "information environment" in which librarians function. In 1902, reference librarians had to perform in an environment of information scarcity, mining their local print collections to answer questions. In 2003, reference librarians must function in an information-rich environment, going beyond local print collections to a wide range of licensed and freely available digital resources.

Educational outcomes research is needed to determine whether learning reference online leads to enhanced performance as a digital reference librarian. At this point, the evidence is anecdotal, based on my experience and feedback from my students. The voice of one student (who worked in an academic library outside Illinois while pursuing her degree via LEEP) concludes this case study. After describing how courses in reference, online information systems, change management, and information storage and retrieval would contribute to her ability to support digital reference services, she continues with some more-general observations about the value of the LEEP experience:

> As a LEEP student, I was mostly reliant on digital reference assistance. I learned what worked for me and what was a frustration. Fast turnaround time (or at least a notification that your request is being processed) is vital. Where the information was coming from was not always clear. Fortunately, the librarians at UIUC are fabulous and I did not have any bad experience.

> By nature of the requirements of the program, [I] had to become comfortable in a digital environment. Learning html coding and xml were very valuable in helping me understand that the person I am assisting may not be seeing the same thing I think I am sending them. [The LEEP technical support staff] are wonderful at helping us learn on the fly. Getting a handle on platforms and formats is a necessary part of long-distance reference. Learning to walk someone through a glitch at their end is a vital skill to learn.

Sitting through the classes in LEEP means that you are interacting with people that you may not have met, so learning to "read" someone from just text turns out to be a skill that still needs exploration, but LEEP students have a leg up in that respect. Of course, the younger generations who do a lot of live text chat room stuff are rapidly developing these skills anyway.

It is also a fine art to steer a conversation in the right direction and make sure everyone is on the same page without visual cues and immediate feedback/correction. Even synchronous sessions have a time delay built in. I also learned that some things require live phone conversations, not just text chats.

I learned many little ways to help online classmates feel more comfortable through watching the styles of various teachers. Some weren't very efficient at keeping up with the text chat while presenting information. Some were fabulous at it. Some of the things that helped were reading the comments and questions out loud before answering them, and constantly mentioning people's names to make sure they are "checked in."

The archived class sessions turned out to be very valuable. Sometimes things fly by so fast, you don't get it all. Being able to go back later and find exactly what you need—usually through the URLs listed—was an excellent tool and something I would hope we will be implementing for those who use digital reference services.

Of course, the best education and preparation was watching [my institution] implement some of their digital reference services—streaming audio for reserves, pdf's for text, the live chat at the university's main reference desk. I used all these services both from a student perspective and from a library employee perspective. So I had the unique opportunity to learn about the architecture of these systems from classes, then see the implementation and de-bugging in a library setting. I also watched and listened as my colleagues [in professional associations] struggled with these issues—hence the [listserv] and the frustrations vented there.

This narrative is a reminder that an online student may have many teachers—professors, fellow students, technology support staff, reference librarians, work colleagues, and professional colleagues. The learning is not confined to what is taught in the basic reference course.

Issues and Challenges in Education for Digital Reference Services

In reviewing the surveys of reference instructors and the current literature on digital reference services, several issues relevant to education for digital reference services emerged. The overarching issue, as expressed by Joe Janes in his response to the survey, is "how we adapt education for reference work to education for whatever reference work is becoming." The following issues suggest needed lines of research to enhance education for digital reference services.

Relative Importance of Tasks

As noted in the discussion of the history of education for reference services, much effort in the past has focused on equipping students to answer ready reference questions. In preparing students for the current workplace, more comprehensive data on digital reference service patterns in different types of libraries would be helpful. What proportion of questions are answered face-to-face, by telephone, by e-mail, by chat? What types of questions are reaching reference librarians in each of these modes? What types of questions are best suited to each of these modes? Janes (2002b, 3) notes that this "may be the last generation of reference librarians who could concentrate on ready reference as a major component of their work lives." Knowing more about the questions that are reaching digital reference librarians would be helpful in preparing students to answer them. As McGlamery observes, "Our remote web-community user leaves a trail of data, transaction logs, database queries and calls to Java applications, which, while not a measure, can be used to take the measure of the user .... This data could be collected and used more effectively than it is at present" (2001, 348).

It is anticipated that the distribution of types of questions will vary by type of library, but it is clear from early reports of real-time reference that the distribution is not what some service providers anticipated. For example, in a case study of instant messaging reference in an academic library, Foley (2002) reports that the majority of questions fell into the information literacy (26%) and catalog (23%) categories. Information literacy questions required the librarian to explain the difference between the online catalog and electronic databases, to suggest a database, or to offer database search tips. The catalog category included questions about specific holdings or catalog terminology. Other categories of questions included requesting help navigating Web pages, inquiries about specific library information such as hours and policies, technical troubleshooting, and electronic course reserves. Surprisingly, only five percent of users asked in-depth questions about a particular subject compared to two percent who asked short, factual questions (more had been expected). In a study of the recently introduced chat reference service at UIUC, Kibbee, Ward, and Ma (2002) report that one-third of questions related to finding specific library materials, 30.5 percent to information about the UIUC library and services, 20.2 percent to subject-based research, 9.1 percent to ready reference, 5.3 percent to technical problems, and 1.7 percent to questions about the service. They conclude that the high proportion of questions relating to UIUC library resources and services calls into question the feasibility of interinstitutional collaboration to answer chat reference questions. The results of both these studies suggest that digital reference librarians, at least in academic libraries, need to be prepared to offer some instruction.

Diamond and Pease (2001) note that the full range of questions found in face-to-face reference is likely to be asked of a digital reference service when libraries do not try to limit questions to ready reference through service policies. Sloan (2002) outlines question categories observed in several different studies of digital reference. Ellis and Francoeur (2001) present a case for applying information competency standards to digital reference services in academic libraries and refer specifically to the Association of College and Research Libraries Information Literacy Competency Standards for Higher Education (http://www.ala.org/acrl/ilstandardlo.html). They suggest that such standards can provide "an overarching framework to understand what it is that students need to know about finding and using information; from this understanding, librarians can then decide what level of instruction they can accomplish in digital reference interactions and can plan their services accordingly" (Ellis and Francoeur 2001, 5). Coffman (2002a) suggests that a digital reference service will prove valuable if it takes into account the types of help people are likely to need on the Web, such as finding authoritative information, finding unbiased information, and going beyond resources that are freely accessible.

Staffing Models and Disintermediation

Related to the distribution of tasks is the issue of roles. What types of positions must digital reference librarians fill, and what tasks formerly performed by reference librarians are being eliminated through the process of disintermediation? Dougherty (2002, 46) contrasts typical reference duties ten years ago with typical duties today: answering reference questions at the desk or by telephone; consulting online catalogs and teaching users how to use them; working on collection development and evaluation of print resources versus face-to-face, e-mail, and Internet reference services; performing technical tasks, including functioning as a Web master; preparing tutorials; learning how to use new software; designing gateways; and training other staff, users, and oneself.

Even within a single digital reference service, there can be a need for role differentiation. Based on their experience with the IPL, McClennen and Memmott offer some guidance on roles and staffing models. They note that "the language used to discuss traditional desk reference was simply not adequate to describe this separation of roles in a new and more complex domain" (2001, 148). They offer a new model to provide a basis for further discussion of and research on the process of digital reference and as a framework upon which decisions about digital reference practice can be made. Roles discussed include: (1) patron asking of questions (need for adequate support of reference interview through design of Web form, e-mail template, or chat script); (2) filterer (apply policy to determine whether questions asked are within scope); (3) answerer; (4) administrator (keep service consistent and running smoothly on a daily basis); (5) coordinator (oversee the "big picture" by defining and implementing policies and procedures that make possible the operation of the service [choose software, develop procedures, train new staff members, make personnel decisions]). Providing a broad view of next-generation information services, Ferguson (2000) defines roles that he terms integrator, collaborator, colleague, access engineer, and leader.

As Crawford and Gorman note, "the history of progress in librarianship is one of decreasing the need for mediation" through such devices as public catalogs, open shelves, and accessible reference collections (1995, 107). As one considers design of digital reference services, the question is thus not the presence or absence of mediation but, rather, the degree of mediation that is desirable and affordable. In an information-rich environment, intermediaries can still play a role in helping users articulate their questions and locate appropriate information sources, whether print or digital. Moreover, reference librarians, by remaining in touch with current users of information, can contribute to new information architectures and help design interfaces that support more skillful information retrieval. Time spent in indirect reference may increase in a virtual environment as librarians develop virtual reference collections, navigational aids, and tutorial material. One indicator of success in this effort may be the complexity of questions coming to virtual reference desks. If the products of indirect reference service enable more straightforward questions to be answered by users themselves, direct reference service may focus on providing responses to more challenging questions and in-depth instruction.

Competencies and Guidelines

Statements of competencies and guidelines, formulated by professional associations, offer guidance in curriculum and course development. (See, for example, the list of educational policy statements at http://www.ala.org/alaorg/oa/educpol.html and the reference guidelines at http://www.ala.org/rusa/standard.html). In what ways do these need to be updated to guide education for digital reference services? In particular, given the importance of the Guidelines for Behavioral Performance of Reference and Information Services Professionals (http://www.ala.org/rusa/stnd_behavior.html) as demonstrated in research reported by Saxton and Richardson (2002), what adaptations are needed for effective computer-mediated communication? What do we need to know, beyond traditional site-based reference, to effectively create, operate, and manage such a service? Experienced providers can be helpful in articulating "skill sets," such as the list provided by Sara Weissman (Lankes & Kasowitz 1998, 131–33) that includes: read domain names of e-mail addresses to identify likely source of a query; use tools such as *American Library Directory* and LibWeb to locate remote patrons' nearest collections; recognize limitations of the query as stated; know when to refer; have the ability to explicate universes of information and to explain limits of different types of information resources.

New Frameworks or Models

Several widely recognized genres of reference books (e.g., encyclopedias, dictionaries, biographical sources) and specific titles (e.g., *Encyclopaedia Britannica;* Webster's *An American Dictionary of the English Language; Dictionary of National Biography*) predate the widespread availability of reference services in libraries (McArthur 1986; Rettig 1992). Thus, it is not surprising that instruction in reference question answering has often been framed along these lines. In a textbook for students of reference, Jahoda and Braunagel (1980) offer this model of the reference process: (1) analyze the query to determine the subject of the request and the type of information needed; (2) determine whether any clarification or amplification of the query is required; (3) identify categories of reference tools likely to contain the type of information needed; (4) select specific titles to search; (5) locate answer (translate query words into language of answer-providing tool); (6) communicate to patron and determine if satisfactory. Experienced reference librarians were sometimes called "Walking Winchells," reflecting their mastery of categories and titles in the *Guide to Reference Books* (Winchell 1951).

The traditional frameworks for thinking about the structure of the reference universe need to be revised. New aggregations are creating new genres of reference sources and thus the need for new strategies for searching. See, for example, the description of Oxford Reference Online (http://www.oxfordreference.com) and Hodgkin's (2002) description of Xrefer.com, which incorporates works from a broad range of publishers and provides a common searching interface to all the resources as well as improved browsing possibilities. Digital reference librarians must become familiar with the "deep Web" (Bergman 2001) of searchable databases as well as the "surface Web" typically probed by widely used search engines. In choosing between print and digital sources, reference librarians must develop an understanding of how well digital reference handles various kinds of questions. Janes (2002a) reports the results of a survey of reference librarians that included an assessment of this, with some differences in the judgment of academic and public librarians as to the types of questions that were best suited to digital reference.

In addition to the type-of-reference-source framework for question answering, librarians have multiple mental frameworks for library research models (Mann 1993).

These frameworks can limit approaches used in locating information. Research is needed to develop new frameworks that will help digital reference librarians determine the best way to answer specific types of questions when several alternate paths are available. The sense of an ordered physical world of published materials was intrinsic to the practice of reference for many years; new conceptual frameworks are needed to address the complexity of the new information environment created by the Internet.

Standards and Cooperation
Topics that have been part of cataloging education for several years, such as the role of standards, are now becoming salient for reference courses (Caplan 2001, 5). Possible areas for standardization include exchange format for queries and answers, interoperability of knowledgebases, standard metrics for measuring service levels, and performance standards for quality of service. Education for digital reference services should include attention to the efforts of standards bodies such as Networked Reference Services: Standards Committee AZ (http://www.niso.org/committees/committee_az.html). Factors related to successful collaboration and cooperation also need to be explored, especially as collaboration in provision of digital reference services extends from the local or regional level to collaboration around the globe. Coffman (2002b) raises a number of questions regarding collaborative digital reference that need further investigation.

Intellectual Property Issues
Point IV of the ALA Code of Ethics states: "We recognize and respect intellectual property rights" (http://www.ala.org/alaorg/oif/ethics.html). As librarians develop digital reference services for reaching patrons at a distance, they must be cognizant of issues related to copyright laws, license agreements, and appropriate use of print and digital resources in a global as well as a national context.

Integrating Relevant Research
Part of educating students is making them aware of the disciplines that may generate research that can contribute to enhancements in digital reference services. This can include social informatics in digital library research (Bishop and Star 1996), computer-supported cooperative work (Twidale and Nichols 1998), computer-mediated communication (Herring 2002), and interface design (Marchionini and Komlodi 1998). On the applied side, the relevance of studies of other e-services (Chidambaram 2001) should be considered.

Communication Skills
Digital reference is currently accomplished using asynchronous or synchronous computer-mediated communication. Education for digital reference services should include becoming proficient in using such tools as electronic mail and chat to handle questions from remote patrons. Abels and Liebscher (1994) note that LIS schools can play an important role in developing instruments for electronic reference interactions and in educating and training information professionals in communicating via electronic channels. As an

understanding of the skills needed develops, they should be integrated into educational programs. Tibbo (1995) offers guidance in interviewing techniques for remote reference, noting that it is unfortunate to treat electronic mail reference just the same as postal service reference. Francoeur (2001) supports further analysis of what is gained and lost when communicating by chat as opposed to communicating face-to-face. He suggests that a close analysis of chat reference interaction that is informed by insights from the fields of communications, linguistics, cognitive science, and psychology would be helpful. Chat communication tips that are specific to reference are beginning to appear (http://www.uflib.ufl.edu/hss/ref/rxchat.html). Although Straw (2000) notes that the key element in making the digital reference interview work is good written communication, those preparing to offer such a service can benefit from more explicit guidance. Smith and Harris (2001) offer a preliminary review, contrasting the skills needed in asynchronous versus synchronous digital reference communication. In particular, synchronous interactions require the ability to interact effectively in a chat environment, speed typing, quick thinking, and mastery of the mechanics of the software employed. Answering questions in both modes depends on knowledge of Web resources and efficient search techniques, rapid evaluation of the quality of Web resources, written communication skills, compensation for lack of nonverbal cues, and the ability to project an online presence in the virtual environment. In addition, it will be necessary to develop specific types of interaction skills, such as dealing with "problem patrons" (Taylor and Porter 2002).

Technological Skills
Published reports of digital reference services suggest that one category of questions received can be characterized as "technology troubleshooting." This raises the issue of what level of technical support should digital reference librarians be prepared to provide and how can they best acquire such knowledge and skills. For example, a recent book on strategies for the "high-tech reference desk" includes several chapters on "the librarian as information technician" (McDermott 2002).

Preserving Values, Added Value, and Evaluation
The final cluster of issues in education for digital reference services revolves around preserving values, adding value, and evaluation. How can the values that underlie face-to-face reference be made manifest in digital reference? What value do digital reference librarians add compared to what the questioner can accomplish on his or her own? And, what are useful metrics for evaluating performance in digital reference services?

In their paper on values-based reference service for the largely digital library, Ferguson and Bunge assert that "Respect for users, in all their diversity and complexity, will continue to be at the center of the library's value system. The constant pursuit of knowledge of users' needs and their information-seeking and use behavior will increase the effectiveness with which informa-tion services are designed" (1997, 262). Furthermore, "the challenge for reference service in the largely digital library will be how to extend this human touch to highly diverse and widely dispersed clients whenever and wherever they want and need it" (p. 264). Similarly, Cullen writes that "the user's time and convenience, the dedication of the system to answering their most complex enquiry and a focus on service quality in service delivery will be the driving values in this new paradigm" (2001, 36). Despite the new structures of knowledge and the new means of communication, human factors and human needs remain. As Nardi and O'Day remark regarding their study of the work of reference librarians, "we were struck by the 'high-touch, high-tech' service librarians provided their clients. The latest technologies were in use, and they were used efficiently and effectively. But right alongside them was the enactment of the librarians' ethic of service. The librarians contrib-uted their special human abilities of tact, diplomacy, judgment, and empathy" (1999, 212). One aspect of education for digital reference services is encour-aging students to consider how to serve the needs of diverse groups of users. What is the applicability of digital reference services to different age groups? Are there digital-divide issues? Are there barriers to use by individuals with disabilities? Achieving principle I of the ALA Code of Ethics ("We provide the highest level of service to all library users through appropriate and use-fully organized resources; equitable service policies; equitable access; and accurate, unbiased, and courteous responses to all requests") means consider-ing the needs of diverse user groups.

More studies are needed to better understand and articulate the added value that digital reference librarians can bring to question answering now that library users have more options for doing their own searching or turning to Web-based question-answering services. Librarians also may add value in indirect reference, creating guides to digital resources superior to those avail-able from other sources. Schneider (2002) discusses the Fiat Lux collective of librarians from Web portals dedicated to planning a major, high-quality Web presence, "a Yahoo! with values and a brain," providing a single place for links to local and global trustworthy content.

As Hauptman (1989) noted, evaluation (by oneself, a peer, a supervisor) can be an important form of education. Thus, education for digital reference must integrate discussion of emerging perspectives on assessing quality. Work by McClure and Lankes (2001) is exploring outcome measures (quality of answers), process measures (effectiveness and efficiency), economic measures (costing and cost-effectiveness of digital reference), and user satisfaction. White's (2001) framework for analyzing and evaluating digital reference ser-vices offers another approach. An interesting development at the level of the reference transaction is the Samuel Swett Green Award for Best Reference Transaction, created to recognize the best transcript of a virtual synchronous reference transaction (http://www.vrtoolkit.net/greenaward.htm). The criteria for this award suggest factors that contribute to the quality of a reference interview via chat. A recently published manual outlines statistics, measures, and quality standards that can be used in assessing and improving digital reference services (McClure et al. 2002).

Recommendations

The challenges faced in developing education for digital reference services are not without precedent in professional education. Thirty-six years ago, Harvey Brooks (1967) reflected on the challenges he saw for engineering education:

> The dilemma of the professional today lies in the fact that both ends of the gap he is expected to bridge with his profession are changing so rapidly: the body of knowledge that he must use and the expectations of the society that he must serve. Both these changes have their origin in the same common factor—technological change.... This places on the professional a requirement of adaptability that is unprecedented" (p. 89).... What does all this mean for engineering education? What kind of faculty? What kind of research? What kind of curriculum and courses" (p. 90)?

The previous section on issues and challenges suggests the growing body of knowledge that a digital reference librarian needs to master. At the same time, the societal context within which libraries function—the publishing and information marketplace, changing modalities of scholarly communication, and evolving capabilities in the user community (Lynch 2000, 60)—is becoming more complex, posing challenges to defining the service boundaries of the library. Education of digital reference librarians must prepare them for a future in which users may ignore institutional and national boundaries in their search for information.

As noted early in this chapter, education for digital reference services may involve five types of activity: (1) formal sequence of courses as part of the master's degree; (2) on-the-job training; (3) continuing education (conferences, seminars, workshops, professional association programs, formal university courses, professional reading); (4) evaluation (self, peer, supervisor); and (5) acquisition of substantive, multidisciplinary knowledge. At this comparatively early stage in the development of educational programs, the goals, scope, and means of each type are still evolving. The Survey Results and Case Study in this chapter provided some insight into current practice in course work for the master's and continuing education. Librarians providing digital reference services may find the need to place increased emphasis on the acquisition of multidisciplinary knowledge. For example, Helman (2001) notes that reference librarians at MIT who formerly could focus on specialized subject areas now had to have some level of familiarity with a wider range of subject areas in order to successfully staff the virtual reference desk. Cross-training sessions cover the basics of each broad subject area. Hill (2001) suggests strategies for acquiring subject knowledge, and Coppola (2001) discusses keeping up with popular culture. Organizations also must give greater attention to ongoing, on-the-job training, using techniques such as those described by Block and Kelly (2001). Completing indirect reference tasks also may enhance skills needed for direct reference service in the digital environment. For example, Mitchell and Mooney (1999) discuss how contributing to INFOMINE, a compendium of Web resources, has provided a valuable continuing educational experience. INFOMINE participating reference librarians, perhaps more so than many reference librarians, have a fully developed sense of how and when to best use the Internet and how to search it effectively. In examining sources for possible inclusion, reference librarians learn how to rapidly and effectively navigate Web sites through the hyperlink mazes that often accompany them and to quickly assess the quality of content.

All forms of education for digital reference need to exploit new resources for educational purposes. The following sections discuss some steps in this direction.

Transcripts as Teaching Tools

The systems that allow for digital communication make it easy to keep a record of the entire interaction with the patron. Such records can be invaluable for subsequent self- and peer evaluation as well as for use as a teaching tool for groups of students (with due consideration for protecting privacy). Carter and Janes (2000) describe their unobtrusive data analysis of IPL question-and-answer sessions. In a presentation at the ALA conference, Cheng (2002) of Wesleyan University discussed her use of transcripts of real-time chat sessions to monitor the work of both new and more experienced reference librarians. She found that newer librarians showed less knowledge of effective use of print sources, whereas some of the more experienced reference librarians tended to make less use of Internet resources. Analysis of this type suggests topics for in-house training.

Research completed as part of a dissertation study using transcripts of verbal interviews between reference librarians and patrons suggests a line of research that could be pursued using text transcripts of digital reference transactions (Smith 1979). The study sought to develop a model of the problem-solving process used by a reference librarian (intermediary) in converting the patron interest statement into a current awareness profile that could be processed against one or more databases. The model was used as a basis for determining what parts of this process could be accomplished directly by the computer or through patron–computer interaction, as well as for identifying intermediary expertise that could not be duplicated easily by machine. Analyzing transcripts to determine what kinds of expertise are being brought to bear in answering a patron's question can provide insights into the preparation needed by digital reference librarians.

Knowledgebases as Teaching Tools
Many libraries maintain question-and-answer files (recall that Illinois students contributed to these as part of their reference course work in the early 1900s), but these files are generally accessible only to the librarians at a given institution. There are a few exceptions, however, such as the more than 1,700 answers to frequently asked or difficult-to-answer questions (e.g., How many muscles does it take to produce a smile and a frown?) compiled by the Science and Technology Department of the Carnegie Library of Pittsburgh and published as *Science and Technology Desk Reference* (Bobick and Peffer 1996). Services such as QuestionPoint plan to build up and maintain a knowledgebase of questions and answers. These can become object lessons in organizing and sharing knowledge as well as illustrating reference questions and answers. Knowledgebases also raise interesting research questions for students: How does a service decide what should be saved? How are saved question-and-answer pairs best organized? What proportion of question-and-answer pairs need to be updated on a regular basis to remain accurate?

Manuals
Training manuals (e.g., Lipow and Coffman 2001) and guides for service implementation (e.g., Lankes and Kasowitz 1998; Maxwell 2002; Meola and Stormont 2002; Lipow 2003) are examples of resources that can be useful in educating future digital reference librarians. Faculty surveyed for this study expressed an interest in developing an instructional clearinghouse as a mechanism for sharing teaching materials for digital reference.

Collaboration with Vendors and Service Providers
To support teaching of online searching, classroom instruction programs have now been established in which vendors provide access to their systems as an investment in training future reference librarians who are more likely to use these systems on the job. Faculty surveyed for this discussion expressed an interest in similar partnerships with vendors of software for digital reference and related service providers. The Digital Reference Clinical Teaching Initiative (http://quartz.syr.edu/education) seeks to bring together the entire digital reference community interested in issues of education and training to create an initiative to share educational materials, educational settings (internships and digital reference services such as the VRD Learning Center and the IPL), teaching approaches, and internship opportunities. It is hoped that this collective expertise can come to consensus on core competencies, educational approaches, and possibly a certification process.

In conclusion, it is interesting to recall one aspect of Licklider's (1965) vision in his book *Libraries of the Future*:

> The console of the procognitive system will have two special buttons, a silver one labeled "Where am I?" and a gold one labeled "What should I do next?" Any time a user loses track of what he is

doing, he can press the silver button, and the recapitulation program will help him regain his bearings. Any time he is at a total loss, he can press the gold one, and the instruction program will explain further how to use the system. Through either of those programs, the user can reach a human librarian (p. 127).

Education for digital reference services must prepare the human librarian to supplement and complement what the user can accomplish with whatever version of "procognitive system" is available. As indicated in the discussion of values and value added, the roles filled by the human librarian will likely include knowledge of a wide range of information sources in print and digital form as part of an information landscape; concern for evaluation and quality of information; facility with tools and techniques for searching; and an understanding of users and their needs.

References

Abels, E. G., and P. Liebscher. 1994. "A New Challenge for Intermediary–Client Communication: The Electronic Network." *Reference Librarian* 41/42: 185–96.

Arms, W. Y. 2000. *Digital Libraries*. Cambridge, Mass.: MIT Press.

Bergman, M. K. 2001. "The Deep Web: Surfacing Hidden Value." *Journal of Electronic Publishing* 7(1). Available online from http://www.press.umich.edu/jep/07-01/bergman.html.

Bishop, A. P., and S. L. Star. 1996. "Social Informatics of Digital Library Use and Infrastructure." *Annual Review of Information Science and Technology* 31: 301–401.

Block, K. J., and J. A. Kelly. 2001. "Integrating Information Professional Development into the Work of Reference." *Reference Librarian* 72: 207–17.

Bobick, J. E., and M. Peffer, eds. 1996. *Science and Technology Desk Reference*. 2nd ed. Detroit: Gale.

Bopp, R. E., and L. C. Smith, eds. 2001. *Reference and Information Services: An Introduction*. 3rd ed. Englewood, Colo.: Libraries Unlimited.

Boyd, A. M. 1943. "Personnel and Training for Reference Work." Pp. 249–66 in *The Reference Function of the Library: Papers Presented before the Library Institute at the University of Chicago, June 29 to July 10, 1942*, ed. P. Butler. Chicago: University of Chicago Press.

Brooks, H. 1967. "The Dilemmas of Engineering Education." *IEEE Spectrum* 4(2): 89–91.

Caplan, P. 2001. "Taking Stock of the Virtual Library: Services and Standards." *Information Standards Quarterly* 13(3): 1–5.

Carter, D. S., and J. Janes. 2000. "Unobtrusive Data Analysis of Digital Reference Questions and Service at the Internet Public Library: An Exploratory Study." *Library Trends* 49(2): 251–65.

Chandler, Y. J. 2001. "Reference in Library and Information Science Education." *Library Trends* 50(2): 245–62.

Cheng, R. 2002. Presentation at ACRL/CLS program, ALA Conference. Available online from http://www.ala.org/acrl/cls/designingservices.html.

Chidambaram, L. 2001. "Why E-Service Journal?" *E-Service Journal* 1(1): 1–3.

Coffman, S. 2002a. "Be It Resolved That Reference Librarians Are Not Toast." *American Libraries* 33(3): 51–54.

———. 2002b. "What's Wrong with Collaborative Digital Reference?" *American Libraries* 33(11): 56–58.

Coppola, E. 2001. "Do You Have Any Information on the Goth Lifestyle? Or, How Does a Reference Librarian Keep Up-to-date? *Reference Librarian* 72: 171–77.

Crawford, W., and M. Gorman. 1995. *Future Libraries: Dreams, Madness & Reality.* Chicago: ALA.

Cullen, R. 2001. "Only Connect…a Survey of Reference Services—Past, Present, and Future. Pp. 3–42 in *International Yearbook of Library and Information Management 2001/2002: Information Services in an Electronic Environment,* ed. G. E. Gorman. Lanham, Md.: Scarecrow Press.

Dede, C. 2002. "Keynote Address: How Virtual Interactions Deepen Learning for Real Students." Paper presented at TeachIT 2002: Teaching with Instructional Technologies, Urbana, Ill., April 12.

Diamond, W., and B. Pease. 2001. "Digital Reference: A Case Study of Question Types in an Academic Library." *Reference Services Review* 29(3): 210–18.

Dilevko, J., and E. Dolan. 1999. "Reference Work and the Value of Reading Newspapers: An Unobtrusive Study of Telephone Reference Service." *Reference & User Services Quarterly* 39(1): 71–81.

Dougherty, R. M. 2002. "Reference around the Clock: Is It in Your Future?" *American Libraries* 33(5): 44, 46.

Ellis, L., and S. Francoeur. 2001. "Applying Information Competency to Digital Reference." 67th IFLA Council and General Conference. Available online from http://www.ifla.org/IV/ifla67/papers/057-98e.pdf.

Ferguson, C. 2000. "'Shaking the Conceptual Foundations,' Too: Integrating Research and Technology Support for the Next Generation of Information Service." *College & Research Libraries* 61(4): 300–311.

Ferguson, C. D., and C. A. Bunge. 1997. "The Shape of Services to Come: Values-based Reference Service for the Largely Digital Library." *College & Research Libraries* 8(3): 252–65.

Foley, M. 2002. "Instant Messaging Reference in an Academic Library: A Case Study." *College & Research Libraries* 63(1): 36–45.

Francoeur, S. 2001. "An Analytical Survey of Chat Reference Services." *Reference Services Review* 28(3): 189–203.

Green, S. S. 1876. "Personal Relations between Librarians and Readers." *American Library Journal* 1: 74–81.

Harter, S. P., and C. H. Fenichel. 1982. "Online Searching in Library Education." *Journal of Education for Librarianship* 23(1): 3–22.

Hauptman, R. 1989. "Education for Reference Work: Breaking the Icons." *Reference Librarian* 25/26: 521–26.

Heilig, J. M. 2001. "E-global Library: The Academic Campus Library Meets the Internet." *Searcher* 9(6): 34–43.

Helman, D. L. 2001. "Bringing the Human Touch to Digital Library Services." *Science & Technology Libraries* 20(2/3): 83–96.

Herring, S. C. 2002. "Computer-mediated Communication on the Internet." *Annual*

Review of Information Science and Technology 36: 109–68.

Hill, K. C. 2001. "Acquiring Subject Knowledge to Provide Quality Reference Service." *Reference Librarian* 72: 219–28.

Hodgkin, A. 2002. "Integrated and Aggregated Reference Services: The Automation of Drudgery. *D-Lib Magazine* 8(4). Available online from http://www.dlib.org/dlib/april02/hodgkin/04hodgkin.html.

Jahoda, G., and Braunagel, J. 1980. *The Librarian and Reference Queries: A Systematic Approach.* New York: Academic Press.

Janes, J. 2002a. "Digital Reference: Reference Librarians' Experiences and Attitudes." *Journal of the American Society for Information Science and Technology* 53(7): 549–66.

————. 2002b. "What Is Reference for? *2002 RUSA Forums.* Available online from http://www.ala.org/rusa/forums/janes_forum.html.

Katz, W. A. 1969. "Reference Services." Vol. 2 of *Introduction to Reference Work.* New York: McGraw-Hill.

Kibbee, J., D. Ward, and W. Ma, 2002. "Virtual Service, Real Data: Results of a Pilot Study." *Reference Services Review* 30(1): 25–36.

Lankes, R. D., and A. S. Kasowitz. 1998. *The AskA Starter Kit: How to Build and Maintain Digital Reference Services.* Syracuse, N.Y.: Syracuse University, ERIC Clearinghouse on Information & Technology.

Lerner, Fred. 1998. *The Story of Libraries: From the Invention of Writing to the Computer Age.* New York: Continuum.

Licklider, J. C. R. 1965. *Libraries of the Future.* Cambridge, Mass.: MIT Press.

Lipow, A. G. 2003. *The Virtual Reference Librarian's Handbook.* New York: Neal-Schuman.

Lipow, A. G., and S. Coffman. 2001. *Establishing a Virtual Reference Service: VRS Training Manual.* Berkeley, Calif.: Library Solutions Press.

Lynch, C. 2000. "From Automation to Transformation: Forty Years of Libraries and Information Technology in Higher Education." *Educause Review* 35(1): 60–68.

Mann, T. 1993. *Library Research Models: A Guide to Classification, Cataloging, and Computers.* New York: Oxford University Press.

Marchionini, G., and A. Komlodi. 1998. "Design of Interfaces for Information Seeking." *Annual Review of Information Science and Technology* 33: 89–130.

Maxwell, Nancy Kalikow. 2002. *Establishing and Maintaining Live Online Reference Service.* Chicago: ALA TechSource. Library Technology Reports 38(4).

McArthur, T. 1986. *Worlds of Reference: Lexicography, Learning, and Language from the Clay Tablet to the Computer.* Cambridge: Cambridge University Press.

McClennen, M., and P. Memmott. 2001. "Roles in Digital Reference." *Information Technology & Libraries* 20(3): 143–48.

McClure, C. R., and R. D. Lankes. 2001. "Assessing Quality in Digital Reference Services: A Research Prospectus." Available online from http://quartz.syr.edu/quality/Overview.htm.

McClure, C. R., R. D. Lankes, M. Gross, and B. Choltco-Devlin. 2002. *Statistics, Measures, and Quality Standards for Assessing Digital Library Services: Guidelines and Procedures.* Syracuse, N.Y.: Information Institute of Syracuse.

McDermott, I. E. 2002. *The Librarian's Internet Survival Guide: Strategies for the High-tech Reference Desk.* Medford, N.J.: Information Today, Inc.

McGlamery, Patrick. 2001. "Monitoring the E-turnstile: Developing Digital Library

User Profiles." Pp. 343–63 in *International Yearbook of Library and information Management 2001/2002: Information Services in an Electronic Environment,* ed. G. E. Gorman. Lanham, Md.: Scarecrow Press.

Meola, M., and S. Stormont. 2002. *Starting and Operating Live Virtual Reference Services.* New York: Neal-Schuman.

Mitchell, S., and M. Mooney. 1999. "INFOMINE." Pp. 97–120 in *The Amazing Internet Challenge: How Leading Projects Use Library Skills to Organize the Web,* ed. A. T. Wells, S. Calcari, and T. Koplow. Chicago: ALA.

Mudge, I. G. 1902. "Illinois State Library School: Instruction in Reference Work." *Library Journal* 27: 334–35.

Nardi, B.A., and V. L. O'Day. 1999. *Information Ecologies: Using Technology with Heart.* Cambridge, Mass.: MIT Press.

Penka, J. T. 2003. "The Technological Challenges of Digital Reference: An Overview." *D-Lib Magazine* 9(2). Available online from http://www.dlib.org/dlib/february03/penka/02penka.html.

Powell, R. R., and D. Raber. 1994. "Education for Reference/Information Service: A Quantitative and Qualitative Analysis of Basic Reference Courses." *Reference Librarian* 43: 145–72.

Rettig, J., ed. 1992. *Distinguished Classics of Reference Publishing.* Phoenix, Ariz.: Oryx Press.

Richardson, J. V., Jr. 1992. "Teaching General Reference Work: The Complete Paradigm and Competing Schools of Thought, 1890–1990." *Library Quarterly* 62(1): 55–89.

Rothstein, S. 1955. *The Development of Reference Services through Academic Traditions, Public Library Practice and Special Librarianship.* Chicago: Association of College and Research Libraries.

———. 1983. "The Making of a Reference Librarian." *Library Trends* 31(3): 375–99.

Ryan, S. 1996. "Reference Service for the Internet Community: A Case Study of the Internet Public Library Reference Division." *Library & Information Science Research* 18: 241–59.

Saxton, M. L., and J. V. Richardson Jr. 2002. *Understanding Reference Transactions: Transforming an Art into a Science.* San Diego, Calif.: Academic Press.

Schneider, K. G. 2002. "Creating a Yahoo! with Values." *NetConnect* (summer): 36–37.

Sloan, B. 2002. "Asking Questions in the Digital Library: Can Users Define a VR Service?" 4th Annual VRD Conference. Available online from: http://www.vrd.org/conferences/VRD2002/proceedings/sloan.shtml.

Smith, L. C. 1979. "Selected Artificial Intelligence Techniques in Information Retrieval Systems Research." Doctoral dissertation, Syracuse University.

Smith, L.C., and L. E. Harris. 2001. "Real-time Virtual Reference Requires Real-time Virtual Reference Skills." 3rd Annual VRD Conference. Available online from http://www.vrd.org/conferences/VRD2001/proceedings/smithharris.shtml.

Smith, L. C., S. Lastra, and J. Robins. 2001. "Teaching Online: Changing Models of Teaching and Learning in LEEP." *Journal of Education for Library and Information Science* 42(4): 348–63.

Straw, J. E. 2000. "A Virtual Understanding: The Reference Interview and Question Negotiation in the Digital Age." *Reference & User Services Quarterly* 39(4): 376–79.

Summers, F. W. 1982. "Education for Reference Service." Pp. 157–68 in *The Service Imperative for Libraries: Essays in Honor of Margaret E. Monroe*, ed. G. A. Schlachter. Littleton, Colo.: Libraries Unlimited.

Taylor, D., and G. S. Porter. 2002. "The Problem Patron and the Academic Library Web Site as Virtual Reference Desk." *Reference Librarian* 75/76: 163–72.

Tenopir, C., and L. Ennis. 2002. "A Decade of Digital Reference 1991–2001." *Reference & User Services Quarterly* 41(3): 264–73.

Tibbo, H. R. 1995. "Interviewing Techniques for Remote Reference: Electronic versus Traditional Environments." *American Archivist* 58: 294–310.

Twidale, M. B., and D. M. Nichols. 1998. "Computer-supported Cooperative Work in Information Search and Retrieval." *Annual Review of Information Science and Technology* 33: 269–319.

White, M. D. 2001. "Digital Reference Services: Framework for Analysis and Evaluation." *Library & Information Science Research* 23: 211–31.

Winchell, C. M. 1951. *Guide to Reference Books*. 7th ed. Chicago: ALA.

Yates, Rochelle. 1986. *A Librarian's Guide to Telephone Reference Service*. Hamden, Conn.: Shoe String Press.

Chapter 9
Exploring the Future of Digital Reference through Scenario Planning

Scott Nicholson
School of Information Studies, Syracuse University

This chapter uses the scenario-planning method to explore several possible futures for digital reference services. Using two dimensions, funding sources and automation, four different scenarios are developed. Common needs across all four scenarios drive a discussion of both current and future research needs and are used to position all components from this digital reference research agenda book in a common context.

Introduction

Throughout this work, the authors have developed a research agenda and laid some of the groundwork toward its exploration. To conclude the book, Schwartz's model of scenario planning (1996) is used to explore the feasibility of the research agenda, the placement of the work presented here, and other opportunities for researchers in digital reference.

To begin the process, we develop several possible future scenarios dealing with digital reference. The goal is not to predict which future will occur but, rather, to explore issues that may drive different futures. The process begins by looking at two types of major forces: those that are predetermined, and those that are uncertain. The uncertain forces are used to develop different scenarios of the future, and commonalities in the scenarios then are explored to present fruitful opportunities (Wilkinson 1998). Finally, the agenda presented in this work will be mapped across these scenarios to confirm what has been presented and to explore additional areas of research.

Major Forces

Some forces will remain constant across all the scenarios. These are assumptions that we are making about the future; these predetermined forces are those that should not change. Some of these major predetermined forces are:

- *Information needs:* People will still have needs for information. In addition, they usually want that information as quickly as possible (or at least want it at their fingertips when they are ready for it). As presented earlier in this book by Lankes and McClennen, it is not useful to separate services into synchronous and asynchronous systems; all that distinguishes the two is the amount of time it takes between steps of the reference process.
- *Need for expertise:* In the future, the need for assistance in finding information will still exist. Whether from a human intermediary or from human expertise captured within a tool, many people will still need assistance in getting from their state of an information need to obtaining the information that will meet it.
- *Digital information:* Most information will be available via some type of digital or virtual form. There may still be a paper/analog/tangible version of the information, but most information will also be available digitally or through visualization tools. This will include nontextual forms of information such as music, video, and objects.
- *Universal networks:* The concepts of the Internet continue to grow and stabilize, and there still is a universal network that allows people around the world with the technology to connect in order to communicate and share information easily.
- *Technology convergence:* As more information is available digitally, the devices that convey and store it will converge. Cell phones that can be used to transfer documents during the call will bring about new methods of telephone reference work, bringing telephone reference into the same domain as live-chat reference. Wireless technologies will allow users to ask for help from any location using portable computers (which may be nothing more than a wristwatch). Users will not be tied to a desktop computer to receive assistance and documents.

However, some forces are uncertain. Combinations of these uncertain forces power the different scenarios presented here. The two uncertain forces used are:

- *Funding:* Will library services as we have come to know them exist in the future, paid out of public funds? Digital reference services may be provided through these public services or paid for by the individuals answering the questions. In addition, a future might exist that mirrors the services of today: Digital reference services are available through both channels of funding. Many commercial information services (such as Onstar and Cellular 411 services) are adding more types of information to assist their customers. Are reference desk services on their way?
- *Automation:* Currently, we have not developed tools that are as good as humans in resolving information needs. However, as standards for agents, question archives, and better searching algorithms are developed, it is possible that there will be tools that serve many information needs better than a human. These tools will be based on the training provided by humans; therefore, human exper-

tise is still part of the digital reference system. The uncertainty is whether the human expert will work directly with the end user or whether the expertise will be captured in a system and delivered to the end user, as appropriate.

Scenarios

To examine these forces, four stories will be told based on different combinations of the uncertain forces. All stories will have the predetermined forces in common. (See figure 1.)

Each of the following scenarios could result from the uncertain forces pushing in a different way. These are not the only possible scenarios from these forces and are not mutually exclusive; they are presented here in order to allow exploration of an appropriate research agenda.

All four stories being the same way: Kendra has an information need. She uses some type of communication device to connect to a reference service via a worldwide network. This device epitomizes the convergence of technology and allows communication via video, voice, text, and file transfer. These devices are available in handheld form and also are integrated into many other devices, such as computers, cars, televisions, and appliances. Therefore, Kendra could be calling from anywhere in a mixed-media communication environment.

Figure 1. Predetermined Forces		
	Funding	
	Public	Commercial
Automation — Human	Digital Reference Desk	Universal Answer Center
Automation — System	AutoRef Library Service	GigaSearch Service

Digital Reference Desk

Kendra contacts her local public library's digital reference desk. A librarian works with Kendra through a traditional reference interview using text, voice, or video. Results and appropriate documents, video, and other items are delivered immediately to Kendra's communication device.

Technical Details

This scenario reflects the possibility that the task of reference may not change considerably. The technology will certainly change, but the concept and model of reference may remain the same. However, if the interactions are archived and indexed, a librarian can use previous questions to quickly answer the needs of new patrons. For many librarians, this is the only future they acknowledge; however, to be prepared, this profession must be cognizant of other possibilities.

AutoRef Library Service

Kendra connects to AutoRef, a service paid for by her local library, and submits her question. The AutoRef searches the history of reference transactions, matches Kendra's questions to previously answered questions, and presents Kendra with a number of topical choices to help her narrow her need to the most appropriate question–answer pairs and information containers.

Technical Details

Because scalability and cost are issues, this type of automated solution may emerge as a way of capturing and leveraging the expertise of reference librarians beyond the single interaction with one patron. This will require advances in search techniques, archiving of interactions, and developments in cross-media searching. A reduction in funding for live human expertise may require this type of solution.

Universal Answer Center

Kendra calls the Universal Answer Center, an extension of the telephone information service offered by telephone companies. This center also can be reached through integrated devices in automobiles, televisions, and computers. For a nominal fee, the Universal Answer Center will connect the user with a librarian who will conduct a reference interview and assist the user with ready reference needs. More advanced research will require an additional fee, and results will be delivered to the user's communication device.

Technical Details

This type of commercial information service currently lives alongside publicly funded services; however, these services are not as ubiquitous as in this scenario. Convenience information services, such as telephone information and OnStar, have expanded their range of services, and these services will continue expand in their offering. As librarianship is the profession best qualified to answer a large range of questions, these services may employ these experts to provide high-quality question-answering services.

GigaSearch Service

Kendra submits her search to the commercial GigaSearch Service. She has previously set up an account with this service, so a micro payment is deducted for her search; however, a version funded through user tracking and product placement is available. Her search is matched to previously created subject guides through a relevance feedback–based process. As she explores these guides, her behaviors modify them for future use.

Technical Details

These subject guides are created by librarians working for GigaSearch. When a user is exhibiting patterns of a search failure, the search is captured and entered into a queue for a librarian to analyze and answer with a new document. The components of the traditional reference process still exist but are broken up and made scalable by delivering results previously created. To stay

competitive, GigaSearch uses many automated techniques for broken connections, out-of-date material, and service management concerns.

Common Research Needs

All four of the scenarios described above have a number of things in common.
They all employ humans at some stage to provide the intermediation needed
to handle a large amount of information. In the automated cases, the human is
involved in the creation of the system in that the knowledge of the expert is
captured and given to the user when appropriate. This difference can be seen
as "just-in-time" reference services as compared to "just-in-case" reference
services; the creation of better storage, metadata, and searching tools will
allow librarians to create storehouses of just-in-case reference transactions.

The research framework presented in this book will support all these
scenarios. Exploration of these research areas will allow reference librarians in
traditional settings to provide appropriate service in future times of convergence and create new opportunities in the commercial sector for digital reference library services. This will require the library to separate the digital library from the digital service as discussed earlier by Pomerantz. (See chapter
2.) Enterprising libraries might look for these opportunities as a way to outsource
services, increase funding, and, most important, stake out territory in new
areas of mediation.

To take advantage of these opportunities, research is needed to lay a solid
groundwork and prepare librarians for the future. The lenses for research
provided by Lankes in the first chapter were policy, instruction, systems, evaluation, and behavior.

Policy research is needed to support these scenarios. User privacy is a key
policy issue, especially when systems provide access to previously asked questions. Another topic for policy research involves the ownership of expertise
provided from volunteer experts on a digital reference system. As Whitlatch
discussed in chapter 5, managers of services are faced with the need to create
new policies to run the service successfully. If libraries outsource reference
services to the commercial sector, new policy explorations are needed to
guide library administrators in this process.

Research involving instruction, as presented in chapter 8 by Smith, will
be needed to develop appropriate methods for teaching reference in this new
environment of information convergence and digital reference. If traditionally nonprofit libraries are going to work more closely with corporate projects,
instruction that prepares librarians to bridge nonprofit libraries and profit-
centered organizations is necessary.

Systems research is needed to provide the backbone of these scenarios. As
more types of information, such as multimedia, are available digitally, standards and systems such as those discussed in this book by Goodrum and
McClennen must be developed to handle these data sources. Protocols for
digital reference transactions, such as the NISO AZ standard (NISO 2003),

will be useful in using question–answer pairs originating in different digital reference systems. Agent-based systems would be useful in helping users/librarians navigate many different database interfaces and other information systems.

Evaluation of services and behavioral research merge in digital libraries because all the behavior is recorded in the system logs. Given the increase in the number and types of users, the complexity of multiple technologies, and multiple access points, advances in evaluation research are needed to give managers and administrators a data-based understanding of their services. The bibliomining process (Nicholson and Stanton, in press) combines data warehousing and data mining to help library decision makers identify patterns of use and create evidence-based measures and reports. However, because the information in the system logs is incomplete and based on the constraints of the system, traditional usability studies and patron surveys can help managers understand what the system is not providing.

Conclusion

Digital reference services are going to change as technologies converge and competitors arise. Librarians can either stay behind their desks, allowing the competition to grow unchecked, or become active players in shaping the future of information mediation. This scenario planning has shown four different futures, but many commonalities. By creating alliances and being prepared through a forward-thinking research agenda, we can place ourselves in the future as the best group for assisting users with information needs, regardless of channel, type of information container, or method of funding.

References

Nicholson, S., and J. Stanton. In press. "Gaining Strategic Advantage through Bibliomining: Data Mining for Management Decisions in Corporate, Special, Digital, and Traditional Libraries." In *Organizational Data Mining: Leveraging Enterprise Data Resources for Optimal Performance*, ed. H. Nemati and C. Barko. Hershey, Pa.: Idea Group Publishing.

NISO. 2003. "Networked Reference Services: Standards Committee AZ." Available online from http://www.niso.org/committees/committee_az.html. Retrieved 8 February 2003.

Schwartz, P. 1996. *The Art of the Long View: Planning for the Future in an Uncertain World*. New York: Doubleday.

Wilkinson, L. 1998. "How to Build Scenarios." *Hotwired*. Available online from http://www.wired.com/wired/scenarios/build.html. Retrieved 4 February 2002.

Index